The Buck, the Black,
and the Existential Hero

The Buck, the Black, and the Existential Hero

Refiguring the Black Male Literary Canon, 1850 to Present

◆

James B. Haile III

NORTHWESTERN UNIVERSITY PRESS
EVANSTON, ILLINOIS

Northwestern University Press
www.nupress.northwestern.edu

Copyright © 2020 by Northwestern University Press.
Published 2020. All rights reserved.

10 9 8 7 6 5 4 3 2 1

Library of Congress Cataloging-in-Publication Data

Names: Haile, James B., 1979– author.
Title: The buck, the Black, and the existential hero : refiguring the Black male literary canon, 1850 to present / James B. Haile III.
Description: Evanston, Illinois : Northwestern University Press, 2020. | Includes index.
Identifiers: LCCN 2019022942 | ISBN 9780810141650 (paperback) | ISBN 9780810141667 (cloth) | ISBN 9780810141674 (ebook)
Subjects: LCSH: American literature—African American authors—19th century—History and criticism. | American literature—African American authors—20th century—History and criticism. | American literature—African American authors—21st century—History and criticism. | African American men in literature.
Classification: LCC PS173.N4 H36 2020 | DDC 810.9352996073—dc23
LC record available at https://lccn.loc.gov/2019022942

To my father, who always showed me the beauty
in life, in things,
and in myself

At night I count
not the stars
    but the dark.
> —Kevin Young, "Obsequies"

And now, each night I count the stars,
And each night I get the same number.
And when they will not come to be counted,
I count the holes they leave.
> —Amiri Baraka, "Preface to a Twenty Volume Suicide Note"

CONTENTS

Acknowledgments	*xi*
Prologue Portrait of a Petit Marionette	*3*
Introduction Etiology of the Black Male Literary Text	*9*
Chapter 1 On Frederick Douglass and the Image of the Negro	*25*
Chapter 2 Ralph Ellison, Fictive Authority, and Existential Heroism: Magic and the Prestige in *Invisible Man*	*61*
Interlude Some Notes along the Way	*96*
Chapter 3 Colson Whitehead's "Dark Matter" Prophecy	*99*
Chapter 4 Cecil Brown: The Functional Negro and the Rise of "Jiveass Nigger"	*139*
Conclusion An Etiology of an Ending	*181*
Epilogue Petit Marionette in the Black Box	*187*
Notes	*191*
Index	*211*

ACKNOWLEDGMENTS

This project has been a long time coming, humming in my head and in my body for years. I would first like to thank my father, after whom I have been named and given a legacy. It is through your image and after your spiritual likeness that I venture out into the world unafraid to be myself and to become the man that I might not even know that I am going to become. I want to thank my mother, who has helped to consciously and unconsciously shape me in ways that I am discovering daily. To my sister, your fearlessness builds in me the kind of intrepidness necessary to speak the truth. And to all those black men with whom I have come into contact, for only moments or for years, you have shown a fortitude that lets me know that I will not always have to wear this armor I have constructed. To Rufus Burnett, I admire your intellect but also your heart and sensitivity. To Jerry Ward, your thoughts beat inside of me and challenge me to always be better.

I thank editor-in-chief Gianna Moser for your belief in the project from the beginning and for all of the hard editorial work you put into the project to see it to its completion—from the development of the project to its twelfth and final edit, it has been a long journey, and you have been steadfast along the way. I would also like to thank the University of Rhode Island and the Center for the Humanities for their support on this project and for seeing it through to the end.

I would like to thank my wife, Shanelle Chambers Haile, who has seen this project from its earliest stages, when it was just a collection of my feelings and experiences in the world and in the profession, to its final and fullest form on the written page. You were with me shooting in the gym, even when you got tired of rebounding my misses. Love you—you're next up, Dr. Haile. And to Hanna, my smallest little joy: every day that I have worked on this and stopped working on this and fallen down, you've made getting up an easy and most pleasant experience.

And to my father's father and my mother's father, my uncles and cousins, my father-in-law, brothers-in-law, grandfather-in-law, and all the nameless and faceless black men, I hope I have written something that resonates truth.

The Buck, the Black, and the Existential Hero

Prologue

✦

Portrait of a Petit Marionette

> I have never felt any attraction to violence. Besides, black violence against white has never been as important as the American press pretends to believe. It is obvious to me that blacks had no chance in an armed confrontation, the odds being 10 to one. It's through acting upon white guilt, and by knowing how far to carry their threats, that Negroes might achieve the greatest revenge.
> —Chester Himes, "Conversations with Chester Himes"

> As we approached the mirror Dr. Bledsoe stopped and composed his angry face like a sculptor, making it a bland mask, leaving only the sparkle of his eyes to betray the emotion that I had seen only a moment before.
> —Ralph Ellison, *Invisible Man*

This a portrait of a man, reckless with self-belief.

His lip is slightly curled, like a coiled spring or the haunches of a cat watching and ready to launch on a small and insignificant field mouse in some middle-class suburban backyard, just below an open kitchen window and in a bed of freshly laid flowers, except his lip was poised to let loose the slow leak of a small and clever phrase, rather than inhale an insignificant pest. Nevertheless, he and the coil and the cat were on the verge of something they thought monumental but were each ridding the world of something it never wanted (to begin with)—a mouse, another clever phrase, more relief of excess tension.

Chester Himes once wrote, "Racism is absurd. Racism introduces absurdity into the human condition. Not only does racism express the absurdity of the racists, but it generates absurdity in the victims. And the absurdity of the victims intensifies the absurdity of the racists, ad infinitum.... Absurdity to combat absurdity. So, it was for me. I thought I had struck a great blow against racial prejudice.... I was arrogant in the belief."[1] Himes thought he had asserted himself, asserted his manhood and taken it back, struck a blow for the cause and, in the process, had become, as it were, a real man, a real Western man, of strength and valor, willing to stake his claim in the world by force—of body or wit—enough to carve out a place among the Great Barons of lore.

This man, like Himes, did not realize that when one wakes up in the morning or releases a curled-lipped claim of wit or justice, what can happen in the span of the day. He did not think that like the field mouse leaving its nest, an anxious spring releasing its exertion, or a cat thrusting itself through an open window, that one's life is but a series of chance occurrences. Rather, this man, like Himes, thought of the world as a scripted rehearsal of stimuli and response, actor and audience, and had become reckless in his very belief in the power of cleverness or the repose of moral outrage to manipulate the actors and actions on the stage. He imagined a landscape where there was (yes!) moral outrage but also manipulation, and he imagined that he, too, could raise children to attend college, move out to the suburbs, and take care of a wife who could bake pies and sit them in an opened window, just above innocuous pests and their own small world of wonder and danger, that he could be a Great Baron of this land—albeit not of an entire country or continent but the thirty by sixty square feet of his own backyard!—unaware that he was not hunting as the cat had done but was being hunted as the equally inane pest.

He has just arrived at his office. His room has air conditioning and is ever-presently chilly, somewhat uncomfortably chilly. This is an achievement, not so much of technology but of the will, for a man is Great only to the extent that he can control his environment and terraform it to his own liking—including the landscape of his own interior life. He wears a buttoned-down dress shirt and a tie, loosened at the neck but still holding its form. He has never actually fastened his tie closed all the way, but its appearance as loosened gives one the idea that it was, at some point, closed and that this man was, at some point, in front of some important people discussing some important matters and that, with the tie's loosening, the man has concluded his business and is in the process of relaxing and attending to new business in preparation for another closed-tie day. There is nothing speculative here, no theory involved, only the reckless nature of self-belief in posturing.

Books by James Baldwin, Franz Fanon, Martin Luther King Jr.—but never Eldridge Cleaver or the "wrong" Baldwin (*Fire*), Fanon (*Wretched*), or King (*Chaos or Community?*)—Sigmund Freud (the collected works only), and pseudo-French, Algerian-born "philosophers" Jacques Derrida and Albert Camus immediately assault your eyes when you enter his office, their spines acutely facing outward near the edge of the floating shelf, close enough to dangle and be in need of a slight extension of an index-fingered push, taking your eyes upward to perfectly lined shelves, with perfectly placed books with unbroken spines that seem to talk, almost organically, to the well-placed and sculpted black-and-white photographs of men who are not in his own family, framed as if they are his loved ones, not quite famous or infamous enough to be in need of asking, "who are they?"—Paul Robeson, older, standing in front of a microphone and an American flag; Jackie Robinson, older, in a high-waisted suit with his wife in arm; an older Duke Ellington, close up and without an instrument for context; older, these men are always older; he knows that the appearance of old age is the perfect balance between artistry and the looming threat of black masculinity.

You can discuss Richard Wright's *The Outsider* or *Native Son* and how the Negro is always outsider, invisible, and see the curl sitting on his lip form as he begins to think of something clever to say about psychoanalysis and whiteness and the construction of the outside and the outsider as the inner projection of the white imago. He is reckless in his usage of these ideas—constructing the innards of whiteness to demonstrate to any learned person that he can outwit and outclass the numerous and vacuous members of those institutions with crests and men who meet once a year to donate monies from their vast fortunes, not enough to retire and establish trusts and grants and named chairs but enough to establish that you must want to be like them, be with them, or at least acknowledge that they are "somebody" and have achieved something Great in this world, of course, on their own merits. And, he, like them, thinks of himself-in-his-collection-of-thoughts-and-ideas—framed on the walls, lining his bookshelves, attached just below his thin jet-black mustache—in his wife, the daughter of an imagined Great Baron of lore, and in his suburbaned-existence pie-on-window above innocuous pests that will, by tomorrow, be exterminated by hired professionals—just one in his collection of professionals—as having achieved something Great and in need of the same sort of recognition that grants one entrance to university clubs and sit-downs with alumnae and board of directors members but not the university president, for who needs this tasteless position of symbolic power when you have plush, soft burgundy and navy Windsor and Queen Anne gold-nailhead-tufted chairs to usurp the president himself? He would be like Martin Luther King, usurping President Johnson, accepting his Nobel Peace Prize!

He will tell you of his upbringing, of his family members one degree removed from either ghettos or prisons or drugs or something that appears in the "urban" section of Introduction to Sociology textbooks, to achieve the effect that he has not lost his way and that he, more than these men in the tufted-nailhead chairs, has really achieved greatness on his own merits and that he, unlike them, still has obligations to these same people of whom these board members and other men do and must donate their monies as tax shelters each and every year. His own tax shelter, though, is those theoretical monies donated to the cause each time he says their names: Michael Brown, Trayvon Martin, and when he wants to be magnanimous, Sandra Bland, as if they are related, and because he knows these men think we are all related, by at least the same horrid conditions, he retains both his pedigree and his identity and places himself to the front of the line in this established era of diversity. He will become a Great Baron of lore through the only means available to black men—deception—transforming that great curse of invisibility and vulnerability into a source of power and persuasion . . . or so he thinks.

He begins his day as he would any other. Awake at 6:30. Breakfast. Kiss the kids—"off to school!" And his wife—"off to work!" Out of the house by 7:30. Unrelenting, unremitting. He will arrive at the office at approximately 8:00 a.m., though he does not have to teach or hold office hours until well after noon. But he wants to get his day started early and be the first to greet the secretary who he knows is well liked at the college and may talk about his daily work habits with other secretaries, who in turn may work for these same men in burgundy and navy chairs. He sits at his desk and looks out the window. He picks up one of three books that he rotates as "browsing" documents and opens to where he left off. He skims a few pages before putting it down to glance over his emails from last night and early this morning—"the usual spam," he thinks.

He thinks about his father and whether he has read his books. And his mother. And his wife and what they must think of him. Of his denial of his father. Of his selling the story of never having known him. Of the audience that bought it without the simple fact-checking that would reveal that, as a third, he was in fact son of a first and second. But given such "sociological" facts as black broken families, it was easy enough to pass himself off as part of this growing crowd of "first-generation, poverty-stricken" folks who line the walls of prestigious universities the ways that heads of deer, buck, and sometimes the exotic boar and bear do an average hunter's wall: a conversation starter ("I didn't know you hunted") and sometimes a defensive wound ("I can't believe you hunt!"). But it was a living, a good living with large suburban homes and wives and open kitchen windows and endless professionals and personal offices and secretaries who speak well of you to other secretaries who in turn tell their bosses who sit in burgundy and navy chairs with you, already having heard of you and your character and your early mornings; and, it is all worth it?

If we were to write about this man, what would we say? Would we pity him? Hate or admire him for his ambition? Find in him a failed bourgeois late-stage neoliberal capitalist? Would we see him as the success or failure of integration and/or identity politics? Would we write about him with the biographical detail of the mouse-turned-man—an individual overcoming circumstance, thwarting all-comers—or perhaps, a man-turned-mouse, to be devoured and, pointlessly so, distracted by the smells all around him, unaware of his surging fate? As one who was willing to be consumed through his self-assertive and reckless attempt to manipulate his identity and therefore circumstance? As one who was being consumed without knowing it—the balkanization of his thought refusing to acknowledge that no black man can actually manipulate his circumstances to become, as it were, the Great Baron of lore?

Or would we fail in our explanation, lacking the language to even begin to think or write about the nature of his recklessness? Would we fail in writing about this man because we fail to understand the nature of his failure or even his limited success? Would our failure to think or write or understand, ultimately, be the result of our failure to see that his self-belief is not the result of hubris, true belief in systemic structures, or his desire to mimic and replicate the Great Barons of lore but its opposite: his behavior and his seeming desire for the power of manipulation is the result of a fundamental powerlessness so central to his existence, which, whether he is conscious of it or not, structures each of his movements and thoughts, gestures and actions? That his existence and the seeming desire for the power of manipulation, whether he knows it or not, is, at bottom, an attempt to deal with the unique fact of his vulnerability—he is at once as embodied as he is conceptual, invisible because he is hypervisible. Would we fail to understand that each quotidian detail of his manicured life is the result of the unique fact that his perceived power and its fundamental threat to Western material, social, political, and psychic life constitutes his vulnerability?

The Buck, the Black, and the Existential Hero: Refiguring the Black Male Literary Canon, 1850 to Present is a beginning statement, not of this particular man's life but of how to begin to think and write about him, how this man's existence challenges traditional concepts, traditional language forms, and storytelling to reflect the diversity and complexity, contradiction and fluidity, that this man himself is and represents. Thinking and writing about this man challenges us to remove normative and regulative ideals that consciously or unconsciously guide our interpretation or reception of certain forms of "reality" as they have always already been presented to us.

The Buck does this, not by thinking and writing about black men but by beginning with what black male writers have said about themselves and how they have structured their narratives and what that structuring "says" or "tells" the reader as to how black men have "seen" themselves and their world. *The Buck* ultimately asks the questions, "What does black male vulnerability look like within narrative form?" and "How does one write about black maleness—how has it been done and how can it continue to be done—in the aesthetic of narrative form that captures and becomes that hypervisible invisibility that is black maleness?"

Introduction

◆

Etiology of the Black Male Literary Text

Andrew B. Leiter begins *In the Shadow of the Black Beast* by recalling a scene from James Weldon Johnson's autobiography, *Along the Way*. In this scene, Johnson remembers walking down the street with a light-skinned black woman, who is taken to be white by a group of white men. Acting as "state militia" upholding "legal and social strictures prohibiting social contact among black men and white women," these men stop Johnson and his companion, demanding they give account of their relationship. Under the threat of violent death, Johnson assures the "white militia" of his companion's "black" heritage and that he has "no sexual intentions."[1] After this defense, Johnson and his companion are allowed to pass. For Leiter, this scene marks not only a critical moment in theorizing the "impact of the black beast image" in the white imagination and in black male existential reality but also a critical moment in the aesthetic structuring of the literary form of black men's writing. Leiter writes, "The 'threat' of black masculinity . . . shapes concepts of white national identity, white communal identity, white femininity, and white masculinity. . . . However, the hostility toward black masculinity and the vilification of black men as it impacted identity surfaced most frequently in literature as crises for African American men."[2] With this statement, Leiter touches on a central feature of black male literary studies: it is not so much just the threat of violence inherent in the very idea of black men but the significance of this identity for narrative construction and for understanding and theorizing black male literature. Leiter's analysis helps to open the galvanizing questions of and for this text as a whole: What does the sort of black male vulnerability described by Leiter and Johnson and in the prologue look like when expressed within narrative form? How does one aesthetically project this intuition, that black men are powerless because they have always already been interpreted as powerful and threatening? In other words, what is the aesthetic nature of black male crisis?

These are significant questions given that black male lives have often been theorized in terms of trauma: from the social death and emasculation of enslavement to the dehumanization of the criminal justice system, black male lives have been largely understood as a sort of living death or a waking nightmare.³ Yet the question of what these historical and social realities mean and how they are not only interpreted but presented and represented in aesthetic form has been of lesser concern. A great example of this is Richard Wright. While he is usually considered within the framework of social and historical alienation, especially when considered existentially, one could and, it will be argued here, should interpret Wright as making an aesthetic intervention within black male crisis itself. In Wright's short stories "Big Boy Leaves Home" and "The Man Who Killed a Shadow," we see the fundamental absence of speech and lacuna of meaning in the main characters, Big Boy and Saul Saunders. These stories are not so much about the compulsion toward self- and world negation, violence, and death or the ways in which each of the main characters comes to represent—or was himself supposed to represent—black male lives within Western modernity as they are about absent presence, or hypervisible invisibility enfleshed within the characters' inability to speak. Yet few scholars have focused on what this absence of speech means for the way Wright is deploying black maleness to discuss black male vulnerability and the way this deployment shapes the narrative structure of the stories themselves—that is, the character and plot development. In these stories, we see Wright answering the sociohistorical and existential questions of who and what Big Boy and Saul are through an examination of where they are. That is, we witness Wright attempting to develop a logic and a language to express a subjective position in which language is absent. At the end of *American Hunger*, Wright offers us a glimpse as to how the deployment of black maleness as an analytic strategy might appear. He writes,

> I picked up a pencil and held it over a sheet of white paper, but my feelings stood in the way of my words. Well, I would wait, day and night, until I knew what to say.
> ... I would hurl words into this darkness and wait for an echo, and if an echo sounded, no matter how faintly, I would send other words to tell, to march, to fight, to create a sense of the hunger for life that gnaws in us all, to keep alive in our hearts a sense of the inexpressibly human.⁴

It seems that the deployment of black maleness reveals a conflict with language itself. Wright leaves us with the question as to why he cannot discover or reveal himself—to either himself or his audience—and why his feelings, of all things, would get in the way of self-expression. Wright, it seems, is confronted with the same problem we have in thinking and writing about our man from the prologue: If the language and the logic we have to think about and write about black men negates their existential humanity, how can Wright write himself past the feelings of linguistic alienation? One is left to puzzle out: Since Wright is alienated in language and is in need of finding a new language to express "the inexpressibly human" in his black male flesh, then, exactly, where is Wright when he writing? Where, exactly, does he go when he cannot speak—where is Wright, the writer and the man, in that moment of pause or silence? That is, what is the existentiality of the pencil hovering over the page? Ostensibly, given that it is the end of the book and not the beginning and given that the book itself is not filled with blank pages, it suggests that Wright has, in fact, written something, that he is, in fact, somewhere, but he is not on the page but also not completely absent from the page. What, then, is the status of what has been written if his feelings "stood in the way" of his words, yet the words are present? How should the reader read the work given this revelation at the end?

What Wright seems to be suggesting is that he is somehow on the page but somehow also not on the page—that he is in between what is already written and what will be written. As such, Wright's writing seems to signal the absence of his actual or futural presence. As we approach Wright's texts, in general, we should read them not so much as philosophical claims to reality but as what awaits a potentiated echoed response.

In other words, our approach to the text should be less of a search for an answer to these questions and more of an approach to what posing them means for how we read black male literary texts. And, as we approach them, it is important to consider that silence or absence do not signify paralysis, as is often argued in response to Wright's black male character types. Rather, silence marks the presence of subjective experience that has been rendered audibly absent in the failure of affective speech-acts—that is, centered on the failure of speech to materially produce effect or to accurately accentuate one's interior life.[5]

In "Big Boy Leaves Home," Wright gives us a concrete example of such failure in Big Boy's inability to speak in the face of his hypervisible invisibility, foregrounding his in-between status as his black male vulnerability. In the story, Big Boy and his black male friends are playing next to a swimming hole on a white-owned farm. Wright presents this scene as fairly normal, though tinged with the threat of violence, for if the boys are caught swimming in the hole, they would be trespassing, a crime of which they are aware but are nonetheless unafraid not only to transgress but to do so with specific language and voice.

> "Ah aint goin in," said Bobo.
> "Done got scared?" asked Big Boy.
> "Naw, Ah ain scared . . ."
> "How come yuh ain goin in?"
> "Yuh know ol man Harvey don erllow no niggers t swim in this hole."
> "N jus last year he took a shot at Bob fer swimmin in here," said Lester.
> "Shucks, ol man Harvey aint studyin bout us niggers," said Big Boy.
> "He's at home thinking about his jelly-roll," said Buck.
> They *laughed*.[6]

What is significant, here, is that Wright underscores the threat of violent death—"last year he took a shot at Bob"—as normalized in black male life. The boys recognize its pervasive existence yet still live the folly of youth. But, what is more, they actually laugh at the prospect of being shot at; they laugh and refuse to flee and laugh about ol man Harvey's obsession with his wife and sex with his wife, that is, "his jelly-roll." Wright's intentional location of ol man Harvey's preoccupation with his wife foreshadows the underlying structure of the story: black men, white men, and the threat of violent death meet at the intersection of white women.

After the boys are done swimming and lying naked in the grass next to the hole, they encounter the white woman and immediately know that this is different than merely trespassing on land. When confronted with the presence of ol Harvey's actual wife and their own naked black male bodies, they freeze and are without language. Instead, "they stared, their hands instinctively covering their groins."[7] As noted earlier, this absence of language or even freezing itself does not entail paralysis but, rather, an intuitive knowledge not only of the meaning of their bodies in relation to the white woman's body, but also of the reality that whatever they may say is irrelevant to their "speaking bodies." They instinctively know, as do ol Harvey and his wife, that when confronted by the body of a white woman, they are silenced by their own black male bodies. Language fails to conquer the sociohistorical fact of the meaning of their existence, and they are trapped between what is and how it seems. It is also significant that their silence comes right before death—first, the death of one of Big Boy's friends, shot in the back by ol Harvey as he attempts to flee; and, second, of ol Harvey himself, who is killed with his own gun by Big Boy. After having killed ol Harvey, Big Boy goes home and is immediately put onto a train out of town. In both instances, in his friend's attempt to run and Big Boy's own family decision, it is significant that black males' silence and instinctive attempts to hide their own bodies prefigure flight.

Similarly, in "The Man Who Killed a Shadow," Saul, a custodian, is confronted by the presence of a white librarian, who insists that he clean underneath her desk, which is but a ploy to bring Saul literally to his knees, for him to discover "her legs . . . spread wide open . . . as though about to spring upon him and throw her naked thighs about his body."[8] In this moment of discovery there is an inversion of perceived and actual reality: the librarian, while remaining silent and appearing disempowered in relation to Saul, speaks her power—to literally and metaphorically bring Saul to his knees—and Saul, though taken to be the hyperaggressive and hypersexual being, becomes the passive and nonsexual observer to his own flesh. And, like Big Boy himself, Saul is made silent. Yet, unlike Big Boy, Saul takes his forced silence to be an insult to his humanity and "without thinking" slaps the white woman and subsequently chokes her to stop her from "screaming a scream that meant [his] death."[9] Saul eventually kills the white woman and attempts to flee the city before getting caught by the police.

In these stories, both Saul and Big Boy are not merely silent; they are silenced—meaning unable to speak or behave in a way to control the meaning of the situation—and, thus, behave instinctively in confrontation with their own black male bodies, which prefigure not only their imaginative transposition into and as black rapists but also violence incarnate. In both cases, it is the white woman's body that activates the potentiated threat of the black male body and necessitates violence to ensure its sanctity and protection. Yet it is not her body as physical object and their bodies as physical objects that Wright is ultimately discussing. Rather, it is the meaning of their bodies, those inexpressible subtextual sets of relation that undergird social and historical action, which belie language and trap Wright between his feelings and the white page.

In both texts, flight becomes an important line of demarcation, one of erasure but also the site line of a new epistemic horizon. Flight in this context, like that of speculation—Where was Saul running? Where was Big Boy going to go? What would happen to them when they got to wherever they were going?—comes to be a response to hypervisible invisibility and an attempt to, more or less, break through the wall of feelings and discover or invent those "inexpressibly" human words of black male existence. As such, flight functions as an ambiguous term of the in-between, for it notes where one has left and the uncertainty of where one is trying to go. It is a term of transition. Linking this concept to silence or voicelessness, it can be surmised in Wright's stories that black maleness when deployed as an analytic concept has the status of transitory becoming.

At the end of *Black Boy*, Wright explicitly represents the transitory becoming of black men in flight as an existential narrative that actively prefigures, in specifically political and aesthetic terms, his concrete decision to leave the South for the North (in larger terms, black migration). He writes,

> I stepped from the elevator into the street, half expecting someone to call me back and tell me that it was all a dream, that I was not leaving.
>   This was the culture from which I sprang. This was the terror from which I fled.
>   The next day when I was already in *full flight*—aboard a northward train . . . I was leaving without qualm, without a single backward glance. . . . My mood was: I've got to get away; I can't stay here.[10]

If one were to read *Black Boy* not so much as Wright's own biography but phenomenologically as a "record of youth," as Wright intended, one would discover that the text is not *his* story or *his* text but *a* text that records black male development. As such, one could read Wright's oeuvre through *Black Boy* as also recording the transitory becoming of black men in search for themselves in the ambiguity, as the ambiguity of where they might go, where they might flee and what might become of them when or if they get there—wherever there is.[11] Wright, in this way, seemed to write ambiguously as a way of both seeking and searching but also waiting, waiting for an echo from others who, perhaps, too, were searching, were in between, were fleeing, were, too, waiting somewhere else for a new reality to arrive or be constructed—a reality that David Marriott terms the black male "dreamwork."

In dreamwork, Marriott introduces us to the conceptual, material, and psychic worlds of black men, which, though they might be invisible in the realm of appearances—that is, silenced—are necessary for understanding the transitory becoming of black men in the development of Wright's characters and narratological form. For Marriott, what makes dreamwork a pivotal concept is its inherent capacity for "speaking our [black men's] most secretive languages and desires." The demarcation of flight, then, signals, along with the transition from past to future, the presence of that which cannot be historically or materially explained, a desire that wells up in black men and offers the possibility, in the face of hypervisible invisibility and vulnerability, for "the wished-for risk and revolutionary hope that by dreaming the unthinkable—namely, wanting, rather than hating, one another"—they can once more become visible.[12]

Our task, then, in decoding Wright and searching for black men's dreamwork is to additionally reveal where Wright and his characters Big Boy and Saul go when they are silenced but their bodies are present. Our task is to see if we can find the entrance for the tunneling between these hypervisibly invisible silent worlds of black men, to reveal the aesthetic dimensions of their dreamwork lives.

The Buck, the Black, and the Existential Negro offers a critical intervention into the problem of language, one that attempts to address Wright's ambivalence to mine how black men have come to think about and write about their own living realities. It will be argued herein that black men do not necessarily write and think of themselves in terms of suffering as such or in terms of these endemic facts. Rather, it will be argued that black men think and write about the existential dimensions of their own fundamental vulnerability—to life itself, to the forces of living.[13] To be clear, vulnerability in this sense does not refer to a systemic lack or even the reality of deprivation in either a social or material sense. The idea of vulnerability enacted here is not simply that of the embodied, sexual, political, economic, and domestic ideations as is present in much of the gender scholarship. Rather, the sort of vulnerability analyzed here refers to the very structure of thought itself, to the very constitution and institution of language that refuses to see or interpret certain bodies as powerless because they have always already been interpreted as powerful. The sort of vulnerability discussed herein refers to the lacuna of meaning and value inherent in traditional perceptions of black maleness in which it is a site of both privilege and power, threat and menace, and whose deployment as both/and occludes both Big Boy and Saul as silenced and themselves in search of a self-expressive language.

Etiology of the Black Male Literary Text

The problem inherent in scholarship surrounding black men and thus in our understanding of black men's literature is that it often fails to account for this vulnerability when deploying it as an analytic concept; rather, the concept is deployed ontologically in a way that bifurcates black maleness between heterosexual and homosexual or queer blackness, locating heterosexual black maleness in league with heteronormativity and thus male dominance and privilege, while locating homosexual or queer black maleness in terms of black queer and feminist studies, thus situating it in contradistinction to heterosexual black maleness. As a result, the black male literary voice is rendered visible only as hypervisibly invisible along these ontological fault lines. However, in this process, we often forget that which undergirds both black maleness and sexuality writ large—that which is prior to each within Western modernity and within U.S. society: consumption.[14]

There are two powerful examples of text that analyze that which is prior to and undergirds identity in Western modernity and U.S. society: James Baldwin's *No Name in the Street* and Harriet Jacobs's *Incidents in the Life of a Slave Girl*. These two texts are intimately tied together around the issue of consumption and black male vulnerability. In both texts, we see black maleness and sexual desire in terms of what Franz Fanon calls the "phobic object," in which black maleness exists beyond sexuality or desire, for the putative difference of black maleness is that which undergirds the possibility of orientation itself. For Fanon, what we think of as sexuality or sexual desire and how it manifests itself in individual and collective behavior, then, is really about a consumptive antiblack logic that produces black bodies and black male bodies in particular.[15] It is in mining these manifest behaviors and the silencing of black male bodies that we discover the "manner of consuming black flesh and *not* just the body, [but] consuming the flesh *as* consuming the primordial relation itself."[16]

In a powerful scene in *No Name in the Street*, Baldwin recalls an encounter he has with an unnamed white southern governor in which the governor, after getting himself "sweating drunk," exposes or allows for himself a "despairing titillation." Baldwin tells us, "With his wet eyes staring up at my face, and his wet hands *groping for my cock*, we were both, abruptly, in history's asspocket."[17] It is this phrase, "groping for my cock," that is instructive to the idea of consumption, for it is not in actually grasping or attaining Baldwin's penis that makes Baldwin pause—it is not in literally consuming his body that causes the horror. Rather, it is in the "groping for" as a kind of roaming, as a kind of desperate searching and seeking to find the foundation for what would normalize their world. It is in this moment in which his penis is transformed into a "cock" that Baldwin understood that they were trapped within a history that was to consume both of them—a history centered on a "primordial relation itself," the relation of force and desire from which sexuality, sexual orientation, power, authority, citizenship, political organization, and individual identity emerge. It was the very "abjectness of it" that constitutes what came to be understood as the very obvious power dynamics undergirding their relationship. Yet, for Baldwin, it was the latent and structuring element of American sexuality and desire—the consumption of black bodies and, in particular, black male bodies—that produced the real terror. He realized that this man, who desperately sought himself in Baldwin's "cock," would enact through his search the constitution of the material order for black people. This man, in other words, who, "with a phone call, could prevent or provoke a lynching," was seeking to institute and constitute himself through grasping for, grasping at, what could not be held.

What language is there to express this latent fact, that, as phobic, "it" goes unnamed, that, as phobic, "it" structures language itself? What is Baldwin to say, where is he to go when the nation itself is held within his penis-as-cock? What and where other than to note, "It is still true, alas, that to be an American Negro male is also to be a kind of walking phallic symbol"; other than to note, "as my identity was defined by his power, so was my humanity to be placed at the service of his fantasies. If the lives of those children were in those wet despairing hands . . . one had to be friendly: but the price for this was your cock."[18] But this is not really saying anything, naming anything that belongs to Baldwin, that captures or attends to his dreamwork. Rather, like Wright's silence, Baldwin is offering a lacuna that appears to be saying something, directly, but is indirect and silent.

Baldwin, thought to be a queer black male writer, references his experience of vulnerability not as merely his own individual experience but within the larger contextual framework of the history of consumption of black male bodies.[19] What Baldwin is noting are the prerational and affective elements of a specifically American logic. But it also must be noted that in this prerational affect there was an exchange, of sorts: Baldwin had to be friendly, had to recognize the governor's power, not for his own sake but because of the "lives of those children" whom the governor would control. A critical aspect of consumption, and what Wright referenced earlier in flight, is the idea of this exchange—one's humanity, the humanity and lives of others, is exchanged, literally and figuratively, at the price of the cock.[20] It is these prerational, affective elements that tie Baldwin's story to Richard Wright's "Big Boy Leaves Home" and "The Man Who Killed a Shadow," for in each case what could be perceived as sexual desire emerges from a more fundamental relation.[21]

Harriet Jacobs's famous slave narrative *Incidents in the Life of Slave Girl* offers a fundamental insight on our point here. Though Jacobs's text is usually thought to be a text about the experiences of black women's relationship to white men under enslavement, there is a critically undertheorized aspect to it. In a critical moment in the text, Jacobs recalls the vulnerability of black male slaves, especially those considered to be bucks, to the plantation owner's daughter. Jacobs writes, "The slaveholder's sons are, of course, vitiated, even while boys, by the unclean influences every where around them. Nor do the master's daughters always escape. . . . The white daughters early hear their parents quarrelling about some female slave. Their curiosity is excited, and they soon learn the cause.... They know that the women slaves are subjected to their father's authority in all things; and in some cases they exercise the same authority over the men slaves. I have myself seen the master of such a household whose head was bowed down in shame; for it was known in the neighborhood that his daughter had selected one of the meanest slaves on his plantation to be the father of her first grandchild. She did not make her advances to her equals, nor even to her father's more intelligent servants. She selected the most brutalized, over whom her authority could be exercised with less fear of exposure."[22]

The importance of Jacobs's claim is not to prove that black men were exposed to similar violations as black women under enslavement; rather, it is to note that what motivated these "unclean influences" that we imagine were imbibed only by the sons—power and authority underscored by consumptive practices—were imbibed by the daughters as well.[23] That is to say, the very idea of slave economy was predicated on the consumption of black flesh, and what differentiated black men and black women was how this consumption landed on their flesh—not the fact of consumption itself. It is important to note the duality and ubiquity of this "primordial relationality"; not doing so works to obscure not only the experiences of black men but also what undergirds the experiences of black women.[24]

Jacobs's description of the daughter of a plantation owner selecting "the most brutalized, over whom her authority could be exercised with less fear of exposure," additionally signals the hypervisible invisible vulnerability of black men, linking Jacobs's narrative to Wright's "The Man Who Killed a Shadow," in which the librarian selected Saul, a custodian, to be the one over whom she would lord her authority, knowing, because of his position and because of her position, that he could not argue with her and had to do his work—which she would define through her embodiment and as the definition of her sexuality.[25] In each case, white women used their perceived powerlessness as a shroud for their exercise of power. But this was only a part of concealment, for it was not just the idea of white womanhood that shrouded their actions but also the always already aggressive black male body that could not possibly be powerless and violated that provided the additional cover. In either case, Jacobs's slave master's daughter or Wright's librarian, it would not make much sense to speak of their behavior as guided by sexual desire or displaying sexual orientation. Rather, it illuminates not only power but the specific consumptive economy that structures this desire for black male flesh and the sociohistorical context that allows this consumption to occur undetected.[26]

It is important that Jacobs references black male sexual relations with white women as coercive and white women as expressing the "imitative authority" of their fathers—that is, the Law/principle/logic of consumptive authority in the United States—for it is here that we can begin to see how vulnerability works within black men who are considered to be powerful yet who are, often, powerless. We see, in both Baldwin's and Jacobs's examples, the fundamental vulnerability of black maleness that prefigures orientation and that betrays a consumption that has little to do with sexual desire and more to do with the modes of authority that structure our social worlds. But, what is more, these examples, and black male literary voices on the whole, allow us to see and to challenge the very categories through which we analyze the social worlds, for within the realm of desire and the various economies at play in the logic of antiblack America, sexuality and sexual orientation do not exist as we have come to think of them—Baldwin's powerful white southerner was no more homosexual than the plantation owner's daughter was heterosexual. Rather, the powerful white southerner and the plantation owner's daughter were both enacting a fundamental principle and a fundamental logic through which both Baldwin and enslaved men were hypervisibly invisible through their vulnerability.

How, then, do we begin to navigate the terrain that belies our historical memory and our conceptual imagination? If what Wright noted earlier is correct—that he must wait for the words to come to break through the wall of his feelings—then are black men not silenced both in their writing and in their bodies? If so, what, then, does this sort of black male vulnerability look like within narrative form? How does it appear? What language does it use? Is it past, present, or future? Does it have a tense at all? Does it linger in the air, like the gossamer of smoke or the entrails of dust when struck by a beam of light? Is it tender, or does it breathe a fire that heats what is below and all around? What sense does it make to talk of a black male literary aesthetics of silenced hypervisible invisible vulnerability?

What *The Buck* is ultimately trying to theorize and thematize is how this hypervisible invisible vulnerability in shaping the narratological structure of black male texts also instructs us, through lines of flight and transitory becoming, not only about how black men write but also about how we are to read their texts and how we are to hear their living.[27]

* * *

While it might seem that *The Buck* is concerned with situating black men as men, or in relation to masculinity (normalized or otherwise) writ large, it is not interested in black men in the sociological sense; rather, what concerns and motivates this study is a challenge set out by Maurice O. Wallace: "Just how *black* masculine subjectivity constitutes itself relative to the masculine hegemony, in other words, or recognizes black masculine subjects as men, in opposition to the putative record noted by [Hortense] Spillers, is a feat of social and psychic wonder that has yet to be definitively named."[28] *The Buck*, in other words, is concerned with the examination of the self-expressive will existing within this specific context "yet to be definitively named," and how it "invert[s] [its] own subjective consciousness, into the highest objective form," as evinced in the literary production that emerges out of it.[29] The task of this book, then, is not to identify the literature written by those persons who are perceived as black men but to learn how to read and hear what is said of black men in their own voice, in what they write and how they write about themselves in the service of discovering their own name.[30] The question to mine for this kind of approach is: How have black men, within the historical and social context of Western modernity, thought about and written about themselves not as men but as those who are vulnerable to the perception that they may are or may not be men or that they may or may not desire the masculine right for themselves?

In addressing these concerns, *The Buck* takes an explicitly phenomenological approach, in that it realizes that the answer cannot be a totalizing grasping of absolute truth—as in the phrase "black men are, or not ____" or "black men believe or do not believe ____"—but must be presented in the mode of seeking or setting forth or discovery. *The Buck* implicitly argues that since black masculinity is intertwined within a sociohistorical context, as Wallace suggests, it needs to be unconcealed or revealed to us and to itself both within this context and beyond it as a means of naming that intersession of "social and psychic wonder." The address, then, can neither evade the context nor be subsumed by it but must take literary production as an avenue for thinking through context. For, as Ralph Ellison instructively notes, "We create the race by creating ourselves and then to our great astonishment we will have created something far more important: We will have created a culture. Why waste time creating a conscience for something that doesn't exist? For, you see, blood and skin do not think!"[31] What this means is that we must first engage with texts directly before bringing to them external theories that seek to explain their meaning, no matter how troubling or offensive we may find these texts to be or how helpful we may find the external theories to be, in order to discover what Charles Johnson has referred to as the "phenomenological perspective" of storytelling.[32]

In the process, what is discovered in this exchange between consciousness and the material world (which produces the literary texts) is itself an argument or its own theory. Part of the phenomenological process is the realization that it is by going through this exchange that we are always seeking, discovering, and creating an ever-unfolding objective form or literary product.[33] *The Buck* seeks to show that, as itself argument and theory, hypervisible invisible vulnerability is the fungible, transitory mode of black male exchange.

The difficulty, though, in this sort of phenomenological approach to literature, and to black male literary text, is that it does not elicit an easily graspable canon. That is to say, it does not elicit a linear narrative of conceptual development. And, though the title of this text might suggest a historical overview of black male literature, *The Buck, the Black, and the Existential Hero: Refiguring the Black Male Literary Canon 1850 to Present* is not an analysis of the history of black male writing, as such. Rather, given its explicitly phenomenological approach to the subject, it resists such temporal organizing for metatheory concerned with the linguistic, conceptual, material, and psychic foundations for reading and hearing the thinking and writing of black men. As such, the four authors chosen for this text—Frederick Douglass, Ralph Ellison, Cecil Brown, and Colson Whitehead—do not represent themselves as such (as this is not an in-depth literary analysis of any of their oeuvres) or historical eras as much as they represent different moments of and approaches to the literary exploration of black male hypervisible invisible vulnerability. The canon, in this sense, becomes not a totalizing historical or literary collective but a mode of analysis and a creative praxis of sociohistorical context and existential introspection and circumspection. Given that it simultaneously seeks, discovers, and creates, it becomes a living, growing document, a temporally discordant cacophonous repository of voices expressing varied and often conflicting black male experiences.[34]

* * *

The Buck, the Black, and the Existential Hero is centered on the following authors and texts: Frederick Douglass's historical fiction *The Heroic Slave* (1852) and his speech "Pictures and Progress" (1861); Ralph Ellison's novel *Invisible Man* (1952); Cecil Brown's novel *The Life and Loves of Mr. Jiveass Nigger* (1969); and Colson Whitehead's novel *Apex Hides the Hurt* (2007).

The reader will notice at the outset that the structure of *The Buck* is theatrical, speculative, and experimental. From the opening prologue, the reader is submerged into the life of a man who finds himself faced with a set of circumstances he imagines he can overcome through the performance of wit and guile. The reader quickly learns that it is not so much this man they will be following throughout the text but what this man will come to stand for and be a metareflection on—that black maleness is always tasked with performing itself (and its negation) on the stage of appearance(s). To read and hear a text both with and against itself, what it is both saying and not saying, both silence and silenced, the reader is tasked with what Ralph Ellison noted may inhibit action: both seeing and hearing around corners.[35] To aid the reader, each chapter begins and ends with a "Stage Direction." The Stage Direction operates to foreshadow the action to take place within the chapter; but, what is more, it offers some insight into the consciousness of the black men under investigation, and by way of dramatic irony, it instructs the reader as to the ultimate reality or conditions that these men will and must face, even if it is one that they will not and cannot actively accept.

Chapter 1, "Frederick Douglass and the 'Image' of the Negro," explores Douglass's speech "Pictures and Progress" and his historical fiction *The Heroic Slave*. "Pictures and Progress" can be thought of as providing the theoretical framework for reading *The Heroic Slave*, in that it offers Douglass's own views of black male self-presentation as the foundation for black political theory and action.

Douglass argues in "Pictures and Progress" that human beings are, essentially, phenomenally sensorial beings, who recognize themselves in both language and image. Both in his own writings and through the replication of his own photographic image, Douglass sought to reconstruct the image of the "Negro" in the nation's imagination—thereby reconstructing the nation's logic, its fundamental relations, and its political landscape. Through the production and dissemination of his photographic image, Douglass can be seen as attempting to navigate between how blackness is perceived and how it is lived.

The Heroic Slave, dramatizes the in-between nature of blackness through fictionalizing a real, historical event—the slave rebellion on the ship the *Creole*. Through its dramatization, Douglass deploys black maleness as a way of exploring and blurring the line between fiction and fact. *The Heroic Slave* is about a black man, Madison Washington, about whom little is known in the historical record. The question that remains is: Why, when telling the story of slave rebellion and, ostensibly, black freedom and black political action, does Douglass make the aesthetic choice to use a figure about whom little is known? There is a certain dramatic irony in Douglass's choosing to write about Washington and the slave rebellion on the *Creole* when he had more well-known cases of Joseph Cinque and the *Amistad* rebellion, Nathaniel Turner and his slave rebellion, or John Brown and the Harpers Ferry rebellion.

In answering this central aesthetically political question, *The Buck* will be tying together critical elements of black literature but also existential elements of black male vulnerability. Like with Douglass's own photographic image, he sought to manipulate the American imagination by creating out of a historical event a character, who is both historical in nature and also the creation of his own imagination, a method of direct indirection. Though this method has been, and still is, omnipresent in black literature, it also must be noted that it reflects something specific about black male vulnerability.

Chapter 2, "Ralph Ellison, Fictive Authority, and Existential Heroism: Magic and the Prestige in *Invisible Man*," explores the theatricality of black male performance as the foundation for black male literary work, arguing that black maleness is much like an up-close theatrical magical act in which the audience is a part of the stage performance. The novel's narrator, like our man in the prologue, pretends to be a nonthreatening Negro but all the while is keenly aware that he might be seen, at any moment, from any action, to be the buck or the nigger. In attempting to navigate who he wants to be and how he might be seen, the narrator becomes, as it were, both that which he is and that which he is not—the living embodiment of blackness and antiblackness.

The first part of chapter 2 is largely centered on the deathbed advice of the narrator's grandfather: "I never told you, but our life is a war. . . . Live with your head in the lion's mouth. I want you to overcome 'em with yeses, undermine 'em with grins, agree 'em to death and destruction, let 'em swoller you till they vomit you or bust wide open."³⁶ The grandfather had presented himself throughout his life as meek and subservient but had, on his deathbed, revealed himself for who and what he imagined himself to be. In a sense, the grandfather is a theatrical up-close magician who revealed the trick to the audience. The narrator is left to untangle the paradox that his grandfather left: How can that which appears to be weak actually be strong? The grandfather, here, inverts the both/and vulnerability of black men, who are disempowered because they are seen as powerful—rather than being weak because he is seen as powerful, he imagines that he is powerful because he is seen as weak. In the tension between the grandfather's performance and the reality of black male hypervisible invisibility, Ellison presents the reader with the "uncontrolled irony" of black male texts. It seems, for Ellison, that uncontrolled irony is even more dangerous and destructive than a gun: while the gun might kill the individual fired upon, uncontrolled irony works its way through generations and eventually implodes a nation. Ellison's novel, then, situates the uncontrolled irony of black male theatricality as the foundation of and for black politics.

The second part of the chapter applies this theorization of uncontrolled irony as a way to discuss the logical structure of both/and black male identity. There are two moments in the novel that are the focus of this part: Ellison's critique of dialectical thinking and Ellison's critique of spiritual faith, both of which are central to American modernity.

Taken together—parts 1 and 2—Ellison's novel can be seen as a field guide for a black male critique of the American imagination and its spiritual and political formation. Ellison's greatest up-close magical act, it can be argued, is not within the novel but *is* the novel itself. Many readers leave the novel not knowing where Ellison lands on blackness, black male identity, or black politics, for, like Frederick Douglass's own work, Ellison's novel presents identities as ambiguous and conflicting.

The "Interlude: Some Notes along the Way" alerts the reader to what was argued in chapters 1 and 2 and thematically ties them together, while foreshadowing what will be argued in chapters 3 and 4 and in the conclusion.

Chapter 3, "Colson Whitehead's 'Dark Matter' Prophecy," is dialectical in nature. It explores metanarrative of language and how language works to shape the reality we experience and the world we navigate as real, but it also speaks to Whitehead's usage of language itself as a metaphor for his narrator, a nameless black man. As the chapter progresses, the reader will see that the ambiguity of language and that of history are also metaphors for the ambiguity inherent in black maleness.

To begin, Whitehead immediately places us into the middle of a historical situation: the descendant of ex-enslaved men and the descendant of a white pre–Civil War entrepreneur are in an ongoing debate over the name of their midwestern town. The descendant of the enslaved want the town to go back to its original name, Freedom, while the descendant of the white pre–Civil War entrepreneur want the town to remain named after their ancestor,

Winthrop. Whitehead places Ellison's uncontrolled irony at the heart of this debate and the center of the novel—the naming debate, thus, the history and future of the town, is to be resolved by a black nameless nomenclature specialist. Whitehead uses this historical situation, these historical actors, and the disagreement over naming to explore larger, metanarrative ideas concerning the aesthetic-politics of memory, history, of naming and of black manhood. The midwestern town, then, is proxy for the construction of the American imaginative landscape and how we have constructed, interpreted, and lived this country and lived its history and meaning through black masculinity.

Whitehead intentionally merges the conceptual, material, and historical together with the linguistic to ask: What does it mean to charge a black man—himself a transitory hypervisibly invisible figure—with naming this midwestern town and thus settling a historical debate over the interpretation and meaning of the past and the future for the American imaginative landscape? Is this where we develop our new language discussed earlier in the introduction? Is this where our new concepts and a new logic will emerge? And, if so, how does this man come to speak this new language to all those who are still within the old-world logical order?

In this sense, Whitehead's novel attempts to answer the dramatically ironic theatrical question of presentation and representation asked by Ellison and Douglass: whether it is possible for a black man to reorganize the logical relations among things and thus reconstitute reality.

Chapter 4, "Cecil Brown: The Functional Negro and the Rise of 'Jiveass Nigger,'" explores the idea that the reconstitution of reality will not be done through dramatic irony or the resetting of the American imagination; it will only come through manipulating, that is, seducing, reality. For Brown, these philosophical ideas of the image or the concept or metanarrativity are themselves but abstract expressions of embodied desires and bodily relations between black men and white women or, more strictly, policing the boundaries around sex itself—insights that are backgrounded by Douglass, Ellison, and Whitehead, but are fully articulated here. Picking up on Eldridge Cleaver's claim that "to reorganize society you have to reorganize fucking," Brown's novel argues that what needs to be considered is how society is replicated, how ideas are enfleshed, how logic and language are formed.[37] In other words, Brown's novel is consumptive and about consumption.

Brown's chapter is last not chronologically but thematically and conceptually, in that it asks the reader parting questions: Can the black male writer ever be heard without the theatrical performance of subterfuge—in the manipulation of images or language? Has being read and heard ever really been the point in coming to terms with black male hypervisible invisible vulnerability? Brown's novel leaves with a challenge: perhaps the only way to approach black male vulnerability is through black male vulnerability. That is to say, if black men are consumed within the totalizing "primordial relation" of black male hypervisibility, can black men ever inhabit this image and ride it all the way home, to the other side of self-recognized literal and metaphorical freedom?

The conclusion, "An Etiology of an Ending" picks up from Brown's conclusively open questions. The conclusion, though, is but a beginning stroke of a new direction, not in that it offers a solution to the questions posed in the text in its entirety or even to Brown's concluding questions. Rather, it suggests a new direction in that it leaves the reader to puzzle them out. In doing so, the reader is challenged to come to terms with what they think they already know and do not know about black men; but what is more, it challenges the reader to come to terms with what they may simply refuse to know.

And so it begins. Like this, every time—just like this.

Chapter 1

On Frederick Douglass and the Image of the Negro

What has been missing from so much experimental writing has been the passionate will to dominate reality as well as the laws of art. This will is the true source of the experimental attitude. We who struggle with form and with America should remember Eidothea's advice to Menelaus when in the *Odyssey* he and his friends are seeking their way home. She tells him to seize their father, Proteus, and to hold him fast "however he may struggle and fight. He will turn into all sorts of shapes to try you," she says, "into all the creatures that live and move upon the earth, into water, into blazing fire; but you must hold him fast and press him all the harder. When he is himself, and questions you in the same shape that he was when you saw him in his bed, let the old man go; and then, sir, ask him which god it is who is angry, and how you shall make your way homewards over the fish-giving sea."

—Ralph Ellison, *Shadow and Act*

For an understanding of the post-slave generations, the history of slave resistance is less important than the legends concerning it, though the two by no means invariably contradict each other.

—Lawrence W. Levine, *Black Culture and Black Consciousness: Afro-American Folk Thought from Slavery to Freedom*

Introduction: Overview of the Case under Investigation

There has been much speculation as to why Frederick Douglass had himself photographed as much as he did in nineteenth century. While it could be argued that Douglass having himself photographed as much as he did might signal vanity or a privileged status in the United States (and in the world at

25

large), it will be argued herein that it, in fact, signaled a fundamental vulnerability, one bound up with his image and the image of the Negro (i.e., the black male) in the American imagination. Through his intentional manipulation of his own photographic image, Douglass attempted to create, more or less, new inner eyes and new speculative possibilities for the Negro.

For Douglass, the image itself held great possibility for the Negro for two reasons: on the one hand, images are that through which we, as human beings, think and consciously construct and navigate our worlds; on the other hand, the specific image of the Negro is central to the nation as a whole, for it is through this image that the nation cultivates and reflects on central concepts such as freedom and the unfree, the citizen and the noncitizen, the human and the nonhuman, and law and lawlessness, as well as how all of these issues intersect, generating notions such as gender (manhood/womanhood) and sexuality (and general mores). As such, within the United States, the very idea of the Negro is itself at once a private, individual phenomenon but also a social and political issue, one that holds tremendous aesthetic value. It is this image that allows politicians, poets, painters, sculptors, theologians, lawmakers, and the like to situate their craftwork on the American Ideal. The Negro, it seems, exists at the intersection—really, is the intersection—of public and private social/political life and the aesthetic configuration of expressive and speculative forms and, thus, is critical for the nation's self-reflection, self-understanding, and self-assertion.

It is, for this reason, that the image of the Negro is at the center of Douglass's personal and professional advocacy. What follows will be an exploration of one of his four photography lectures, "Pictures and Progress." This chapter is principally concerned with addressing Douglass's views on the social and political importance of photography in constructing the image of the Negro and its potential power for the abolition of enslavement in America. In addition to mining this text, this chapter also analyzes how this lecture on photography and the photographic image both theoretically and materially grounds Douglass's only fictional historical novella, *The Heroic Slave*.

This chapter at once seeks to dis-cover Douglass's phenomenological vision and the power of the image in his photography lecture and how this lecture, alongside his fictional historical novella, helped to shape new possibilities for how to think and write about "the Negro."

Part 1: Frederick Douglass, the Negro, and the Photographic Image

On December 3, 1861, Douglass delivered an address on the value and enduring quality of photographs as part of the Fraternity Course lectures at Boston's Tremont Temple. Departing from his usual subject matter, Douglass also deviated from his customary speaking procedure by reading a prepared lecture. The Boston correspondent of the *Springfield (Mass.) Republican* thought it "came near being a total failure; the Speaker only saved himself by switching off suddenly from his subject, and pitching in on the great question of the day"—slavery and the Civil War. The adoption of a new topic prompted the conclusion that the "closing part of the address, though disjointed and rambling, gave evidence of some of Douglass's old power, and the audience applauded, . . . relieved from what they feared would be . . . an evening without result."

> I am at liberty to touch the element out of which our pictures spring. There are certain groups and combinations of facts and features, some pleasant[,] some sad, which possess in large measure the quality of pictures, and affect us accordingly. They are thought pictures—the outstanding headlands of the measuring shores of life and are points to steer by on the broad sea of thought and experience. They body forth in living forms and colors, the ever varying lights and shadows of the soul.
> —Frederick Douglass, "Of Pictures and Progress"

[*Stage direction*] A Negro is alone on a stage. He is seated on a stool before the new technology. It is as if he is seated in front of a time machine. He will be cast himself both into the past and into the future. He takes photograph after photograph, in countless moments of replication. In some photographs, he opens his hands; in others they are closed. In some photographs, he looks down into the camera; in others, past the camera; and in still others, straight through the lens. His clothes are usually pressed, but sometimes the inlay of his suit vest is left (intentionally?) crooked and wrinkled, peaking through austerity with a slight hint of vulnerability. All the while he knows. . . . *We all get (in the end) what we (have) come for.*

Frederick Douglass was the most photographed man of nineteenth-century United States of America.[1] He controlled and captured his image—arrested the frame and told (and foretold) his legacy. The image of the Negro in this century, perhaps more than at any other previous time, was being contested. At the center of the issues of slavery, states' rights, federalism, and the fate of the nation as a whole was the *idea* of the Negro—as chattel, as man, as Christian, as brother, as servant, and as citizen. For Douglass, photography was central in the narrative telling of the Negro and the nation; it articulated equally the aesthetic and political dimensions of presentation and representation. But, what is more, photography, for Douglass, tapped into that deeply moral aspect of human life and, as such, had more moral and social influence than even that of laws. For Douglass, it is in the merging of the aesthetic and political with the social and moral that photography ultimately could be revelatory, disclosing and activating the highest ends of humanity: self-improvement through self-conscious recognition of human dignity—in short, liberty, freedom, and liberation. In the broadest of strokes, then, the *idea* and the *image* of the Negro was at the heart of the nation itself and could, if properly expressed, transform the nation.

Maurice O. Wallace and Shawn Michelle Smith begin their edited collection *Pictures and Progress: Early Photography and the Making of African American Identity* with the following insight, "To be sure, photography was a watershed invention. So profound was the influence of photography upon antebellum and postbellum American life and thought that, like today's digital technology, early photography shifted the very ground upon which the production and circulation of knowledges, scientific and philosophical, had set only a half century earlier."[2] They argue that this new technology, in particular, the daguerreotype, shaped our phenomenologically centered modern visual-material culture.[3] They go on to clarify what they mean: "The deep impact of war, emancipation, mechanization, expansionism, and late-century immigration on American social life and identity was in no small way secured by the aid of early photography and its rapid advance over the century."[4] Here, Wallace and Smith echo the insights Douglass offered in his speech, delivered in Boston's Tremont Temple, on the relationship between art, morality, politics, and abolitionism, "Pictures and Progress," in which Douglass notes,

> Byron says, a man always looks *dead*, when his biography is written. The same is even more true when his picture is taken. There is ever something statue-like about such men. See them when or where you will, and unless they are totally off guard, they are either serenely sitting, or rigidly standing in what they fancy their best attitude for a picture.
>
> The stern serenity of our photographic processes, in tracing the features and forms of men, might deter some of us from operation, but for that most kind of natural Providence, by which, most men easily see in themselves points of beauty and excellence, which wholly elude the observation of all others. ("Pictures and Progress," 455)

What Wallace and Smith's and Douglass's quotations share in common is the insight that the phenomenological truth—that is, lived or living truth—of photographs is their capacity to generate an *emotional reality*; this, they argue, is what has the capacity to transform both the individual and the nation. The image generates an emotional reaction, emotional facts of reality, and comes to constitute not only what is true but also the manner in which and through which this truth and reality come to be interpreted as such. And the photograph, like the word, because it can be staged, can be controlled; and, thus, its truth element can also be controlled. Like words, pictures work to freeze an image, a moment of temporal existence, for the individual and for their circumstance, to either contradict or confirm (live up to, down to, or within) popular depictions of material and existential reality. Douglass believed that most of the nation did not directly know of the horrors of slavery because the drawings and etchings circulated in magazines, newspapers, and pamphlets depicted enslaved men, women, and children as not only well taken care of but also blissfully happy.[5] The photograph, though, unlike the drawing or etching, for Douglass, could not lie. Although it could be staged, the photographic image could cut through propaganda to reveal the living conditions and physical scars of enslavement.[6]

African Americans, in particular, black men, have often suffered from having their image constructed from the outside, by white inner eyes, the white imagination, and the logics of a white framework. While this image was useful for propaganda—for obscuring the harsh treatment of enslaved Africans in the generation of the nation's wealth—it was more than mere propaganda, that is, more than a mere tool to justify abhorrent treatment of enslaved Africans. Rather, this image was necessary for the construction of the nation itself, in that it provided the background against which white Americans could reflect an idea of themselves, and the nation as a whole, as inherently moral and democratic. Part of this American white self-image was the image of enslaved and happy Africans, but it was also the barbaric Africans who, through enslavement, could be brought to modernity, civility, and Christianity—that is, moral, social, and economic betterment. John Stauffer reminds us in his book *The Black Hearts of Men: Radical Abolitionists and the Transformation of Race*,

> Most white Americans in the 1850s believed that blacks were innately inferior, incapable of self-government, and thus unable to participate in civil society, and they used pictures—though usually not photographs—to show it. Scientists as well as artists resorted to pictures. In 1854 the respected ethnologists Josiah Knott and George Glidden published an influential and popular book called *Types of Mankind*. In it they included numerous engravings that evoked a strong affinity between blacks and gorillas. The first printing sold out immediately, and the second edition, published the same year as Douglass' *My Bondage and My Freedom*, featured an engraving that compared the heads and skulls of a "creole negro," a "young chimpanzee," and a *statue* of the white *Apollo Belvidere*.[7]

The significance of the photographic image, then, for Douglass cannot be understated. The same year he published his autobiography depicting his enslavement and liberation, the height of both Negro civility and ingenuity, Knott and Glidden published a text on the barbarity and inhumanity of the Negro, each text featuring images of the Negro—Knott and Glidden, drawings of the Negro; Douglass, his famous frontispiece portrait. These two texts presented competing images of the Negro and competing ideas of the place of the Negro within civil society. At the center of this debate was the question: Who or what *is* the Negro, and how is he to be depicted within social, political, aesthetic, and narrative form?

Douglass, though, saw great possibility in the photographic image, in that it allowed African Americans to participate in the debate—to create, re-create, and curate their own image and to directly combat the prevalent image and idea of the Negro reified in many of the national tropes. Humanity, for Douglass, could be affected either negatively or positively by images, but what could not be debated was that humanity was both directly (or consciously) and indirectly (or unconsciously) affected. The image worked on both the physical eye and the inner eye, on the social and spiritual self of the individual. Douglass writes,

> I have said that man is a picture making and a picture appreciating animal and have pointed out that fact as an important distinction between us and other animals. The point will bear emphasis.
>
> It lies directly in the path of what I conceive to be a key to the *great mystery of life and progress*. The process by which man is able to invert his own subjective consciousness, into the highest objective form, considered in all its range, is in truth the highest attribute of man's nature. ("Pictures and Progress," 461; emphasis mine)

Douglass here is operating on the existential level—the level of the individual—while keeping in mind the effect individuals have on their social worlds. So, while it is true and important to note that humans create and appreciate pictures, see the world and ourselves through images, it also must be noted that these images hold the key to the great mystery of life of social and political progress. At the center of Douglass's social and political rumination and philosophy is this phenomenological insight: social and political progress best occurs through the image, and the cultivation of the proper image—the one most representative of material and historical fact—is the "highest attribute of man's nature." For Douglass, the social, political, and moral and spiritual are intertwined in the aesthetic production of images.

Yet, like all aspects of human nature, the capacity to produce and consume images—the inversion of one's own subjective consciousness into a higher objective form—can be misused, and that which is meant to liberate can actually enslave. Douglass continues,

> This picture-making faculty is flung out into the world like all others—subject to a wild scramble between contending interests and forces. It is a mighty power, and the side to which it goes has achieved a wondrous conquest. For the habit we adopt, the master we obey in

making our subjective nature objective, giving it form, colour, space, action and utterance, is the all important thing to ourselves and our surroundings. It will either lift us to the highest heavens or sink us to the bottomless depths. ("Pictures and Progress," 461)

One can return to the frontispiece portrait of Douglass in *My Bondage and My Freedom*—his austere pose, clean shaven, seated with restrained balled fists in his lap at the double-breast closure of his jacket—and compare it to the drawings of Knott and Glidden's *Types of Mankind*: a drawing of a Negro man with protruding nostrils and thick, upturned lips next to a drawing of a skull with a sloping forehead, nestled between, on the one side, the image of a Greek man, drawn to represent beauty, next to a drawing of a fully formed human skull and, on the other side, the drawing of a young chimpanzee, suggesting that the Negro is somewhere between human and animal. This comparison helps one understand both visually and conceptually that what is being presented in the conflict of images is a social, political, and spiritual war over the natural order of society itself. It is a war over how society is organized but also over the logic of the organization itself. Who is going to decide what constitutes law? Who is going to decide the adjudication of law? Who is going to decide on the social and moral culture and conscience of the nation—what its beliefs are, what its concepts are, and how to apply these to material circumstances? All of this is up for grabs within these two contested images of the Negro. For Douglass, seated before the camera, having his photograph taken over and again contests the thousands of drawing and etchings of the Negro. There is a perversion in the very nature of humanity itself, a person's capacity to present, represent, and *properly* consume an image at the very moment one must argue for or against, for example, whether the Negro is not-animal or not-quite-human.

Photography, then, can be understood as a method through which humanity *may be able to* reach its fullest capacity. It highlights our capacity but does not guarantee our morality. Photography in itself only offers possibility and, in either success or failure, reveals four key insights: (1) it is that in which and through which we know ourselves, reflectively, as human; (2) the human is itself, fundamentally, speculative; (3) presentations and representations are mapped onto and become the axis point for understanding or shaping reality; and (4) we are able to, in making and appreciating photographs, elevate our humanity toward its moral perfection.[8]

The political commentator David Brooks argues that photography not only reveals these four aspects of the human but also highlights an important insight regarding history—historicity and its interpretation. That is, photography, in its capacity to alter human consciousness and thus how we organize ourselves socially and materially, allows us to see and "see"—to utilize both our physical eye and our inner eyes of judgment—that no arrangement is settled and permanent and that our existence is continually unfolding. The image has this capacity to reframe perception and perspective and allows us to understand that perspective *is* perception, and vice versa. Brooks writes,

> We are often under the illusion that seeing is a very simple thing. You see something, which is taking information in, and then you evaluate, which is the hard part. But in fact, perception and evaluation are the same thing. We carry around unconscious mental maps, built by nature and experience, that organize how we scan the world and how we instantly interpret and order what we see. With these portraits, Douglass was redrawing people's unconscious mental maps. He was erasing old associations about blackness and replacing them with new ones. . . . He was taking an institution like slavery, which had seemed so inevitable, and leading people to perceive it as arbitrary. He was creating a new ideal of a just society and a fully alive black citizen, and therefore making current reality look different in the light of that ideal.[9]

The connection between the physical eye and the inner eye is critical here. For the inner eye is what constructs what the physical eye sees—that is, what the physical eye takes in and processes as the constitutive element of reality. But it also decides what is elided as outside or contrary to reality—this is what Brooks means when he writes, "perception and evaluation are the same thing," for one cannot see—perceive—what one does not "see"—apperceive as constitutively real. For Douglass, the photographic image, once seen, could not be denied, and thus, the constitution of inner eye either would be confirmed or would have to be altered. If one saw enough images of enslaved Africans and the real conditions of their enslavement and enough photographs of Douglass himself, both dignified and defiant, one would be forced into the view that enslavement is not only brutal but also inhumane, for Douglass's photographs would prove the humanity of African American persons.

But Douglass was not speaking of photography, specifically, that is, beyond or outside other aesthetic forms of experience, presentation, or representation. Rather, photography was just one mode of revealing the expressible human element, of transforming and rerouting our unconscious mental maps. It is not, then, a surprise that Douglass relates photography with other forms of aesthetic expression, in particular, literature and music—for images come in many forms, as do presentations and representations to give humanity a holistic picture of truth. That is, for Douglass, the photographic image, as well as the written word and the song, moves the human soul and sets it on the inner-eye construction of reality. Douglass notes, "As to the moral and social influences of pictures, it would hardly be extravagant to say of it, what Moore has said of that of ballads, give me the making of a nation's ballads, and I care not who has the making of its Laws. The pictures and the ballads are alike, if not equally social forces—the one reaching and swaying the heart by the eye, and the other by the ear" ("Pictures and Progress," 456). The significance of this claim cannot be overlooked. For Douglass, an abolitionist, to claim that photographic images and songs and ballads are more significant to the building a nation than are its laws tells us how Douglass understood law. For Douglass, it seems, law is merely a concrete, material expressions of another, more fundamental organizing logic—the logic of relationality, the logic of our "unconscious mental maps." As noted earlier, if we could shift these maps or the inner eye, we could reconstitute the world at the level of its logic, which is more fundamental and profound than statutes alone. Douglass continues, "Dry logic and elaborate arguments, though perfect in all their appointments, and though knitted together as a coat of mail, lay down the law to empty benches. But he who speaks to the feelings, who enters the soul's deepest meditations . . . will never want for an audience" ("Pictures and Progress," 462).

Humans are inherently *feeling* creatures, whose reason itself is not outside or separate from emotion but is constituted within emotion or feeling. For Douglass, emotion or feeling is the governing logic—or organizing principle—through which the world is ordered and on which reason signifies in the formation of its laws. We can situate Douglass here counter to the intellectual positivist tradition that deemed the world an inherently ordered space, which reason alone could penetrate, understand, replicate, and eventually master. Yet Douglass is not arguing, as Maurice Merleau-Ponty does in *The Visible and the Invisible*, that "we see the things themselves, the world is what we see," but "if we ask ourselves what is this *we*, what *seeing* is, and what *thing* or *world* is, we enter into a labyrinth of difficulties and contradictions,"[10] for Douglass, as a Negro, was entering the world that Merleau-Ponty inherited, in which reason and experience were in tension. Douglass's entrance to the world where perceptual faith is problematic to reason itself, where concepts have been separated out from phenomenal experience, was through witnessing white Americans, for the most part, either flatly deny (as in the South) or apathetically ignore (as in the North) what, for him, was clearly present before their own physical eyes—Negro humanity. The photographic image could change all of this—it could reject the denials and animate apathy.

Douglass, the Negro seated before the camera, existed in a world dominated by inner-eye constructions that determined what the physical eyes took in as either inevitable (in the sense of northern apathy) or natural (in the sense of southern racism) facts. In this world, Douglass argues, there is no need for *more* reason, for this kind of reason was in conflict with the world that Douglass lived and perceived. Douglass argued that a world constituted by these oppositional poles was a world at odds with itself. In this world, neither argument can actually be victorious, for the premise on which they are in debate is a false premise, one that contradicts the very nature of humanity itself.

It is in *this* world, Douglass argues, being confronted with the image—in the photograph, in the singing voice, in the written word—can have more sway than reason, dry logic, or even law itself. It is this world that the inner workings of the moving machinery behind the face need to be reanimated, brought back to conscious life in critical reflection of the old habits of obeying what has been taken to be objective historical fact, rather than misguided subjective speculative expression ("Pictures and Progress," 465). For arguing the humanity of the Negro with reason alone is like stating that Niagara Falls is a "river of this or that volume falling over a ledge of rocks two hundred feet" or that thunder is "a jarring noise"; neither are "fitly described when it is said to be." Rather, for Douglass, the phenomenal truth of Niagara Falls, thunder, or universal humanity is a truth that is revealed in the fullness of "its sublimity and glory" ("Pictures and Progress," 462).

In the world that Douglass sought to bring about, the dichotomies of reason and phenomenal experience, reason and feeling or emotion, would not exist; rather, these dichotomies would merge into a union where they would be mutually supportive—reason confirming phenomenal experience, feeling or emotion confirming reason.

Yet Douglass recognized that he lived in a world of enslavement wherein the contested idea and image of the Negro offered resistance or apathy to the abolitionist cause and made the possibility of mutually supportive relationship between reason, feeling, and phenomenal experience, in the search of the glorified object of truth, difficult to achieve. The topic of enslavement, though, was not of central concern in his photography lectures, as it is elsewhere; rather, it is the world out of which the institution emerges and the fact that it is not individual persons who constitute this world-order-meaning-logic but the government itself that has constituted this order-logic in shouldering the burdens of slavery. Slavery as an institutional truth concealed larger epistemic problems in phenomenal world constitution. Obedience to the phenomenal world presented as given, inevitable, and natural was the problem. Such obedience, though, was only possible through the image of the Negro, for this image, more than any other, came to represent the nation as a whole. And if, as Douglass argued, "every great pillar in our national temple is shaken" and the nation finds itself in a "dreadful calamity," it was because the nation was unable, due to government-supported false images of the Negro, to face the truth, obvious to Douglass, about reality ("Pictures and Progress," 464).[11]

This false idea of the Negro, even when appointed toward noble ends, actually stood in the way of the nation achieving its full glory of itself and "the sublime mission of man" in his quest of the "*discovery of truth*—and all conquering resistance to all adverse circumstances whether moral or physical" ("Pictures and Progress," 472). For example, Douglass was known to be a moving orator, speaking with fire and eloquence on the conditions of enslavement and the subject of abolitionism. He had become known for his speeches, and both subject matter and rhetorical pathos were expected. For Douglass, an image of himself had been created, as had expectation in the white abolitionist audience, the habit of seeing what they expected to see. Douglass's photography lecture was "almost a total failure," his audience showing frustration in not getting what was expected by booing, Douglass only saving himself "by switching off suddenly from his subject, and pitching in on the great question of the day." Whether the image of the Negro is positive or negative, if it does not affirm the fundamental issue of human liberty, rather than spectatorship, it cannot offer spiritual, emotional, social, and political perfection, in the individual or the nation.

The image of the Negro thus represented spectacle and held within it expectations demanded to be met. This image, for Douglass, was critical, for it is in it that we can see a particular moment in the aesthetic experience of the human, for this image represented life "*both as it is* and *as it seems*" ("Pictures and Progress," 461–62; emphasis mine). The duality of this phrase is key in understanding our earlier discussion in the introduction to the text on the both/and fluidity of blackness and black maleness, for it is the image of the Negro that both confirms and disconfirms, asserts and negates, and represents American life as it is and as it seems. It is also this image of the Negro in its duality that presents and represents the lacuna of knowledge inherent in the ambiguity of the both/and, where one cannot quite tell what *is* from what *seems to be*, suggesting that life is at once speculative but also certain, mutable but also immutable. It is this ambiguity that at once charges Douglass's autobiographical works and his fictional historical novella with their narrative form and creates deep anxiety and also causes white American audiences to cling tightly to images that produce stable notions of truth, fact, and history.

Douglass, in his own life and in his written work, utilizes this lacuna to curate his own image, to influence and navigate the space between truth, fact, and history. His fictional historical novella captures each of these elements, as Douglass utilizes the lead character of this work to explore how the impact of images and the both/and fluidity of the Negro work to shape how he wrote about freedom and liberty, resistance and violence, and the possible morality of rebellion and insurrection.

The task, then, in what remains is to discover how to read Douglass himself and his works in the way that the Negro is both seen and "seen" as perception and perspective. Reading as seeing and "seeing" means interpreting Douglass and his work both intratextually (with regard to itself) and extratextually (with regard to the larger social, political, and historical worlds), reading his fictional historical novella *The Heroic Slave* within itself but also alongside his photography lecture "Pictures and Progress," as well as alongside his more well-known autobiographical work *Narrative of Frederick Douglass: An American Slave* (1845).

Julia Faisst has gone as far as to note that Douglass's *Heroic Slave* is pivotal for understanding both his lecture on photographs and his autobiographical works. In her essay "Degrees of Exposure: Frederick Douglass, Daguerreotypes, and Representations of Freedom," she writes,

> From its inception in 1839, photography was taken as an essential metaphor behind the democratic aesthetic. Douglass' autobiographies and speeches, and in particular his first and only foray into fiction from 1853, "The Heroic Slave," were products of this increasingly ocular time.... Having undergone a life-altering transformation from slave to free man, Douglass embarked on a literary journey which necessitated a threefold revision of his autobiography. In it, he takes the kind of liberties with re-writings and re-interpretations of a life-story that is generally associated with fiction writing—and produced his piece of genuine literature, "The Heroic Slave."[12]

More will be said of *The Heroic Slave* later. As for now, what is significant to note is that Douglass cultivates three main images of the Negro—the photographic image, the written image, and the oral image—and that this fictional historical novella brings all of these elements together.

Part 2: *The Heroic Slave* and Douglass's Literary Technique

> Irony and absurdity are not only thorns in the briarpatch in which they themselves were bred and born but also precisely what literary statement is forever trying to provide adequate terms for!
>
> —Albert Murray, *The Hero and the Blues*

Frederick Douglass begins his fictional historical narrative *The Heroic Slave* with a description of our heroic slave as chattel. He writes,

> The state of Virginia is famous in American annals for the multitudinous array of her statesmen *and heroes*.... Let those account for it who can, but there stands the fact, that a man who loved liberty as well as did Patrick Henry—who deserved it as much as Thomas Jefferson—and who fought for it with a valor as high, an arm as strong, and against odds as great, as he who led all the armies of the American colonies through the great war for freedom and independence, lives now only in the chattel records of his native State.[13]

Heroism, it seems, in part is the constitution of liberty. If we remember, the first governor of the state of Virginia in 1775 at the Virginia Convention, in opposition to British taxation, exclaimed, "Give me liberty or give me death," a remark held in American lore to be a swaying remark of the Revolutionary War. Such liberty, as Patrick Henry exhibited, was only a fraction of that of the chattel given no more status than that of a horse or an ox. Ironically, as Henry's heroism seems to be in part also tied to his relationship to the greatness of his birth state, the greatness of the bourgeoning American freedom, and idea of the sacrifice inherent in the necessities of human imagination and human action, a man, given over to the status of chattel but who bears these same elements (of birth state, of the greatness of freedom—and the bourgeoning act of emancipatory independence—and the idea of ultimate sacrifice) is also denied the status of heroism. Emergent out of a fundamental and primal liberatory act—understood as the Revolutionary War—the very *idea* of freedom also gave rise to the idea of American exceptionalism—that very essence that was to define our difference from other nations on the Earth. Tied together, liberation, freedom, and exceptionalism were all defined by this emancipatory act of independence.

It seems that the concomitance of these traditional American features—of liberty, freedom, emancipation, and independence—confronted by another traditional American feature, chattel enslavement, gave rise to the necessity of Douglass's narrative telling as fictional literature, revealing the true nature and meaning of heroism and the heroic condition. In other words, it was the very conflict of these traditions borne out in the actions of an enslaved man, Madison Washington, that, for Douglass, came to define heroism and heroic action in the American context. For Douglass, Washington and Henry's actions were tied together, one defining the other, American heroism requiring both what is written in the historical record and that which is not written; that which is the marker of a new constitutional system of law and that which contradicts this system. Douglass's penning of the slave as heroic links Patrick Henry to Madison Washington ironically through the metaphorical similitude of their liberatory acts—Henry's act of independence through words and Washington's through marronage.

What is interesting about Douglass's fictional story is his noncommitment to classifying Madison Washington's status with reference to his escape. As we will see later, Douglass does not reveal to his reader exactly how Washington liberates himself from enslavement; he is just emancipated without a definite act marking his freedom. What Douglass does allow the reader to see is that Washington, while set against his enslavement is also unable to leave his enslaved wife, giving him, rather than the clean break from oppression, that Henry thought he had, a sort of status in between "petit" and "grand" marronage—what can be referred to as an ambiguous state of liberty.[14]

What allows Douglass to depict Madison Washington's liberty status ambiguously is the fact that little is known of Madison Washington, and, as such, how Douglass presented and represented a social, political, and aesthetic choice. As Cynthia S. Hamilton highlights, "Douglass' use of a historical figure about whom so little is known appears a somewhat quirky choice. On closer examination, however, the choice of hero becomes explicable, and the subtleties of Douglass' narrative strategy begin to emerge."[15]

Douglass had alternatives to Washington to construct a narrative about the critical issues of freedom and liberty, emancipation and independence, and the moral questions of resistance and violence, rebellion and insurrection, struggle and heroism: Toussaint Louverture, Denmark Vesey, Nathaniel Turner, Joseph Cinque. But he chose Madison Washington; this choice of Washington signals Douglass's commitments and should shape how we read the narrative arc of the story as a whole.[16] As such, "Douglass' narrative strategy" to choose Madison Washington as the central figure was an act that was neither accidental nor insignificant. Rather, it signaled how Douglass was going to handle these critical issues in the novella and how, in his handling of them, he would construct an image—that is, presentation, representation—for and of enslaved Africans, in particular, enslaved African men. The "quirky choice" to use Washington thus reifies the earlier discussion of the phenomenology of the image of the Negro and the subjective constructive elements of historical and objective fact. In the framework of this narrative, Washington becomes less a character and more of an image, not for the physical eye but a thought image for the inner eye.

Madison Washington, then, as a figure of whom little is known and of whom little is made, is less a historical figure and more a literary technique. It can be argued that Douglass's choice of Washington was a literary decision *because* less is known of him and *because* he is less of a figure of controversy; so more could be imprinted onto him, and through him Douglass could paint a more fluid narrative without the problems of historiography and historicity. Not only does Douglass use Washington to tell a narrative of freedom and liberty, emancipation and independence, and the moral questions of resistance and violence, rebellion and insurrection, struggle, and heroism; he also uses Washington to tell a metanarrative about subjectivity, aesthetic approximation of fact, phenomenological reality, and the meaning and value of history and historical truth.

As literary technique, Madison Washington is an ambiguous figure, both conceptually and materially, allowing Douglass to craft a historical fictive narrative alongside a metanarrative, which addressed the aforementioned core issues. Madison Washington's ambiguous status allowed Douglass to speak but not speak, to write but not write, ultimately to occupy an ambiguous position with regard to his own thoughts on freedom and liberty, emancipation and independence, and the moral questions of resistance and violence, rebellion and insurrection, struggle, and heroism, while addressing these ideas in written form. More will be said of this later.

Immediately, there is the ambiguity of the name itself: Madison Washington—conceptually, a blending of two names: president James Madison (1751–1836), the fourth president, who, though conflicted over the morality of the institution of slavery, owned slaves, one of whom, Paul Jennings, after purchasing his freedom from Daniel Webster, penned his own White House memoir in 1865, *A Colored Man's Reminiscences of James Madison*; and president George Washington (1732–1799), the first president of the United States, who himself owned slaves and who, though his views on the institution were to change over the course of his life, still could not, in the duration of his existence, bring himself to see their liberation. Madison Washington's own name metaphorically represents the internal struggle not only within the nation but within each of the men—Madison and Washington had each argued at times for slavery but had privately questioned the institution but nevertheless denied the liberty of the enslaved. Madison Washington represented this both/and status in his name but also in his embodiment and actions—as a man who through his actions liberated himself at a time when his liberty was denied and fought against the institution that denied him the capacity for resistance.

Secondarily, there is ambiguity of voice. *The Heroic Slave* is broken into four parts, surrounding two key scenes. The initial scene places Washington in the woods, confessing to God about his enslaved condition, the enslaved condition of his wife, and the in-between status of his marronage liberty. The last scene places Washington on the ship *Creole* in the midst of a slave rebellion, eventually commandeering the ship and sailing it to the British Virgin Islands and to his own freedom. What is curious, though, is *who* Douglass elects to narrate these two critical, bookend events, for it is in these two events that we learn the details of Washington and his views on his enslavement, his wife's enslavement, and his own marronage condition. It is not Madison Washington or any other black character whom Douglass elects to voice these pivotal scenes but two white characters: Mr. Listwell, a northerner traveling through the state of Virginia, voices the first scene; and Mr. Grant, a seaman aboard the *Creole*, narrates the second. But, what is more, it is in these two critical scenes that Douglass also directly addresses the core issues of freedom and liberty, emancipation and independence, and the moral questions of resistance and violence, rebellion and insurrection, struggle, and heroism.

It seems odd that Douglass would allow two white men to shape how readers see and "see" Washington and these critical issues, when Douglass could have allowed Washington himself to be the voice addressing them. The strangeness of this decision is especially heightened once readers realize that this fictional historical account was published in 1852, in between Douglass's two pivotal autobiographies, *Narrative of the Life of Frederick Douglass, an American Slave*, published in 1845, and *My Bondage and My Freedom*, published in 1855. Readers must ask, What does it mean that Douglass would pen a fictional account of the issues discussed in both autobiographies—was it meant to signal something about narrative storytelling generally and autobiographies in particular? And why would Douglass pen a fictional historical account of freedom and liberty, emancipation and independence, and the moral questions of resistance and violence, rebellion and insurrection, struggle, and heroism, and allow white men to control this narrative? Once again, readers are confronted with what seems to be a literary decision, one that is critical to the construction of the narrative. Why does Douglass obscure what seems to be the most important details of the narrative by voicing them through white characters?

What follows is a short synopsis of the first critical scene:

Imagine a man, standing alone in the woods; imagine another man, watching this man, in these same woods. The first man, it seems, imagines he is alone; the second man knows that he is not. The first man—enslaved—is confessing to God, in the form of a conversation, in the structure of a soliloquy, of his wretched condition as a slave; the second man—a white man—listens, spellbound, to the confession. The second man had never considered the personal weight of enslavement before this moment; but, after this moment, he is forever changed, swearing when returning home to do something about the institution. The first man, upon confessing, is also changed, swearing to never again be enslaved, swearing too to never allow his wife to be enslaved. Both men are witness to a sea-changing event. Or so it seems.

Listwell, traveling horseback through the woods, stops near the edge of a dark forest to allow his horse to drink from a stream, when he hears a voice. Tying up his horse to a nearby tree, Listwell journeys into the forest for a closer listen and to see who was speaking. It was Madison Washington, alone, speaking. Listwell, hiding behind a fallen tree, hears the following:

> What is freedom to me, or I to it? I am a slave—born a slave, an abject slave—even before I made part of this breathing world, the scourge was platted for my back; the fetters were forged for my limbs . . . But here am I, a man—yes, a man!—with thoughts and wishes, with powers and faculties as far as angel's flight. . . . No—no—I wrong myself—I am no coward. *Liberty I will have, or die in the attempt to gain it.* . . . This cringing submission to insolence and curses! This living under the constant dread and apprehension of being and transferred, like a mere brute, is too much for me. I will stand it no longer. . . . My resolution is fixed. *I shall be free.* (*Heroic Slave*, 12–13; emphasis mine)

Readers are to understand this as a pivotal moment of transformation. Washington began questioning his relationship to freedom and ended with the resolution that freedom belonged to him. Setting aside the irony of Patrick Henry's phrasing of liberty and death, we see Washington transforming from a slave questioning freedom to a man willing to die to attain it. Douglass, in *Narrative of the Life*, undergoes a similar transformation through his violent confrontation with the slave breaker Edward Covey. In *Narrative of the*

Life, though, Douglass does not actively reflect on his enslaved condition in relationship to freedom, as he does in this fictional scene, but he nevertheless makes the same declaration at the end: he was no longer a slave but a man, a free man.[17] The question is why Douglass would pen his own transformation from enslavement to freedom and manhood in his own voice but pen Washington's transformation in the voice of Listwell.

As it stands, what Washington actually said in the forest remains unknown without Listwell's testimony, and what stands out then is not so much *what* Washington may have said but *how* Douglass decided to retell it. The *what* becomes *how* and subsequently *where*. As noted earlier, in our investigation into blackness and black maleness, we are not so much concerned with question or investigation into the who or what of blackness and black maleness but where, as in, Where can black men go to articulate themselves and the world, from what location does one hear this voice? And given that Washington, from Listwell's accounting, imagined himself alone in the woods yet still unable to speak for himself, we see this issue as a critical concern.

As Washington becomes an enigma, his voice and words a lacuna of meaning, we come to see and "see" Madison Washington vulnerable in that where he speaks remains hidden, and he himself remains hidden—readers do not hear his voice but its approximation; in short, we hear Listwell's voice-as-Washington's-voice. And given that Douglass was well aware of the argument that Africans lacked the interior or subjective life—and thus humanity—to write their own stories, to situate themselves existentially, self-reflectively, one must ask why Douglass chose to replicate this idea by making Washington's transformational moment hearsay? Douglass here seems to be attempting to say something, both about freedom and liberty, emancipation and independence and the moral questions of resistance and violence, rebellion and insurrection, struggle, and heroism, and also about something else entirely. This literary technique and analytic strategy in writing about an issue to write about something other than the issue, by speaking by not speaking, revealing as concealing, lies at the heart of black literature and reveals something about Douglass's deployment of blackness and black maleness. If, in fact, this scene is about these issues and not about these issues, what then is being revealed with their deployment?

Once we eschew the central concerns assumed to be present, what stands out immediately in this scene is the dynamic between the watcher and the watched. It is a phenomenal exchange but of an ironic sort. Within traditional motifs of Western existential phenomenology, phenomenological exchange happens either within the individual (as a sort of internal solipsistic monologue) or in intersubjectively. Yet in this scene, neither and both occur. There is the phenomenal internal exchange of Washington's soliloquy, but this exchange is narrated through a secondary party, reporting to readers what he has heard, negating the existential authenticity of the moment. On the other hand, the intersubjective phenomenal exchange is only partial, in that

Listwell "stealthily drew near the solitary speaker . . . concealing himself by the side of a huge fallen tree" (*Heroic Slave*, 12), negating the authenticity of an intersubjective exchange where each subject is affected by the presence of the other. And yet something phenomenal is being exchanged in this moment. The question is, What?

Listwell imagines himself invisibly watching Washington and, thus, watching a genuine existential moment of discovery and self-possession as Washington migrates from reflecting on his condition as enslaved to the resolution of his manhood and freedom. In this moment, Listwell witnesses the phenomenal reality of self-recognition and self-possession outside the normative framework of law or societal expectation. We can see Washington presented as both outside the law (as an escaped slave) and at the same time beyond the law (in declaring himself free). In this moment, Washington's black male both/and fluid identity becomes starkly clear—he is at once god-like in his self-creation ex nihilo (or creation from the nothing of enslavement and social death: ex negrolo?); he is also beast-like in his refusal to acknowledge the normative law that negates his self-possession or self-assertion. In both cases, readers recognize that Washington does not need society to confirm or disconfirm his existence or identity.

Interestingly, Douglass has Listwell remark on both of these aspects when describing Washington's both/and fluid black male existence. Listwell notes,

> Madison was of manly form. Tall, symmetrical, round, and strong. In his movements he seemed to combine, with the strength of the lion, a lion's elasticity. His torn sleeves disclosed arms like polished iron. His eye, lit with emotion, kept guard under a brow as dark and glossy as the raven's wing. His whole appearance betokened Herculean strength; yet there was nothing savage or forbidding in his aspect. A giant's strength, but not a giant's heart was in him. A broad mouth and nose spoke only of good nature and kindness. . . . He was just the man you would choose when hardships were to be endured, or danger to be encountered—intelligent and brave. In a word, he was one to be sought as a friend, but to be dreaded as an enemy. (*Heroic Slave*, 13–14)

Washington is compared at once to beasts (a lion and a raven) and also a (demi) od [god] (Hercules). We see in this description both beastly and godlike elements as well as natural elements—Madison is both of this world and beyond this world, both made of the stuff of existence and beyond the bounds of material existence. He is to be feared because he is somewhere in between the normative bounds of law, boundlessness outside law, and fundamental boundedness within nature. Yet Douglass is quick to note that "there was nothing savage or forbidding" about him and that he was additionally "intelligent and brave"—that is, both autonomous and moral—to help situate

Washington as man/not-man and beast/not-beast and god-like, on whose shoulders and arms a child might play or dance. Washington, with all his power, was inherently gentle and kind but threatening, only if challenged and only for the sake of justice.

What is the narrative strategy of presenting Washington in this light? Is it similar to Douglass himself sitting before a camera, having himself photographed, it seems, to alter the image of the Negro from beast-like to dignified? If that were the case, why creation ex nihilo? Is Douglass making of Washington a folkloric character? And, if so, why have Listwell offer the description instead of an omniscient narrator? Perhaps we are not asking the right question: perhaps this scene and the description of Washington are not about Washington at all but really about Listwell and how he can be utilized to carry forward a story seemingly about a black man.

Douglass here seems to be conducting a sleight-of-hand narrative strategy, placing into Listwell's mouth both Washington's words and also his own words in description of Washington. It must be noted that Listwell's description of Washington directly follows his reporting of Washington's words—adding to the seamlessness to these two moments. In placing Washington's words and his description in Listwell's mouth, Douglass is distancing himself from the claims, all the while still making the claims but from a more relatable and reliable source. If we were to think of slave narratives as analytic tools deployed to shift the inner eyes of white America and thus to shift the image of the Negro, then one would need a literary technique to do so; it turns out that Listwell, not Washington, might be Douglass's own literary technique.

Yet there exists another possibility for Douglass's literary technique: Douglass places Listwell in the forest to hear Washington as a constructed image for Listwell to consume. Within this interpretation, Washington's self-creation ex nihilo was not internal but external. That is, Washington's internal alteration and transformation, wherein "that moment he was free, at least in spirit," was meant to be interpreted by Listwell as Washington's having "just solved a difficult problem, or vanquished a malignant foe," but was a theatrical deployment of blackness to act on and transform Listwell's soul (*Heroic Slave*, 13). Perhaps Washington was deployed by Douglass as a literary technique to waken Listwell—and apathetic white readers—into abolitionism and activism (*Heroic Slave*, 16).

* * *

Douglass opens part 2 of the narrative five years removed from the incident in the forest. Listwell is in his home in Ohio with his wife and dog. All three are seated around a fire; outside a wind and rainstorm brews. The year is 1840, which is a vital piece of information to remember. Washington, lost in the forest, cold and tired, approaches Listwell's house seeking refuge from the weather. As we will come to find out, it is the light inside the house, glowing through the lattice, that compels Washington's approach. It is not clear, in this moment, if Washington interpreted this light through the lattice as a sign of a safe house or if he merely approached the house, as Douglass seems to suggest, without knowing its occupants, simply wanting refuge for the night. Listwell seems to know Washington is coming. Douglass offers the following dialogue:

> Slightly hesitating, the traveller [Washington] walked in, however, without regarding his host with a scrutinizing glance. "No, sir," said he, "I have come to ask you a great favor."
> Instantly, Mr. Listwell exclaimed, (as the recollection of the Virginia forest scene flashed upon him,) "Oh, sir, I know not your name, but I have seen your face, and heard your voice before. I am glad to see you. I know all. You are flying for your liberty—be seated—be seated—banish all fear. You are safe under my roof." . . .
> Thus assured, the stranger said, "Sir, you have rightly guessed, I am, indeed, a fugitive from slavery. . . . I am on my way to Canada. It was my purpose to have continued my journey till morning; but the piercing cold, and the frowning darkness compelled me to seek shelter; and, *seeing a light through the lattice of your window, I was encouraged to come here and beg the privilege named.* You will do me a great favor by affording me shelter for the night."
> "A resting-place, indeed, sir, you shall have; not, however, in my barn, but in the best room of my house. Consider yourself, if you please, under the roof of a friend; for such I am to you, and to all your deeply injured race." (*Heroic Slave*, 19–20; emphasis mine)

The year is 1840. By this year, the 1793 Fugitive Slave Law was rapidly growing weak, with a number of whites refusing to participate in the returning of slaves and because of a federal ruling that nonslave states did not have to, by law, offer aid in the hunting or capturing of enslaved persons. With this information in hand, which Douglass surely would have known, we see him constructing narrative possibilities. He leaves open the possibility that Listwell, after hearing Washington in the forest, was now turned abolitionist and placed the lantern in the window to indicate this. Under this reading, then, it is not at all surprising that Listwell "felt all the evening as if somebody would be here to-night"—someone but not necessarily Washington (*Heroic Slave*, 19).

But there is another possibility for Washington's arrival on Listwell's doorstep. In having Washington visit Listwell's home, Douglass was enacting uncontrolled irony, asking readers to suspend their critical, historical eye for the sake of the narrative. Readers are tasked with not looking too closely into why Washington would not only knock on a stranger's door, enter his home without a "scrutinizing glance," but also fully confess both his maroon status and his plans to continue north to Canada. Douglass, though, does try to balance his story, making Washington initially hesitant. "The timidity and suspicion of persons escaping from slavery," Douglass writes, "are easily awakened, and often what is intended to dispel the one, and to allay the other, has precisely the opposite effect" (*Heroic Slave*, 19). But Douglass does not tarry long on this point; rather, he mentions it and in the very next line moves away from the issue, telling his readers, "Quickly observing the unhappy impression made by his words and action, Mr. Listwell assumed a more quiet and inquiring aspect, and finally succeeded in removing the apprehensions which his very natural and generous salutation had aroused" (19–20). Douglass does not tell us *how* Listwell convinced Washington of his good intentions. He does not let us in, in this pivotal moment of suspicion-turned-trust, in the same way that he does not let us into the head of Washington himself in his forest soliloquy. Instead, there seems to be a lacuna of information as to what occurred in the moment between what is said and what is not said, which Douglass never addresses.

We see a similar example of this uncontrolled irony and the suspension of critical analysis in Douglass's *Narrative of the Life*, where he writes about his fight with Edward Covey. In the fight, Douglass asks his readers to consent to the idea not only that a young boy could physically defeat a slave breaker in the presence of other white men but that a slave breaker, having been defeated in front of other white men, would accept Douglass's humanity and Douglass's freedom, never touching him again. In each moment, Douglass can be seen as deploying blackness and black maleness theatrically for the impact it might have on readers. Recalling Douglass's photography lecture, where he notes, "he who speaks to the feelings, who enters the soul's deepest meditations, holding the mirror up to nature, revealing the profoundist mysteries of the human heart to the eye and ear by action and by utterance, will never want for an audience," we can begin to see how the theatrical deployment of black maleness in the narrative possibility of uncontrolled irony can be enacted for the purpose of constructing the inner eye of his readers, who, it seems, Douglass hopes will be transformed like Listwell hearing Washington's forest declaration.

Whether for the sake of narrative possibility or uncontrolled irony, Douglass, in placing Washington at Listwell's doorstep, is asking his readers to suspend critical analysis, while leaving them within a narrative lacuna. It does not matter that these pivotal scenes appear internally disjointed. It does not matter that it is curious that Washington, an escaped slave, who, Douglass observed, "loved liberty" so much that he absconded into the woods to relieve himself of his chattel status, would be as careless as to confess his marronage, right out in the open, in the clearing of said forest. It makes little difference if we are to believe that a man, hiding for years in said forest accustomed to hearing the slightest sound, would have allowed Listwell, a man not himself trained in capture or evasion, to sneak up on him unbeknownst. It matters little that five years later Washington just happened to choose Listwell's home for his stop to request "a great favor." Just as it does not really matter why Washington went from skeptical maroon to trusting friend in the span of a sentence.

Taken together—in the forest, at the doorstep—neither of the two critical moments speak to an authentic, straightforward existential bildungsroman narrative of enslavement to freedom, nor are they meant to do so, just as Douglass's fight with Covey was not meant to be taken literally. Rather, readers are led in one direction to point in another direction. In Listwell's retelling of Washington's forest speech and in his description of Washington, we see and "see" Douglass at once manipulating readers' perception, by placing Washington's voice in Listwell's mouth, but we also we see and "see" Douglass using Listwell as a credible source to give Washington a sense of dignity that he might not receive on his own as black and male. In Washington's choice of Listwell's home, we see Douglass utilizing the theatrical deployment of blackness for readers' own consumption interest.

In both interpretations of the phenomenological exchange—Listwell placed in the forest; Washington placed at Listwell's doorstep—readers can see and "see" Douglass making literary decisions. Readers are also led to wonder if in these two moments of exchange, Douglass is not saying something additional about black liberation, black male vulnerability, and the status of black heroism. On the one hand, Washington's forest transformation could be interpreted as Douglass's claim that black liberation was not social but spiritual, internal and outside white recognition. On the other hand, Douglass does place Listwell in the forest to overhear and narrate this transformation—was it necessarily for Washington's benefit or solely for Listwell's own benefit of his own self-transformation? In placing Washington at Listwell's doorstep and having Listwell aid in Washington's escape, is Douglass saying that white aid is essential to black liberation—but only to social and political liberation, not spiritual? Is Douglass alerting his potential audiences of both/and—for his white audiences, cajoling their activism; for black audiences, not to depend on white recognition for self-liberation? What, though, in these exchanges is the status of heroism?

Listwell was a literary technique deployed by Douglass to speak objectively and from a position of authority about the both/and fluid status of blackness and black men and how this status itself solidified the Negro as citizen and equal. On the other hand, Washington was a literary technique deployed to liberate Listwell from his own apathy. Listwell was deployed for the sake of Washington's liberation; Washington was deployed for the sake of saving Listwell's soul. In both cases, Washington and Listwell were literary decisions made by Douglass and manipulated images of Douglass. In either interpretation, Douglass's hero is a manipulated self-image by and of the Negro himself.

Does this discovery of Douglass's potentially doubling and embedding messages, and deploying a black man to do so, say anything about the precarious and vulnerable position of black men? Douglass, it seems, was unable or unwilling to directly state his intended claim; rather, through lacuna of narrative information and through a disjointed plotline of seemingly inauthentic existential expression, he makes his claims indirectly. This is at once a literary technique and a literary decision but also points to his own vulnerability in his own inability to say directly what he wished. Douglass here replicates the idea of the manipulation of images to the end of truth and social justice, and like himself poised, hands clenched at his waist, jacket slightly opened to display a small wrinkled section, we see in his fictional history a small moment of vulnerability within poised defiance.

Part 3: The Heroic Status of Mr. Washington

I

Perhaps we learn something more about Douglass's literary technique and his literary decisions in his presentation and representation of Washington as a heroic figure. As noted earlier, Washington occupies multiple, seemingly conflicting positions, due to his both/and fluid identity. He is at once a liberated man, beyond-man, a fugitive from law, as well as a subperson and nonman. But we also learn that Washington is a husband and a father, and these additional elements of his identity also weigh on the literary choices Douglass makes in portraying him. Seemingly, it was not sufficient to portray Washington only in reference to enslavement, liberation, freedom, and abolitionism; Douglass additionally needed to present him emotionally as a husband and father. I say "needed to" because, given that much was not known of Washington, Douglass did not have to add this additional wrinkle, unless it served some larger purpose.

We learn about Washington's family only after he trusts the Listwells and opens up about his marronage status: "I gathered up the few rags of clothing I had, and started, as I supposed, for the North and for freedom. I must not stop to describe my feelings on taking this step. It seemed like taking a leap into the dark. The thought of leaving my poor wife and two little children caused me indescribable anguish; but consoling myself with the reflection that once free, I could, possibly, devise ways and means to gain their freedom also, I nerved myself up to make the attempt" (*Heroic Slave*, 22–23). Douglass here juxtaposes the flight of marronage with the emotional connections of family. It is important to note, from our conversation earlier, that while freedom and liberty may be transformative spiritually, their emotional aspect is unclear: What is the status of emotion in Douglass's articulation of Washington and his deployment? In juxtaposing marronage and emotion, we learn that Douglass's deployment was incomplete.

While Listwell had described Washington as beast-like, god-like, humane, intelligent, fearsome, and gentle, he did not describe his emotional state, outside of "agony" and "triumphant." With the additional elements of his wife and two children, we see and "see," perhaps, a glimpse into Douglass as a man and a writer. This scene may remind readers of Douglass's own narrative about his mother, whom he only saw "four or five times" and never "by the light of day."[18] Douglass tells us, "My mother and I were separated when I was but an infant—before I knew her as my mother," but she nevertheless traveled twelve miles each way to see him. Whether it is true that Douglass's mother traveled twelve miles "after the performance of her day's work" is not relevant.[19] What readers are to gather from this story, as from the above example of Washington and his own children, is something about the intuitive emotional truth of a narrative. While the two opening scenes—Washington in the forest and on Listwell's doorstep—were not meant to generate emotional truth, for each seemed untrue with regard to our reflective intuition, the last scene was meant to do just that: a father's or mother's desire for one's children is intuitively emotionally believable.

With this aforementioned example, Douglass alerts us to the idea that sometimes a narrative is meant to convey larger ideas concerning social, political, and spiritual truths, transforming some readers along the way while signaling to others subtle arguments about revolution, liberation, and freedom; at other times, it is meant to convey some intuitive emotional truth. The difficulty, though, with Douglass's *Heroic Slave* is that he mixes these elements in one narrative, potentially confusing readers: *Which* elements are meant to be spirit altering, *which* elements are meant to signal readers to radical liberty and freedom, and *which* elements are meant to carry the emotional truth of the narrative?

The difficulty with Douglass is that commentators have often confused these elements, taking the spirit-altering ones or the subtle revolutionary ones as the emotionally true ones (and vice versa)—for example, scholars have taken his fight with Covey as being deployed for intuitive emotional truth rather than for the sake of being spirit altering for white readers or signaling to black readers something about liberty and freedom. This makes Douglass often difficult to read and to follow and makes commentators want to give only a singular reading of his work.[20]

The multiple, conflicting deployments in *Heroic Slave* are meant create an overall image of blackness and black maleness and are meant to present Washington as a heroic figure, as noted in the title. There is one more critical scene to discuss in Douglass's narrative: the enslaved rebellion of the *Creole*. Sections II and III will discuss the slave rebellion and how Douglass depicts the role Washington played in it as a way of prefiguring his view of heroism and heroic action, but also the role of the heroic in Douglass's own narrative construction. As we will see, it is not merely that Washington was aboard and said to have led the slave rebellion on the *Creole* that makes Washington a heroic figure, for if this were the case, Douglass would have begun and ended the narrative in part 4. The other three parts were meant to create a synoptic image of black male heroism, not as the "stagolee," bad-nigger image, not as the manipulative beguiling Negro, not as the father and husband willing to risk life and limb for his family, but *all* of these and *all* of the literary devices, literary techniques, literary decisions, lacuna of knowledge, uncontrolled irony, ambiguous both/and status of blackness and black maleness.

II

Much of how Washington has been interpreted by scholars depends on the last scene of the story, which is, strangely enough, the one with the least amount of information: mutiny aboard the slaving vessel *Creole*. How Washington is viewed depends on how one sees and "sees" and reads the lacuna of information in the scene: one can read Washington as (1) a strong liberator willing to kill for freedom or (2) a devout, nonviolent figure unwilling to kill on the principle of life—in this case, the principle of life being of a different sort than the principle of liberty. And, adding difficulty, each of the readings is present in Listwell's initial description of Washington: beast-like, god-like, with Herculean strength, gentle, intelligent, a great friend, and a terrible foe.

But to fully get a range of the dimensions of Washington as heroic, we should get a full range of how Douglass depicts him in the story. Let us tell the rest of the story. We left off with Washington hiding in Listwell's home. The next day, Washington is helped by Listwell in escaping to Canada. Upon arrival, Washington cannot bear the idea of his wife and children still enslaved and decides to place his freedom in jeopardy, returning to give her liberty as well. Upon his return, he is caught, and she is murdered.[21] He is transported to the slaving vessel *Creole*, which is to take him farther south, never to return. Prior to boarding the vessel, he is aided, again, by Listwell, with a file. With the aid of the file, Washington leads a revolt, takes hold of the ship, and steers it to Nassau, a British protectorate. Upon arrival, he and the enslaved crew are now free. This is how Douglass portrays him:

> The leader of the mutiny in question was just as shrewd a fellow as ever I met in my life, and was as well fitted to lead in a dangerous enterprise as any one white man in ten thousand. The name of this man, *strange to say*, (ominous of greatness) was MADISON WASHINGTON. In the short time, he had been on board; he had secured the confidence of every officer. The negroes fairly worshipped him. His manner and bearing were such that no one could suspect him of a murderous purpose....
>
> The attack began just about twilight in the evening.... I put my hand quickly in my pocket to draw out my jack-knife; but *before I could draw it*, I was *knocked senseless* to the deck. When I came to myself,... there was not a white man on deck. The sailors were all aloft in the rigging, and dared not come down. Captain Clarke and

> Mr. Jameson lay stretched on the quarter-deck—both dying—while Madison himself stood at the helm unhurt. . . .
>
> . . . I told them that by the laws of Virginia and the laws of the United States, the slaves on board were as much property as the barrels of flour in the hold. At this the stupid blockheads showed their ivory, rolled up their eyes in horror, as if the idea of putting men on a footing with merchandise were revolting to their humanity. When these instructions were understood among the negroes, it was impossible for us to keep them on board. They deliberately gathered up their baggage before our eyes, and, against our remonstrance, poured through the gangway—formed themselves into a procession on the wharf—bid farewell to all on board, and, uttering the wildest shouts of exaltation, they marched, amidst the deafening cheers of a multitude of sympathizing spectators, under the triumphant leadership of their heroic chief and deliverer, MADISON WASHINGTON. (*Heroic Slave*, 64–65)

We see in this depiction, narrated by Mr. Grant, a seaman aboard the vessel, that Washington again encompasses all the elements described earlier: intelligent, a terrible foe, god-like, both man and beyond-man, both legal property and beyond-law. What is interesting, in addition to Grant's depiction of Washington, are the discursive strategies Douglass deploys, similar to those used earlier but for a different effect. Like earlier, Douglass uses an unreliable source to be the main voice of Washington's actions. Douglass can, again, be seen and "seen" as he distances himself from settling on a side in a debate—in the first part, Douglass distanced himself commenting on the physical, moral, and spiritual character of a fugitive slave by having Listwell relay it to the reader; now he distances himself from commenting on the physical, moral, and spiritual nature of a proper liberatory act by placing the description of the mutiny in the mouth of Grant.[22]

Readers are unclear as to what exactly happened aboard the ship and about Washington's role, for Grant, whom Douglass chose to tell this story, could be considered less than honest in multiple ways. On the one hand, Grant was knocked unconscious just before the revolt began; and when he awoke, Washington was at the helm of the ship. On the other hand, Grant was narrating these events to a skeptical white audience who was accusing him of dereliction of duty, if not complicity in the mutiny itself and in stealing the "property."[23] Either way, Douglass is, again, narrating Washington's actions in an indirect manner.

Douglass's ambiguous indirect manner of speaking about slave rebellion, mutiny aboard a slaving vessel, and the possibility of armed and violent resistance, foregrounding liberation, does not allow readers to gauge Douglass's own views on the matter. While Douglass obscures Washington's role and thus the question of whether he is a strong liberator willing to kill, a level-headed leader defending life, or a devoutly nonviolent man, he also obscures his own position on these matters. We can recall that Douglass was well versed in the stories of Toussaint Louverture, John Brown, Nathaniel Turner, and Joseph Cinque—all of whom led violent events of slave rebellion—so one can surmise in Douglass's choosing Washington to discuss slave rebellion, he was, in a sense, expressing his own unwillingness to take a side on the issue. Or so it seems.

Is the title of Douglass's fictive historical narrative ironic, given that Douglass leaves a lacuna of information within the narrative structure, making Washington's heroism unknowable? Or does the title signal that Washington's heroism does not lie in whether he was violent or nonviolent, the leader of the revolt or a passive participant? If the revolt scene was not central to Douglass's understanding of heroism and to Washington's heroism, what is central to the concept, and why include it at the very end of the narrative?

III

Douglass offers something of a glimpse as to what might be at stake in understanding black male heroism, in the various lacunae throughout the story. Given that blackness and especially black maleness is situated in both a black and antiblack world and that black men could not directly demand liberty or freedom through physical confrontation and were forced instead to use guile, moral suasion, indirect discourse, and the deployment of black maleness in various forms, it should not be surprising that the heroic slave was a story about which nothing certain could be said and whose actions toward liberation and freedom were equally as ambiguous. Perhaps Douglass is stating that black male heroism is but indirect direct action, ambiguous social, moral, and political identity wherein the image constructed—both internally and externally—is the only one seen and "seen." Perhaps he is stating that it is, in fact, nothing at all.

In one of the last scenes, Douglass recounts Washington's conversation with Grant about liberty, freedom, morality, and violence, where it is unclear exactly what Washington's or Douglass's position is on the matter. Douglass writes,

> "I [Tom Grant] will state the fact precisely as they came under my own observation. . . . I was completely weakened by the loss of blood, and had not recovered from the stunning blow which felled me to the deck; but it was a little too much for me, even in my prostrate condition, to see our good brig commanded by a *black murderer*. . . . You murderous villain, said I, to the imp at the helm, and rushed him to deal him a blow, when he pushed me back with his strong, black arm, as though I had been a boy of twelve. . . . I started towards Madison again. . . . The rascal now told me to stand back. 'Sir,' said he, '*your

> *life is in my hands. I could have killed you a dozen times over during this last half hour, and could kill you now.* You call me a black murderer. I am not a murderer. God is my witness that LIBERTY, not malice, is the motive for this night's work. . . . We have struck for our freedom. . . . We have done that which you applaud your fathers for doing, if we are murderers, so were they.'" (*Heroic Slave*, 61–62; emphasis mine)

Grant initially describes Washington as a "black murderer." Douglass here is making a subtle point: blackness intensifies all things, in this case murder, for it is the blackness that becomes the ontological marker determining the morality of the action undertaken. Despite the ambiguity in Washington's words—"I *could* have killed you," "*We* have struck for our freedom," "*We* have done that which you applaud"—Grant still situates Washington's actions as murderous, for Washington's blackness disallows him to seek his freedom through liberation.

Douglass's deployment of the lacuna of knowledge here reveals to readers that actions themselves are meaningless absent the particulars of context. Black maleness, it seems, alone is sufficient for crime, especially that of murder. In this scene, it does not so much matter what Washington's actions were aboard the ship; it is his very blackness itself that ontologically determines the morality of his actions or his inactions—he is guilty, even if he is not guilty. This ontological horizon is strong enough that is disallows Grant to "see" what he, in fact, sees: "I confess, gentlemen, I felt myself in the presence of a superior man; one who, had he been a white man, I would have followed willingly and gladly. . . . It was not that his principles were wrong in the abstract; for they are the principles of 1776. But I could not bring myself to recognize their application to one whom I deemed my inferior" (*Heroic Slave*, 64). Grant, an everyman character, represents the everyday racist, just as Listwell, also an everyman character, represents liberal apathy. The deployment of these white character types perhaps says what Douglass will not directly say about black heroic action in relationship to the white racist and the white apathetic: while moral suasion might be sufficient for the latter, the possibility of violent action might be necessary for the former.[24]

Part 4: Of Mr. Murray and Negro Heroism

> I invite you to imagine a rather comically American scenario. The intellectual, a promising young man of color, has made his way to one of the great capitals of Europe. . . .
> He had planned to write during his year abroad (indeed the first he has ever had) a study of Black American intellectuals who came of age after the great wars. He had thought to pay

On Frederick Douglass and the Image of the Negro

> homage to that generation of male artists and critics to whom he felt most indebted, those who had grappled most assiduously with matters of race, gender, and sexuality, those who had been celebrated in his childhood as fine examples of genius, Black, American, genius. He finds himself stifled, however, distracted as he has said, because the work of celebration, of historical recovery, has become suddenly, if not inexplicably, a rather more complicated matter. The gift, the challenge that was given from that earlier generation to his own, was not, he believes, simply an impressive body of literature nor even the heroic and largely successful struggles to advance the civil and human rights of not only Black Americans but indeed much of the human community. It was not even that American people with crinkly hair and brown skin more or less similar to his own crinkly hair and brown skin have come, in some quarters, to be associated with the advance of liberal society. The even more profound gift, the warmly glowing coal that burns with a throbbing, impersonal heat when examined too closely is the knowledge that the Black American has not only had a great hand in the creation of America and thus the world but also and importantly that the Black American, quiet as it's kept, has had a substantial role in the creation of himself.
> —Robert Reid-Pharr, *Once You Go Black*

[*Stage direction*] The Negro is back on stage. The camera and the stool are gone. He stands, appearing to get himself ready for a monologue. He raises his hand in a grand, subtle gesture. Paul Robeson, Frederick Douglass, Booker T. Washington, and countless other black orators present themselves. He begins to elocute. He is erudite. He is the Existential Negro. He is our Hero. *An eruption of applause.*

Albert Murray, staunch critic of "social science fiction fiction" and progressor of the Negro image in the idea of aesthetics and the blues tradition, author of *Omni-Americans*, wrote, at the beginning of his seminal text *The Hero and the Blues*—"originally presented at the University of Missouri, Columbia, in the form of three public lectures on October 7, 8, and 9, 1972"[25]—the following:

> Storybook images are as indispensable to the basic human process of world comprehension and self-definition (and hence personal motivation as well as purposeful group behavior) as are the formulas of physical science or the nomenclature of the social sciences. Such basic insights as may be derived from the make-believe examples of literature are, moreover, as immediately applicable to the most urgent problems of everyday life as are "scientific" solutions.

> With this premise, it might not be too much to say that the most delicately wrought short stories and the most elaborately textured novels, along with the most homespun anecdotes, parables, fables, tales, legends, and sagas, are as strongly motivated by immediate educational (which is to say moral and social) objectives as are the most elementary.[26]

For Murray, stories and the storytelling process are indispensable for what it means to be human. Similarly, Douglass argues that the replication of the image—produced and consumed, spoken and heard, written and read—is that through which "man is able to invert his own subjective consciousness into higher objective form" ("Pictures and Progress," 461). It is an educative process in which the producer is instructing the consumer on not only *what* to see and "see" but also *how* to see and "see." Together, the producer and consumer are creating their mutual world. As such, the phenomenal object—the photographic image, the song, the written word—is the material proof of this phenomenal exchange, this phenomenal agreement as to the nature and meaning of reality. As such, the phenomenal object and the phenomenological exchange are as central to creation and functioning of society as are scientific solutions, for they alert us to imaginative possibilities and foretell the most basic and urgent problems of everyday life. In this sense, stories and storytelling help us to interpret the world as objectively real and help to institute ourselves as figures in that world.

In traditional stories, there is a hero—usually the central character, usually identifiable by the narrative progression. The hero as a character is usually indispensable for carrying forward the thematic structure of the story and delivering its message. For Murray, the hero is not always easily detected or immediately known—to themselves or to readers. The hero sometimes is the one not born heroic but elected from circumstance—elected by what they are called on, at least in the moment, to *become* in order to *be* themselves, in the most fundamental sense—to meet its requirements. In this way, heroism, the hero, and heroic action are as much concerned with the solvency of circumstance as the individual's response to it; both are elemental to the existential double unfolding (of self and context). As such, when framing the hero as central to storytelling, it must also be noted that heroism is relational. Murray writes,

> It is the writer as artist, not the social or political engineer or even the philosopher, who first comes to realize when the time is out of joint. It is he who determines the extent and gravity of the current human predicament, who in effect discovers and describes the hidden elements of destruction, sounds the alarm, and even (in the process of defining "the villain") designates the targets. It is the storyteller working on his own terms as mythmaker (and by implication, as value maker), who defines the conflict, identifies the hero (which is to say

the good man—perhaps better, *the adequate man*), and decides the outcome; and in doing so he not only evokes the image of possibility, but also prefigures the contingencies of a happily balanced humanity and of the Great Good Place.[27]

Murray is not asserting that heroism or the constructed narrative is ethical in any straightforward way or that the storyteller is inherently moral. Rather, he is highlighting that the narrative that the storyteller constructs prefigures or sets the determination of what will be considered the good and the bad or the adequate-to-the-moment (good) or inadequate-to-the-moment (bad). The writer as artist decides, that is, takes measure and depicts, the outcome of this moment and, in doing so, aesthetically centers the balance of reality.

One can see in Douglass's photography lecture and his fictional historical narrative that he is prefiguring and setting forth an image of the Negro but also a concept of the heroic Negro, even amid the narrative lacuna and overall ambiguity. The hero, for Douglass, becomes a gesture, an analytic strategy deployed, a constructed idea of the balance of reality. Douglass serves as an example of black writing, for his offers both an image and its subtextual qualities, which are elements of African American literary aesthetics but especially black male literary works. He talks back and forth between and across different audiences, at different registers, with different messages attached to the same deployed black male character.

Murray, though, complicates matters a bit more, offering nuance to the category, for there are three kinds of heroes: (1) the tragic hero, "whose problem is his own contamination (his own flaws, mistakes, choices, or whatever)"; (2) the comic hero, "whose problem is his naiveté, or lack of perception"; and (3) the melodramatic hero "of some sagas, of some medieval romances, and the scientific success story purifies society. He overcomes his inadequacies . . . by following the proper instructions and acquires the magic formula which cures and saves an ailing body politic."[28]

In many readings of black male literary figures we see a sort of narrative and character construction that follows a mixture of these three kinds of heroism but from within a larger structural arc of a traditional bildungsroman tale. Within this assumptive prefiguration, the hero, through his own flaws, which include his unfailing belief in a social order that is set to his death, is able to show to himself and to the society as a whole its internal flaws and thus, in sacrificing his consciousness (and often his body), helps to purify society, in the process becoming a new man and ushering in a new social order. As noted earlier, many scholars have read Douglass himself as this sort of heroic figure, and Madison Washington could certainly seem to be of this sort as well; but this is a mischaracterization of the deployment of blackness and black maleness.

This idea of the hero, whose very prescience purifies society, is seen over and again, from Douglass to Du Bois, Franz Fanon to Ralph Ellison—one cannot help to see and "see" the DuBoisian double-conscious hero, whose naiveté is his contamination but whose "dogged strength" allows him to overcome his condition by way of a unique sense of clarity, whose mystical and supernatural origins offer him, and only him, the gift by which the nation can be saved, bridging the Negro and Anglo-Saxon with his individual talents.[29] One cannot help but to see and "see" Ellison's narrator, invisible, because "others refuse to see him," but nevertheless comes to the realization that he still must engage society as "even an invisible man has a socially responsible role to fill"[30] or the Fanonian alienated hero who overcomes his racial malady through the scientific process of examining it.[31] Within this framework, Douglass the man and Douglass the writer are transformed into an impulse for reconciliation through his inner heroic strength, his own narrative becoming a transformational moment for his progenitors, which his very being enacts for us. Douglass becomes, as all black heroic figures in this framework, what Murray refers to as the sacrificial goat, wherein we retrace the steps "leading to destruction" and through enacting or deploying the sacrificial goat figure perform a "purification ritual in imitation of the life process itself."[32] Douglass reminds us, like all black heroes, where things went wrong so that we will not repeat them—but, as Murray notes, this desire for reconciliation is not literature or about literature in that it does not teach us anything but offers catharsis.

Which is to say, much of the scholarship on Douglass, as on black intellectual existential figures, tends to be centered on the purification role that he performs, in particular, the almost singular focus on his fight with and victory over the slave breaker Edward Covey as the transformational moment to discuss freedom and liberty, resistance and violence, and the possible morality of rebellion and insurrection, struggle and heroism. In the pivotal scene, Douglass quite literally beats Covey and, by proxy, the slaving system itself and transforms himself from a Negro into a MAN, one whose physical, psychic, and moral prowess cannot be denied. Douglass writes of his fight with Covey,

> Whilst I was obeying his order to feed and get the horses ready for the field, and when in the act of going up to the stable loft for the purpose of throwing down some blades, Covey sneaked into the stable, in his peculiar snake-like way, and seizing me suddenly by the leg, brought me to the stable floor, giving my newly mended body a fearful jar. I now forgot my roots, and remembered my pledge to stand up for my own defense. The brute was endeavoring skillfully to get a slip-knot on my legs, before I could draw up my feet. . . . While down, he seemed to think he had me very securely in his power. He little thought he was—as the rowdies say—"in" for a "rough and tumble" fight; but such was the fact. Whence came the daring spirit necessary to grapple with a man who, eight-and-forty hours before, could, with his slightest word have had me tremble like a leaf in a storm, I do not know; at any rate, I was resolved to fight, and, what was better

still, I was actually hard at it. The fighting madness had come upon me, and I found my strong fingers firmly attached to the throat of my cowardly tormentor; as heedless of consequences, at the moment, *as though we stood as equals before the law*. The very color of the man was forgotten.... He held me, and I held him....

Covey at length (two hours had elapsed) gave up the contest. Letting me go, he said—puffing and blowing at a great rate—"Now, you scoundrel, go to work; I would not have whipped you half so much as I have had you not resisted." The fact was, he had not whipped me at all....

Well, my dear reader, this battle with Mr. Covey—undignified as it was, and as I fear my narration of it is—was the turning point in my "life as a slave." It rekindled in my breast the smoldering embers of liberty.... I WAS A MAN NOW. It recalled to life my crushed self-respect and my self-confidence, and inspired me with a renewed determination to be A FREEMAN.[33]

It is interesting to juxtapose the clarity and the detail with which Douglass describes his fight with Covey with the opacity of Washington's mutiny on the *Creole*, where Douglass could have elaborated in the fashion he did of his fight with Covey but chose instead to occlude its details. When one reads these two depictions next to each other—two depictions of mutiny, freedom, and liberty—and takes notice that they were published but *two years apart* (1853 and 1855, respectively), one must ask why two different rhetorical strategies were used for two quite similar thematic scenes. What is Douglass telling us about heroism? Was Washington heroic, while Douglass himself was not? If black male heroism is but indirect direct action, ambiguous social, moral, and political identity, wherein the black male hero both saves the soul of the apathetic and perhaps violently punishes the racist, can we simply read Douglass enacting two different rhetorical strategies, which are not in conflict with each other?

If Douglass is enacting two different strategies, not in conflict with each other, where there are parallel narratives that are also perpendicular—as in the case of Washington himself—it seems that reading Douglass's works in themselves but also across his oeuvre, one might realize some evidence of what Murray terms a "farce." Murray defines a farce in the following manner: "Essentially, a farce, which always involves subversive intrusion, is a capricious or goat-like song and dance symbolizing disorder. As such it is a ritual reenactment not of goat sacrifice or of sacred totemic copulation but rather of the absurd and outrageous and inexorable resurgence of nature itself.... Farce breaks the spell of ritual.... It protects human existence from the excesses of the imagination and operates as a safeguard against the overextension of ideas, formulations, and formalities."[34] Seemingly, the farce and the goat sacrifice are quite close, with the exception that the farce is aware that sacrifice itself will not save society or the individual from disorder, because order is an illusion. Douglass's literary technique of uncontrolled irony offers conflicted narrative structures and contradictory emotional truths, which offer little in the way of one clear synoptic vision but many visions working together. This disorder that refuses order but presents elements of order brings together the comic, tragic, and melodramatic narrative structures and heroic types, for it is in the farce that the myth comes to its true force—the world turned upside down is resignified, not in another false order but within the chaos that it itself always already was. One can think of the various scenes in *The Heroic Slave*, from Listwell's overhearing of Washington's wooded confession, Washington's choice of Listwell's home, the ambiguity of the mutiny aboard the *Creole*, the ambiguous narrator of the mutiny itself, to see that Douglass's narrative offers a farcical account of history and historical documentation. In each of these scenes the ideas of reconciliation, through which readers may feel triumph (the Negroes are free at the end of the narrative!) or resolution (the white man does, in the end, do the right thing!), are disrupted with the unknown and with a narrative structure that has little emotionally intuitive truth.

As a way of reordering reality, Murray's definition of the farce is connected to what he refers to as a "counterstatement"—which counters the ritualistic practices of ideology (or that which is asserted to be true) with another narrative arc, one that deals with disorder without resolution and allows the chaos to be itself without subsuming the individual or their life within it. Imagining the Negro as conquering his condition, though, is neither farcical nor a counterstatement; it is a signifier for and to the linear cosmological force of a specific mythmaking praxis. It is, in short, the Negroid version of what Murray terms "the hegemonic fusion of Marxian-Freudian complex,"[35] only slightly tilting the axis of reality from the topside to what is *underneath*.

In the bildungsroman framework of the tradition of black male heroism, there is, in addition to desire for order, unity, and reunification, an anthropological and psychological assumption about individuals and their relationship to their environment. Such an assessment normalizes the subject in very specific ways through mythmaking about the nature of subjects and subjectivation. For example, the narrative mythical arc of Douglass's *The Heroic Slave* read through European existentialism would center recognition as the basis of the relationship between Washington and Listwell. Listwell's recognition of Washington's humanity is what set forth and foregrounded the possibility of Washington's eventual liberty and freedom. If one were to take a farcical view of the text and read it against this dominant view, then one would not center the narrative construction on recognition but on false narration as counterstatement to the straightforwardly given narrative of linear character development of either going through or overcoming certain odds. In this case, it would be Listwell's absence that grants Washington his actual liberation.

For Murray, the problem of these traditionally straightforward formulations is that they are not the work of literature or the imagination but the articulation of specific modes of a modern social science narrative wherein the heroic individual is less a character and more of an explainer to the audience of all of the social ills of reality.[36] What Douglass offers by way of a counterstatement is not so much a prognosis but a paraconsistent frame of reference. As such, the function of the hero is not only that of critique (of the prevailing system) but should be one of counterstatement through which the world can be remade but never simplified. Thus, if we take Murray seriously and take his claim seriously, we have to read Douglass not so much as an extension of the European existential and literary traditions but as establishing a new tradition of farcical black literary expression, where each moment is layered with multiple, parallel, and perpendicular meanings, presenting what is true as inauthentic and what is false as authentic.

Situating Douglass's fictional text within his photography lectures and Murray's notion of the counterstatement, Douglass's fictional and nonfictional works provide perspective but also "specific instruction and general education" as to "what happens in given circumstances and why it happens, but, perhaps most fascinating of all, how it happens."[37] To regard Douglass as a writer in this sense is to regard Douglass as both subject and object; it is to regard Douglass in his own autobiography similarly to how we regard Madison Washington—as a saver of souls, a self-liberator, and an abolitionist for whom violence is sometimes necessary. But more than anything, Douglass's fictional narrative and his photographic writings inform us that Douglass, himself, is an illusion—one of his own self-creation, an illusion meant to convey something about reality, a mirage set deep into the horizon of possibility. Douglass's fictive narrative shows that the hero and black heroism are illusions but no less real deployments of ideas sent into the world to reconstruct it.

[*End of scene.*]

[*Stage direction*] The Negro has finished his first recitation, turns abruptly and leaves the stage. The stage is now empty; the spotlight remains but slowly begins to fade. The dress lighting comes on, awaiting the second act to begin.

Chapter 2

✦

Ralph Ellison, Fictive Authority, and Existential Heroism

Magic and the Prestige in *Invisible Man*

> just because you
> cant see d stone dont
> mean im not building.
>
> you aint no mason. how
> d fuck would you know
> —Ishmael Reed, "dragon's blood"

> "Could we," I said, "somehow contrive one of those lies that come into being in case of need of which we were just now speaking, some one noble lie to persuade, in the best case, even the rulers, but if not them, the rest of the city?"
> "What sort of a thing?" he said.
> "Nothing new," I said, "but a Phoenician thing which has already happened in many places before, as the poets assert and have caused others to believe, but one that has not happened in our time—and I don't know if it could—one that requires a great deal of persuasion."
> "How like a man who's hesitant to speak you are," he said.
> "You'll think my hesitation quite appropriate, too," I said, "when I do speak."
> "Speak," he said, "and don't be afraid."
> —Plato, *Republic* (414b–c)

Theatrical Magic and "Real" Magic

[*Stage direction*] The Negro reenters the stage. The spotlight pops on. The dress light fades, and the audience settles in for the Second Act. The Negro is now dressed in an Oxford shirt (or maybe it is from the Cambridge collection, but it is a blue pinpoint either way), untucked, gray slacks, and is holding a striped university tie in front of his face, examining it closely. He turns up the collar on his shirt, reaches into his pocket for collar stays, and begins to tie a Windsor knot. He finishes his knot, puts his collar down, and undoes his pants and tucks in his shirt. He is getting ready for the world. The Hue and the Cry. He is steadying himself for an up-close theatrical magic act; he is steadying himself to be the hero; he is, in other words, preparing himself to lie.

> I knew that I was composing a work of fiction, a work of literary art and one that would allow me to take advantage of the novel's capacity for telling the truth while actually telling a "lie," which is the Afro-American folk term for an improvised story.
> —Ralph Ellison, introduction to *Invisible Man*

We are trading and tanning the explorers ... "to tan," to put on, to jive, to haze, as it were, through physical or mental testing; "the explorers," those who are not indigenous to a region or an area, those who wander, and through their wandering come to look upon themselves as wanderers (and extol this as a virtue). We are tanning the explorers, and we do so by trading ourselves.

[*Setting*] For those of you who do not know the story, *Invisible Man* is a novel about a nameless Negro youth traveling to the American South—from where is not really relevant—to attend a Negro college after having won a scholarship in a Battle Royal boxing competition. Through a series of events, he is suspended from the college and made to work in the North (New York City, to be exact) to pay for his education. While in New York, he encounters a series of figures: a black storefront preacher, a Rastafarian black nationalist, members of a communist organization, an evicted black couple, and a series of white philanthropists. Through these events and these figures, he learns about himself and the world—most abjectly, that the world and people are never what they seem. At the end, after having learned this lesson, our nameless Negro youth is ready to face the world. Or so the story goes ... *Invisible Man* is not so much a novel but a case study in the theatrics of black male existential aesthetics.

Invisible Man is a theatrical novel. Ellison himself has gone as far to say, "When American life is most American it is apt to be *theatrical*."[1] *Invisible Man* is an American novel, about the American experience, an experience, Ellison instructs, "in which the possibilities are many."[2] Specifically, *Invisible Man* is a novel about what becomes possible when the line between appearance and reality—"between the discontinuity of social tradition and that sense of the past which clings to the mind"—becomes blurred, and all that is left is the mask of reality, codified by ritualistic acts of concealing and revealing the joke of the present.[3] In other words, *Invisible Man* is not so much about race, racial authenticity, democratic equality, marginalization, or the existential claims to the lived experience of being black. Ostensibly, it has these elements, but they are all mere ruses for something else, for the joke of these. And, by direct indirection, Ellison is telling us something about the manner, method, mode, and articulation or disarticulation—that is, deployment—of the joke in the theater of appearances that is America.[4] The novel is, in short, an examination of "what was really happening when your eyes were looking through."[5] In this sense of the joke, of the play between appearance and reality in the presence of the mask and its theatricality, *Invisible Man* is a novel that at its heart is concerned with magic.

Straightaway, it is important to make clear just what sort of magic is being referred to here: namely, secular magic. Simon During offers us helpful clarification of the concept in his introductory comments to *Modern Enchantments: The Cultural Power of Secular Magic*. He writes, "The magic I mean is not the magic of witches or Siberian shamans—not, in other words, what one writer on the subject of the occult calls 'real and potent magic'—but rather the technically produced magic of conjuring shows and special effects. This magic, which stakes no serious claim to contact with the supernatural, I will call 'secular magic.'"[6]

Secular magic, while not conjuring the other side of reality or encountering the metaphysical realm, nonetheless *is* sublime. That is to say, secular magic works, fundamentally, because the performer and audience know that what is being witnessed is not real, and the experience of witnessing the non-real as real causes an effect of awe. And, it is this element that must be kept in mind. As such, when referencing secular magic, what is of interest is not any particular trick (card tricks, sawing a woman in half, flying in the air, etc.) but the experience of the knowing ruse, or the knowing lie that constitutes the phenomenological exchange between performer and audience, and the ritual of the show itself. When an audience attends a magical act, a certain implicit and explicit contract is enacted in which there are certain parameters and certain expectations that, together, constitute its social and cultural elements of space and time. That is to say, in the space of the performance, the usual time and space elements are suspended so that a man can fly or a woman can be sawed in half.

It is important to note, though, that a secular magic act is not the evasion or avoidance of reality; something very real is being enacted in the space and time of the performance. The secular magic act simply reveals the necessity of the ritual of belief in the construction of a shared, socially recognized reality, which is important to remember in thinking about America. It is the collective believability of the act that makes the experience *an experience*, that allows for the enjoyment; but it is also this exchange—believing in the magical act while also still believing in the ordinary laws of reality—that makes for a vertigo-like experience and the sublimity of the performance. As Darwin Ortiz notes, the magic act is not "simply about deceiving. It's about creating an illusion, the illusion of impossibility."[7] It is in the impossible experienced as possible that makes for the experience, for no one in the audience actually thinks something metaphysical has occurred—we would, then, be in the realm of the occult.

The exchange between the magician and the audience is, really, a contract of contradiction, which is what allows the antinomic phenomenal experience—an experience of the impossible as possible—to occur. In this experience, there is a necessary and active relation between audience and performer: the audience agrees actively *not* to suspend belief in reality in order to have the experience of secular magic, for the suspension of belief would break the exchange and the magic act, and the antinomic phenomenal experience would end. Additionally, the magician must not break the ruse and show his hand by disclosing the nature of the trick. What is important in the phenomenological exchange is not only the continuance of belief but also its continuance within the experience of its rupture.

The audience—in the context of *Invisible Man*, the reader—must understand that, for Ellison, what occurs in the American landscape are not merely random events but scripted moments of this exchange. As such, these scripted moments are not necessarily to be followed in terms of a journey through consciousness but truths to be discovered within the confines of an antinomic phenomenal exchange that is the narrative. What we are to discover, along the way, in these scripted moments are the tanning (the magician never quite showing the audience the trick) and the trading (the audience returning for another sublime encounter).

What is important in reading Ellison's novel is to understand that reading is like seeing in that one never reads what is on the page, as one never sees what is before the physical eye. Rather, both reading and seeing are phenomenal exchanges of expectation, in which what is experienced is constituted by the sets of rituals enacted to constitute one's reality. The secular magic act, like reading and seeing, demonstrates the deployment of this phenomenological exchange and what is being concealed and what is being revealed; what is being traded and who is being tanned; and just what the joke is and on whom. For, as Ellison notes, reading and seeing are not passive but active engagements in which the audience and performer have responsibilities, not so much to each other but to the very principle of their exchange—to the sublimity of the ritual of human existence against the backdrop of human folly. That is to say, within the ritualistic construction of reality, sometimes a secular magic act can demonstrate to the audience the limitation and inaccuracy of their own expectation; sometimes the magic act and the performer can take on the role of educator. For, if the audience is not educated and does not really understand the nature of their reality, they will not quite get why the act is so sublime, or they may take the magician's assistant to be the trick itself. The audience has the responsibility of not being naïve but holding firm to an understanding and a belief within a rational framework, while, all the while questioning that framework.

Ellison's novel is concerned with the exchange between the audience and the performer—reader and novelist—on the stage of representation and ritual that is the social order. In Ellison's context, Americans trade and tan one another from within the specific modes of social and cultural exchange—race, racial authenticity, democratic equality, marginalization, and the lived experience of being black are the terms of this particular secular magic act. In this context, it is the black male who is the performer; his audience is the larger American context—of symbols, rituals, meaning, history—through which white Americans are born and borne and through which they see and "see" and judge reality. The black male deploys himself as hypervisibly invisible to his audience to be consumed as the sublime spectacle of consciousness; he constitutes and consummates the theatricality of the American contract.[8]

One can think back to the discussion in chapter 1 about Douglass's deployment of theatricality and irony in his depiction of Madison Washington—both in his description and in his literary or analytic strategy. Douglass as a writer creates the sublime image of a heroic slave, Madison Washington. What is disorienting about Douglass's writerly performance of Madison Washington is his comparing slave rebellion to the American Revolution. Douglass's audience is well versed in the ritual belief in the principles of 1776 and well versed in the mythology of the liberation and the Declaration of Independence. Douglass is aware of and counts on this knowledge, such that when he makes mention of Madison Washington enacting these principles, it creates a sublime experience in which his audience is forced to review their own principles in light of Douglass's writerly theatrical performance. As such, the impossibility of black freedom becomes possible in Douglass's narrative, and the audience, who have agreed *not* to suspend their belief in ordinary reality, are confronted with the paraconsistence in the simple phrase, "We [the enslaved on the *Creole*] have done that which you applaud your fathers for doing, and if we are murderers [in overthrowing our enslavers], so were they."[9]

But, if the audience is naïve and is unaware that they are in fact participating in a secular magic act, if they are unaware of their ritualistic construction of reality, they will not experience their world as reversed and may only experience the vertigo without reason and think of Douglass as merely a conjurer of images or as merely a mode of entertainment without the educative element. But there is more still here. As part of a theatrical performance, the black male artist, as performer, cannot merely be thought of as presenting his act straightforwardly. It must be remembered that part of the secular magic act is the distraction necessary for the act itself. And it is this that necessitates an educated audience so that they do not take the distraction for the act. In black male performance, this distraction can, and does, take many forms.

The question of the what and where of the distraction and the what and where of the core elements remains. This is the theatrical element of Douglass's fictional essay. Douglass does not use his own voice to narrate this story.

He uses the voice of two white male narrators to discuss black liberation. This other voice through which we hear Douglass's voice is akin to the magician's assistant; the assistant provides just enough cover and just enough time for the magician to perform the trick without the audience watching too closely. Douglass has declared black liberation through a white speakerly voice.

As noted in the introduction of this book, the context of America is paraconsistent in our definitions of black and white, which are but two sides of the same coin—one cannot theorize freedom, for example, in the American context without thinking the unfreedom inherent in the enslaved. As such, what is considered antiblack or those elements meant to constitute blackness as nonhuman and noncitizen actually relies on blackness to constitute itself. It is this black/antiblack American context—of symbols, rituals, meaning, history—that Ellison refers to as theatrical and in which one can only understand in terms of secular magic: the paraconsistence of actual reality constituted in the unbelievability of the magical act itself. In the case of Douglass, one can only understand the relationship between liberty and death through understanding that the two concepts are reversed in the chattel experience. As such, when Patrick Henry shouted, "Give me liberty or give me death," he reified the white-Anglo *and* enslaved realities, and when Douglass mirrored this formulation, he reified their inversion—he was not reifying the same social and logical order but engaging in a secular magic in which the blackness of whiteness is revealed.

The black male performer, then, must deploy the joke of American rituals and American reality while not alerting his audience that this is in fact what is being challenged through the secular magic act. (It would be akin to sawing a woman in half as the distraction, and what is really being challenged here is the treatment of women, whom one can view as cut-in-half as theatrical and without horror.) In the case of both Ellison and Douglass, their black male literary secular magic act deployed the joke but not necessarily just that of American ethos only but also in how black men must appear within this ethos. Ellison informs us in the opening paragraph of *Invisible Man* that he is an invisible man. But that is not meant to say that he is not a physical presence, "a man of substance, of flesh and bone, fiber and liquids," just that he is invisible in that he must perform himself before an audience that has reified certain constructions of him through the ritualistic practice of seeing only his "surrounding, themselves, or figments of their imagination—indeed, everything and anything except [him]" (*Invisible Man*, 1). It must be remembered that it is Ellison writing about not being seen—he must see himself not being seen, as a mode of seeing himself not being seen. The second rendition is the theatrical magical act, while the first iteration is what is termed the double-consciousness of black male existentialism.

The black male performer, like any magician, knows the expectations of his audience and their view of reality—he must in order to perform the act. And, as such, he knows that in order to play on these assumptions, to create an antinomic experience, his audience must negotiate them right along with him. As Douglass informs us in *The Heroic Slave*, "Madison was of manly form. Tall, symmetrical, round, and strong. In his movements he seemed to combine, with the strength of the lion, a lion's elasticity. His torn sleeves disclosed arms like polished iron.... His whole appearance betokened Herculean strength; yet there was nothing savage or forbidding in his aspect."[10] But it must be remembered that it is not Douglass who makes these remarks but a white man, Mr. Listwell. At the same time, it *is* Douglass that makes these remarks, for he is the writer; Listwell, a white male character, is deployed as a black male literary distraction to the real trick being attempted: the inversion of reality alongside reality—for the white audience might trust the words of a white character. The doubling here is the twin ideas inherent in black manhood: on the one hand, the necessity of black male perfection and god-like (or demigod) status in order to be considered human and nonthreatening; on the other hand, the necessity to see black men as elemental (iron) and animalistic (lion) in order to carry forth material and labor exploitation. In a word, the black male magician must know this duality and must know that his audience, too, knows it and that, in order to enact his act—and consummate his exchange with the audience—he must be, or appear to be, animal, mineral, and god-like; that is, he must become the heroic, virtuous Negro.

Both Ellison's and Douglass's titles of the works reflect this secular magic act of both/and black male identity: the invisible man, one who can be invisible and still have a mode of existence; and the heroic slave, one that can be enslaved and still heroic and virtuous. In other words, the performance of black manhood is theatrical in nature, is paraconsistent in experience and fact. Sometimes he may appear as the "Negro," erudite, refined; sometimes middle class (in fact or orientation), lawful, a true believer, virtuous. Sometimes he may appear as the "Nigger," malcontent, badass, breaker of law, and that vast and infinite possibility for aggression, violence, chaos, sexual assault. As Ellison notes, the black man is "Brother-taboo-with-whom-all-things-are-possible" (*Invisible Man*, 400). The difficulty, then, is discovering what has appeared, how it is being deployed, and for what purpose; an educated audience must know who they themselves are and their own landscape of context to really understand which black man has walked onstage.

At the height of theatricality, though, both the "Negro" and the "Nigger" show up in the same person, in the same performance! This is witnessed as a paraconsistent doubling or as an uncontrolled irony of the super- or suprahuman where the performer is seen and "seen" and read and "read" as being of superior strength, superior intellect, and superior *and* inferior morality. Throughout the history of black male literary work, there have been deployments that range between these two poles—that is, the folkloric legend, the entertainer, the bawdy liar, the vaudeville performer, the Great Integrator, the misguided true believer, the Historical Actor, the trickster, the musician (bluesman, jazz man, band leader), the Afro-American, the African American, the black American, the citizen equal, the brother-builder-partner of the nation. The black man is all of these; the black man is none of these but is always counted on for infinite fungibility in his capacity to punish, be punished, *and* forgive.

The difficulty of the black male performance is the fact that the audience, while they are willing *not* to suspend reality in engaging in the performance, are willing to experience paraconsistent vertigo, knowing that all the while they can leave the performance space at any time and that the performance will eventually come to an end. What must not be forgotten is that a theatrical performance is a chosen event—the audience purchases a ticket, shows up to the theater, and awaits an experience. They can, at once, enact the mask, the joke inherent in the performance, and not be fully responsible for the paraconsistence because it is a paid event, with tickets and a marquee. This is the difficulty that Douglass experienced when giving talks—recall that during one of his lectures on photography, his audience started to turn on him, insisting that he begin to talk about slavery, to give them what they came to see in him. In this way, the performance, while a phenomenal exchange, is equally up to the audience with regard to what they want to "see." And, as Douglass discovered, it takes a skilled theatrical magician to give the audience what they think they want to see, while giving them what he wants them to see.

In the American context, the secular magic act and the ritualistic phenomenological exchange are at once invisible and hypervisible, necessary and demanded by an audience that require, as part of the reification of their self-imagining and self-fashioning, the mythology of their context as necessarily independent from the performance itself. What constitutes the sublimity of the performance is the fact that it can only really be consciously experienced and accepted when its sublimity is rejected, either through the naiveté of the performance or by avoiding the very context of performance. And this, it seems, is what Ellison means when he writes, "When American life is most American it is apt to be *theatrical*." At its *height*, American life involves the secular magic act, the performance of magician, and the avoidance or naiveté of the audience.

It is this expectation that the audience will not and cannot tarry with the both/and experience of witnessing the negation of reality alongside the existence of the real that creates the paraconsistent discomfort of bearing witness that reveals why the trick is a trick and just what reality has been upended. For just as the audience cannot come to terms with the fact that they are Mr. Listwell looking at Madison Washington or that the values reversed by Douglass are their values or that they are the ones who have constructed the "mirrors of hard, distorting glass" that surround Ellison's narrator, projecting onto him what the audience sees and "sees" in him, the audience also cannot come to terms with the values that are being critiqued in presenting

Madison Washington as heroic or Ellison's narrator as invisible, that they are their values, are themselves. Instead, the audience—in this case, the reader—thinks of Douglass and Ellison as extensions of themselves, as participating in *their* values and beliefs and structural modes of existence alongside them.

But what Ellison alerts us to in the opening sentence of the novel is that the black male performer must always be self-aware and nevertheless participate in the ritualistic act of the performance, knowing that his audience may not be equipped to tarry with the both/and experience of witnessing the negation of reality alongside the existence of the real that creates the paraconsistent discomfort of bearing witness and the undercurrent of avoidance and naiveté. As Ellison noted about the French existentialists but as is also central to the American audience and experience, "The French had to dive from the height of their philosophy into the deep pool of reality; black Americans spent their day-to-day lives underneath the surface of the water."[11] In other words, the secular magic act is neither a distraction from nor an abstraction of experience; rather, it further allows the audience and performer, in their exchange, to really understand the laws of reality by calling them into question through creating the illusion of breaking them. The secular magic act, in other words, reveals why the trick is a trick and just what reality is by upending it.

The American context, through the performance, becomes a joke that reflects on itself, offering only the dizzying experience of a complexity that is at once the seriousness of racism and racial violence, on the one hand, and a tongue-in-cheek aesthetics of the telling lie or a lying truth, on the other. When reading Ellison's *Invisible Man* or Douglass's *Heroic Slave*, the reader or audience has to at once deal with the irreverence of telling a joke about a serious matter, on the one hand, and the seriousness of the literary technique in the crafting of a narrative about a serious matter through the telling of the joke, on the other. In particular, their texts about an invisible man or a heroic slave cannot reveal a knowing subject, because the subject, as we traditionally understand it, is absent. The joke is then that you have a story about a disembodied nonsubject who is nevertheless subjected to racism. The who or the what of their texts, then, cannot be constituted in the traditional space and time referent of Western modernity but has to, like that of the secular magic act, exist in but also be upended by these narratives. As such, the nonsubject subjected invisible man and heroic slave are not disclosed as the who of rational, bildungsroman narrative structures or even the disinheritance of poststructuralism but the when and where of dissemblance, in which a story is told somewhere and sometime by no one.

And this is the dizzying aspect of the performance. Once the audience has reflected on it, they come to realize that no one really knows—or can know—the performer. The performer does not really exist; he merely occupies the position of he who challenges and supplants but does not overturn reality. He is but a conduit of and for a suspended reality, a conduit or what might be called a conjurer of another reality overlapping and intersecting their own reality. And, like Ellison's narrator, who disappears behind what Ellison wants his audience to see as a naïve black man—or Douglass, who disappears behind Washington disappearing behind his white narrators—the performer is not really in front the audience, though he is physically present.¹² He is both there and not there, both present and absent—present as absent. Like Ellison's narrator, he is but a reflection of the distorted mirror surrounding him; and as in the traditional subject, who comes to know itself through the existential process of self-awareness in choice and responsibility, becomes the performer, who is neither known nor self-known but is at once subject*less*, process*less*, and choice*less*. He is, in a sense, a refusal of existential subjectivation or formative subject-making altogether—yet he must seem as normal as an ordinary pack of cards.¹³

Take, for quick example, one of the early scenes in *Invisible Man*. The narrator sits with his family at his dying grandfather's side. His grandfather is a man whom the narrator thought to have been meek, a bit of an "Uncle Tom," a misguided true believer, who, having been himself born a slave, was nevertheless thought to have believed in the principles of democracy so much that he refused to fight for his rights and land during Reconstruction, instead giving up his gun. Yet, at the end of his life, he reveals himself as a malcontent, with the vast and infinite possibility for aggression, violence, chaos, and lawlessness. When his family is gathered around, he tells them, "Keep up the good fight. I never told you, but our life is war and I have been a traitor all my born days, a spy in the enemy's country ever since I give up my gun back in the Reconstruction. Live with your head in the lion's mouth. I want you to overcome 'em with yeses, undermine 'em with grins, agree 'em to death and destruction, let 'em swoller you till they vomit or bust wide open" (*Invisible Man*, 16). The grandfather had lived within the theatrical space of the performer, having convinced his audience and his own family, who had themselves bought into the greatness of the American context, that he had not only forgiven the nation but had believed so strongly in the nation that he was willing to give up the protection of himself, his family, and his land rights to become the brother-builder-partner in the American project of democracy. Yet, at the end of his life, at the end of his theatrical act—what in theatrical secular magic is termed "the Prestige," the moment of reveal when the magician takes the woman out of the box whole or brings the coin back from its invisibility—rather than bringing out the woman whole, he flipped the box on its side, revealing the trick to the audience; he revealed himself as a spy, a traitor. In other words, he was no longer willing to mask or play the joke.

"The Negro's masking," Ellison tells us, "is motivated not so much by fear as by a profound rejection of the image created to usurp his identity. Sometimes it is for the sheer joy of the joke; sometimes to challenge those who presume . . . to know his identity."¹⁴ The grandfather ceased fulfilling his role in the magic act. He showed the viewing audience the trick, breaking the contract and ending the phenomenological exchange between himself as performer and his family, the viewing audience; and, like any audience, his family was shocked, appalled at his refusal to participate in the joke. "They thought the old man had gone out of his mind. . . . The younger children were rushed from the room, the shades drawn," and the narrator was "warned emphatically to forget what he [his grandfather] had said" (*Invisible Man*, 16). Significantly, the grandfather died immediately after these words, giving neither the narrator nor his family the chance to ask why, after all these years, he revealed himself and revealed the trick. The performer revealed the trick and then immediately left the stage, leaving his last words as a riddle to be solved.[15]

Or take for example the opening lines of *Invisible Man* in detail. Ellison informs readers, quite directly, that they are to be part of an elaborate theatrical magical act. His writes,

> I am an invisible man. No, I am not a spook like those who haunted Edgar Allan Poe; nor am I one of your Hollywood-movie ectoplasms. I am a man of substance, of flesh and bone, fiber and liquids—and I might even be said to possess a mind. I am invisible, understand, simply because people refuse to see me. Like the bodiless heads you see sometimes in circus sideshows, it is as though I have been surrounded by mirrors of hard, distorting glass. When they approach me they see only my surroundings, themselves, or figments of their imagination—indeed, everything and anything except me. (*Invisible Man*, 3)

Revisiting these lines from our discussion earlier, notice that much of the language concerns perception—the perception of the viewing audience on the black male performer. The audience "sees" what they want—they are willing participants in whatever image or figure emerges from the other side of their projected perception. And there is the black performer, a man of substance and consciousness; we, the viewing audience, are not quite sure how he "sees" himself. What we know is only by inference: he is *not* a spook, and he might even possess a mind. The distance between the certainty of how he is "seen" and how he "sees" himself leaves the narrator, at the outset, as ambiguous but also creates the sense of a distorted mirror. We, the viewing audience, who imagine ourselves as sophisticated and having figured out the meaning of the novel, reflect back on this opening paragraph and conclude, along with much of the extant black male literature, that these lines depict white racism and the forced invisibility of black people within it. We see the line "I am invisible simply because they refuse to see me" as concrete and the novel as an existential meditation on tragedy, for it reveals the fact that though invisible, our narrator, in fact, wants to be seen and "seen." But, if we look at these lines as distortions themselves, then Ellison's claim that he is surrounded by distorting mirrors may ring as disingenuous, for he is the one who is really distorting reality, presenting the narrator as naïve, as ignorant, though Ellison seems to know and be in control of the narrative and the narrator—and his invisibility—the whole time.

Very few commentators look at this opening scene in relationship to Ellison's essay "Change the Joke, Slip the Yoke" and his deployment of the image of the mask as the ritualistic mechanism for concealing and revealing—just as virtually no commentators on Frederick Douglass's slave narratives also focus on *The Heroic Slave* and the role of irony in Douglass's work overall. Rather, many commentators of Ellison and Douglass read their work as they would read any Anglo-American or European text: as a straightforward narrative about the relationship between normative subjectivity, rights, and liberties.

The doubling in Ellison's and Douglass's work that is so critical to the ritual of the performance is also essential to antinomic experience of their theatrical act, for those images seen and "seen" in the mirror of the text are identical to those of the reality of their audience, only they are reversed; the reality of their audience is represented as its identical opposite, creating the feeling of vertigo. What, really, is Douglass's view of the American Revolution? Is it really an event to be revered or something to be mocked? What does he think of Anglo-American values? How should the reader understand Ellison's narrator given that it is unclear if the narrator really thinks himself invisible? How should we understand Ellison's politics—or the politics of his novel—given that he seems to be mocking values of assimilation and forgiveness? Perhaps there is something more profound occurring, something subtextual in Ellison, as there is in Douglass. Reading the genre aesthetic of black male literature as secular magic act necessitates that we "see" presentation as representation and reality as an inverted distortion—not in the sense of a simulacra but of an illusion.

There are two main antinomic moments in Ellison's novel that will be discussed for the remainder of the chapter: Ellison's inversion of dialectical thinking and Søren Kierkegaard's *Sickness unto Death*; and an expansion of the earlier discussion of "The Grandfather's Riddle." But before we begin, more needs to be said about western European existentialism and black existentialism as it relates to antinomic phenomenal experience.

Scene One: Existentialism and Heroism

> I always come this far and open my eyes. The *spell breaks*. . . .
> It's so long ago and far away that here in my invisibility I wonder if it happened at all. Then in my mind's eye I see the bronze statue of the college Founder, the cold Father symbol, his hands outstretched in the breathtaking gesture of lifting a veil that flutters in hard, metallic

folds above the face of a kneeling slave; and I am standing puzzled, unable to decide whether the veil is really being lifted, or lowered more firmly in place.

—Ralph Ellison, *Invisible Man*

He knows the stories. He has read Franz Fanon and discussed at length theories of alienation and his blackness. He knows how he is supposed to feel. He knows what is expected of him and what he must say. He has served, many times, as emissary and translator of his foreign world. He is the Existential Negro, our black hero.

"Insofar as it is genuine, *what* is said [i.e., what one is interpreting the thing as] should be derived *from* what is being talked about." That is, the concepts used in the interpretation should be *appropriate* to the thing one is interpreting, i.e., that they should *illuminate* it, not distort it.

—Edgar Boedeker, "Running Commentary to Being and Time"

Franz Fanon once noted in his critique of Jean-Paul Sartre's claim that black consciousness—or the idea of utilizing a racial identity as the formative structure of self-identification or self-recognition—was in bad faith, "My Negro consciousness does not hold itself out as a lack. It *is*. It is its own follower."[16] Ralph Ellison once famously noted that "the true subject of democracy is not simply material well-being, but the extension of the democratic process in the direction of perfecting itself. The most obvious test and clue to that perfection is the *inclusion*—not assimilation—of the black man."[17] And Lewis Gordon reminds us, "A mistaken view of Africana philosophy and black thought is that they are parasitic of Western philosophy, and that they are so in a way that limits its legitimacy as an area of *thought*." Gordon continues with an important concluding remark: "This formulation is from a longstanding assumption that Africana and black peoples bring experience to a world whose understanding finds theoretical grounding in European, often read as 'white' thought."[18]

What each of these thinkers is arguing, in different ways, is the failure of conceptual integrity when it comes to theory created by and through black people. That is, as both Ellison and Gordon note, the true task of reading—that is, interpreting or, in Ellisonian terms, seeing,—black philosophy is to do so not through another lens but through itself as it is self-articulated.[19] As Fanon notes, his blackness "is its own follower"—that is, it sets before itself its own intellectual project, within its own historical becoming, and does not look outside itself to justify its own recognitive, reflective idea. This does not mean, though, that there is no such thing as influence; Ellison himself is keenly aware of the consequences of claiming that one lives strictly in a "black world."[20] It is simply to note the distinction between causation and correlation.[21] More will be said of this subject in the next section.

What, then, could we possibly mean by "black existentialism"? As just discussed, it cannot be merely the application of existential terms to black life but must be something else. But what? Is it the understanding that all knowledge is historically, socially, and culturally grounded and emergent from this grounding and that in order to properly seek something, to properly name something—as a spatial and temporal designation—we first need to adjust our seeking, our thinking, our speaking to what is under investigation? Critical to this analysis is the idea of "black" that is reified.[22] And, while I will not fully follow the path of analyzing "blackness" or the meaning of "black" existence within an antiblack world, what I am interested in, in this chapter and in this book as a whole, is to note the distinction between blackness as it is seen and "seen" and how those persons who are seen and "seen" as black manipulate this distinction and play within this gap. In other words, given Ellison's claims of the theatrical performance of Americanism and race, it is important to note that there is a great distinction between being seen, seeing yourself being seen, and seeing yourself being seen being seen. It is in this latter sense in which blackness is never where and when it is seen but always sometime and somewhere else—in the performance of distance and the distance of the performance.

And it is in this performance of the distance and distance in the performance that black existentialism is being deployed as a metadiscussion of how we are to engage in and with that which is where and when we are not looking. But, what is more, in this analysis, it is also important to note how black men have constructed, curated, and circulated their existence. What makes black existentialism significant for this project is the fact that it highlights human expression as the artifact (material and intellectual) of a specific anthropology.[23]

* * *

Existentialism has long been thought of as a postwar intellectual and cultural phenomenon of western Europe. Following the internal war among the modern European states and the transfer of power from the European powers to the United States of America, existentialism was thought to have been both a radical critique of tradition and the establishment of a new mode of living beyond tradition, beyond the historical past, establishing what Walter Kaufmann termed "an anti-tradition tradition."[24] Within this radical "anti-tradition tradition" we see the denial of what are thought to be certain tropes of European intellectual life—that is, the idea of absolute forms of living, absolute forms of knowing, forms that become mooring posts to shape approaches to political, economic, social, and scientific lives and worlds. In this transformation, the structures of thought were opened up onto this new realm of possibility. Figures such as Martin Heidegger, Jean-Paul Sartre, and

Albert Camus, to name a few, forwarded ideas that human existence is without external, substantive meaning. Instead, meaning within human existence is something that has to be established *by* human existence, by the lives we as humans choose to live. At the moment in which choice becomes the determinative feature of the human, the possibilities for kinds of living expand, and we are freed from the traps of history, tradition, culture, and religion. Or so it seems. . . .

Even within disavowal, traditional existentialism nevertheless emerges from and out of a certain cultural and historical framework of interpretation and meaning. Famously, Heidegger instructs, "The question of existence never gets straightened out except through existing itself. . . . The question about that structure aims at the analysis of what constitutes existence."[25] Sartre also instructs, "we are now upon the plane where there are only men," and what that means is simply "man chooses himself, . . . [and] in choosing for himself he chooses for all men. For in effect, of all the actions a man may take in order to create himself as he wills to be, there is not one which is not creative, at the same time, of an image of man such as he believes he ought to be."[26] Following Heidegger's instruction, it seems that the ontological task of existentialism is analyzing the question of existing itself—for once we have discovered the structure of existing, we can understand the meaning of existence. Interestingly, Heidegger distinguishes between "existing" and "existence," the latter understood through the former: the only way to understand what or who we are is to understand what we are already doing, which beg the questions, How do we reveal existing itself while we are, in fact, existing? And, What does it mean to reveal existing to existence or the existing or doing parts of ourselves to those critically reflective that are experiencing what we have already been doing?

These questions are, for Heidegger, ontological in scope and hermeneutic in direction, meaning that they do not reveal themselves in traditional philosophical form—in syllogistic explanation or rational deduction. Rather, given that they concern our existing, they can only be answered inductively from piecing together the meaning of what we have already been doing prior to critical self-reflection. If we are to take Heidegger seriously—and take into account existing to understand existence—we must not take human existence as a general or universal category emitting general or universal concepts; rather, we need to look at concepts as the artifacts of existing and those things through which human beings exist. In other words, to perform an existential analysis, we must take into account the meaning and interpretation of the history of concepts themselves—where they come from and how they have been used within the existing lives and worlds of the human beings enacting them to reify their reality.

So much of black self-reflective intellectual life has been littered with European and Anglo-American concepts repurposed without taking seriously the ontology of concepts as existing elements of human existence. To perform a black existential analysis—in other words, to deploy blackness as a critical and formative element—we must ask the question of historicity and the ontology of thought enacted in the world (and vice versa). We are to ask ourselves, Is the phrase "black existentialism" or "existence in black" meant to signify that there are universal human elements that can be extracted across divides of time and space and the modes of human existing we call culture? Or is it to mean that we think through the constructed elements of human living through choice? What does and can that mean for black people, in particular, black men, who, in the literary genre under investigation, articulate these narratological choices subterfugally? It is to ask, subterfugally, what are we to hear in black existentialism—in black existential analysis in the meaning of black life?

When Heidegger tells us, "The often heard expression 'Western European philosophy' is, in truth, a tautology" because "philosophy," being Greek not just in origin but in its nature, "first appropriated the Greek world, and only it, in order to unfold," are we to hear this in our earlier discussion of understanding existence through existing?[27] Are black existential philosophers to hear in Heidegger's methodological praxis a specific cultural spiritualism? Are we to ignore the ontology of this method and its ideas? Are we to hear that "philosophy" and "existentialism" are not ontological terms with a specific history and a specific culture even though they are clearly marked as such? Are we to ignore this ontology yet take seriously the project as ontological, one in which we can substitute *our* ontology such that the existing elemental structures of "Western-European philosophical" existence can be retrofitted into the self-reflective existence of black human beings? What would justify such an evasion?[28]

When Sartre instructs us that "the point of departure there cannot be any other truth than this, *I think, therefore I am*, which is the absolute truth of consciousness as it attains itself," and "every purpose, even that of a Chinese, an Indian or a Negro, can be understood by a European. . . . In every purpose there is universality, in this sense that every purpose is comprehensible to every man,"[29] are we not supposed to hear that critical self-reflection, though it may include the other—Negro, Chinese, and so on—as centrally European or Cartesian in nature since it is through this methodological reduction we generate the framework of reference? Are we not supposed to hear Franz Fanon's critique that "Sartre forgot the Negro suffers differently in his body" and realize that the other is embodied in a situation and that the European provides the intellectual framework—the elements of existing—to theorize this embodied existence? Are we also not supposed to understand the critical historicity out of which Cartesianism sprang—the battle between the church and science, a battle that not *all* of humanity fought—which necessitated a new intellectual approach, direction, and foundations for the sciences that would not be revelation? Should we not hear Descartes's plea to the church, "although it is quite enough for us faithful ones to accept by means of faith the facts that the human soul does not perish with the body, and that God exist, it certainly does not seem possible ever to persuade infidels of any religion, indeed, we may almost say, of any moral virtue, unless, to begin with, we prove these facts by means of the natural reason"?[30] Are we not to recognize that the fear of excommunication motivated the structure of the text and realize that Sartre, try as he might, cannot extract Cartesianism from *this* ontology—this history, this culture?

Would this evasion constitute a kind of intellectual theatricality that, if understood properly—that is, self-reflectively—would constitute the tragicomic aspects of human folly but, if not properly understood—if taken to be universal—would then become only tragic? If we did, though, understand the theatricality of the performance, would it unravel our concepts by showing their relative historical truth? This, in a sense, is what Ellison's narrator is navigating and what is at stake in Douglass's usage of white narrators to narrate Washington's own critical appraisal and usage of concepts such as liberty—concepts that are used explicitly with reference to the historicity of the Revolutionary War. This is what is at stake and what they are doing: pulling at ontological threads and unraveling modern Western notions by revealing their relative historicity through the deployment of black maleness.

Scene Two: Dialectical Thinking?

The first of these moments to be unraveled is Ellison's inversion of Hegel and Kierkegaard. These are critical moments, because they allow us to understand (1) Ellison's own intellectual commitments and (2) his fundamental critique of "Western-European" philosophy and the illusion of its usage for the American context.

Though many scholars have commented on Ellison's usage of Western philosophical themes and Western philosophical ideas in *Invisible Man*, one must be careful and clear about overlaps and departures, because the fit between the two will not be seamless. That is, one must be cautious with the usage of alternate epistemological frameworks. While they may be and often are useful, it must be kept in mind that they are also anthropological markers, and this idea must be taken seriously. As noted in the previous section, existentialism, as an intellectual tradition, marks out that the construction of the world and its meaning—whether arbitrary or inherent—is constituted within a specific cultural or spiritual frame, and thus our analysis and usage of it must first engage this fact. For it is one thing to claim that a figure is engaged in and with certain intellectual ideas; it is quite another to claim that his or her analysis is consistent with or emerges *from* these ideas.[31] For one can engage *through* critique.

I am not, though, suggesting that Ellison is not influenced by the Western canon—in particular, Marxism, Freudianism, and Hegelianism—but that these traditions, when run through the black American tradition, become inverted, distorted, convex, and concave. In other words, though they may appear similar to the traditional ideas, when one looks closer, they are in fact markedly different. It is my contention here that though Ellison does engage with the Western intellectual canon, his Americanism and his blackness anthropologically mean that he will not interpret the world the same way as these other figures; and, therefore, he will not come to the same conclusions as those other intellectual traditions.

Take, for example, the first moment: Ellison's inversion of Hegel's dialectical thinking and dialectical history comes early in the novel and takes place with the narrator already underground, describing his "hole." Ellison writes,

> My hole is warm and full of light. Yes, *full* of light. I doubt if there is a brighter spot in all of New York than this hole of mine, and I do not exclude Broadway. Or the Empire State Building on a photographer's dream night. But that is taking advantage of you. Those two spots are among the darkest of our whole civilization—pardon me, our whole *culture* (an important distinction, I've heard)—which might sound like a hoax, or a contradiction, but that (by contradiction, I mean) is how the world moves: Not like an arrow, but a boomerang. (Beware of those who speak of the *spiral* of history; they are preparing the boomerang. Keep a steel helmet handy.) (*Invisible Man*, 6; emphasis in original)

Here we can see Ellison doubling, layering meaning in indirect language, alluding to intellectual traditions, offering critique and corrections. He is "taking advantage" of us because, at the beginning of the novel, readers might not be aware of this doubling language, that they are part of a theatrical magical act in which nothing is what it seems to be and is somewhere in between the thing itself and the image, reversed and distorted in the mirror. But how and in what way are we being taken advantage of? What doubling is going on?

The narrator begins like any magician, showing you what you take to be an ordinary circumstance: an ordinary pack of cards, an ordinary box. He tells us, sure, Broadway in New York is full of light. Who would contest that? But the claim, like the pack of cards, like the box, is about to undergo a radical transformation of meaning. The definition of "light" and "dark" are about to be changed without clear indication: the magician is about to somehow change the condition in which the ordinary becomes extraordinary while still appearing to be ordinary.

When he claims his hole is bright, one of the brightest spots in all of New York, he does not literally mean bright as in that light which the physical eye takes in. Rather, the concept of light here is related to the inner eye referenced in the first chapter—not the physical eye but "those eyes through which they look through their physical eyes upon reality." For as the inner eye is that which constructs reality and that through which reality appears as both concrete and stable, the light is that which enlightens or reveals the reality that has been constructed or the inner eye itself. As noted earlier, if the only way to understand existence is by existing itself, then the light is that element which reveals our existence. For Ellison, then, the light, in showing our existence, is also the mode in which we exist—it is civilization itself.

When Ellison notes, then, that his hole is "full of light," that it is "brighter" than all of New York, he is referencing the civilization out of which New York City emerges as a concrete, real, and stable place. His hole, his living quarters constructed from his inner eye, is more enlightened or reveals a fundamentally different civilizational ethos than the beacon of Western modernity—the hyperindustrial city. To say that this hypercity is a "dark spot" means simply this: the hypercity reveals or enlightens that it belongs to and is the product of a Western industrial modernity that itself is dark. In other words, *it is the light that reveals the inner eye, which is dark*; the hyper-technologically-advanced city reveals the decadent civilization.[32]

But Ellison does not stop there. He qualifies even further: a civilization is but the collected artifacts of a particular culture, which is why civilization can be understood as our existence, which can only be understood through our existing—what we *are* is revealed in what we *do*. Culture itself is what we do; civilization is what we, in fact, are. The hyperindustrial, technologically advanced, decadent city is what America, in fact, *is* and is the result of a series of historical and ongoing choices and actions: the "mask" of civility and progress, which both projects the future and preserves the past, is why in our "absolutely technical state . . . only a god can save us. The only possibility available to us is that by our thinking and poetizing we prepare a readiness for the appearance of a god, or for the absence of a god in [our] decline."[33] Or so it seems. Maybe what we are awaiting is a different civilizational model. But, again, "that is taking advantage of you"; maybe what we are awaiting is not a different civilization or a different culture but the one we already have; maybe what we are awaiting is what America already *is*, not decadent or in decline but "black" and in denial, at odds with itself, which is why it appears decadent.

This idea is represented in the opening sentences of Ellison's novel, where it appears that the narrator is telling readers *his* story when he writes, "*I* am invisible man. . . . *I* have been surrounded by mirrors of hard, distorting glass," but it is not the narrator's experiences that he is telling in the story but the audience's, for it is the audience who "sees" the reality in terms of the distorted mirror; it is the audience who *is* the distorted mirror, for they are the ones whose existence is predicated on such distortion as a mode of existing; it is the audience who is holding the mirror, constructing its cracks, and presenting the image, *their* image, as distorted. Just as the performer does not create the context of the performance but only reveals the context of antinomic vertigo, through revealing to the audience the context of their own belief or disbelief, readers are not reading the narrator's story; it turns out that the narrator is telling readers, the audience, *their* own story. He, in this sense, is not invisible; rather, his audience is invisible to themselves, which necessitates his existence as invisible for the audience to situate itself as his audience. "What else could I do?" the narrator asks us. "What else but try to tell you what was really happening when your eyes were looking through?" (*Invisible Man*, 581).

In switching the subject or perspective from the performer to the audience, Ellison not only unmasks white American existence, but in playing with meaning, form, structure, and context he creates new concepts and a new vernacular that illuminates rather than distorts black male existence. Ellison's deployment of invisibility is the joke—the blackness of white American existence—the context and content of and for the performance in which America is understood as "a land of masking jokers," whose mask both projects the future and preserves the past, preparing us to live in a present.

White Americans for Ellison are thus in conflict with themselves, their own historical and cultural framework in the guise of blackness. It is this internal conflict, Ellison notes, that engenders white Americans to imagine what America would be like without blacks. Yet, for Ellison, white Americans could not think of themselves at all without this presence; in a direct way, for Ellison, white American existence is not predicated on the existing structures of western Europe but the existing structures of blackness itself. In the American context, white Americans, rather than recognizing their own masks—their own existence as the inversion of "Western-European philosophy"—reduce the performer, that is, the black male, "to a sign . . . to repress the white audience's awareness of its moral identification with its own acts and with the human ambiguities pushed behind the mask."[34] For Ellison, this means that although blackness is necessary for the construction of the audience's reality, the audience are either naively or consciously unaware of their reliance on the performer for their own sense of self and unaware that the mask, "although it resembles the role of the clown familiar to Negro variety house audiences, . . . derives not from the Negro but from the Anglo-Saxon branch of American folklore. In other words, this 'darky entertainer' is white."[35]

It is here that the boomerang comes to its full significance, for it refers to what is cast out and/as what is called back. This, though, differs significantly from the Hegelian dialectical readings of Ellison's novel, which argue for the progressive unfolding of the narrator's consciousness as the structure of the novel.[36] Within Hegel's formative structure, consciousness becomes historical, but history itself, or absolute knowing, becomes its content. Yet, for Ellison, history does not emerge from or for consciousness as its object and its content; rather, it is what happens to consciousness as it engages with and in the material world as its ordered control. The boomerang, thus, is a relic of Hegel's failed attempt at reconciliation, and history is the name for this failed event.

There are two formative moments in the failure of history: one is the death of Clifton; the other is the presence of the zoot suit boys. In Clifton's death scene, the narrator and the collective group of which he and Clifton are both members, The Brotherhood, is searching for their comrade who has disappeared. While The Brotherhood is usually thought to be a stand-in for communism, I want to argue that it is actually a stand-in for the Hegelian dialectic and the idea of a rational understanding and control over history.[37] It is important to note that the headquarters of The Brotherhood is called Chthonian, which is not just about the chthonic or the underworld but is directly concerned with that which dwells in the underground, the Cthulhu, a fictional god-like creature, "a monster of vaguely anthropoid outline, but with an octopus-like head whose face was a mass of feelers, a scaly, rubbery-looking body, prodigious claws and hind and fore feet, and long, narrow wings behind," which, while trapped underground, always threatens to return—to be called back—to the surface and consume.[38] While not much has been made of Ellison's reference to this fictional character and this fictional underground world, when understood in terms of its relatively unknown and mythical origin, equally worshiped and threatening to take one down into its underworld and to consume, the connection between it and reason and its construction of history and absolute knowing becomes clearer. Similar to the fictional character, the dialectics of reason and history of equally unknown origin, is equally beguiling and equally threatening to take one under and consume one into itself, that while being banished threatens to always return. Within this context, it is understandable why this scene with Clifton is troubling for the narrator, who attempts over and again to normalize himself in a world that he always already knows refuses his totalization but will only—*can* only—consume him as a mode of his participation in history or as a historical subject.[39]

What is significant in this scene is the idea that Clifton has left The Brotherhood and is now engaged in the selling and proliferation of relics from the past, relics that the dialectic should have overcome to move on to another phase of consciousness. And yet the narrator finds Clifton, who like himself has been immersed in dialectical training instead of overcoming or sublating the past, *returning* to the past. The dialectic, in the moment, has regressed—the narrator asks himself, Why would Clifton have left the order, have left the structured and rational understanding and control of history for the chaos and madness of the past—this past of racialization? "Why," the narrator wonders to himself, "should he [Clifton] choose to disarm himself, give up his voice and leave the only organization offering him a chance to 'define' himself? . . . Why did he choose to plunge into nothingness, into the void of faceless faces, of soundless voices, lying outside history?" (*Invisible Man*, 438).

The theatricality of this moment cannot be overstated. In this scene, Clifton has disappeared, and The Brotherhood is searching for him. He has not been taken but has, by all accounts, simply left. The narrator finds Clifton on the sidewalk selling "Sambo dolls," a throwback to another time of "racist" Americana long thought abandoned by the progress of history, a facsimile of human action, a facsimile of life brought to life by an agent of history. Readers can hear along with Ellison's narrator Clifton's theatrical performance of these dolls:

> *Shake it up! Shake it up!*
> *He's Sambo, the dancing doll, ladies and gentlemen.*
> *Shake him, stretch him by the neck and set him down,*
> *—He'll do the rest. Yes! . . .*
> "Follow little Sambo around the corner, ladies and gentlemen," Clifton called. "There's a great show coming up." (*Invisible Man*, 431, 434; emphasis in original)

Clifton here is foreshadowing his final conflict, his final dance—the big finale, the "great show." History has returned to Clifton and the narrator but not as one might think. This is the function and action of the boomerang. History as the totalizable project of reason emerges and returns to close up loose ends, to foreclose possibilities of ruptures to inform us as to what it is and how it functions. It is here that the narrator is confronted with his role in history in how Clifton dies: he is shot by the police after a violent confrontation over the Sambo dolls. This death, what amounts to a kind of choreographed death, is precipitated by a dance. The police, the arbiter of Right, the absolute embodiment of authority and law, the enactment of reason onto the material plane, brings order, that is, historical necessity, to an unreasoned chaos. It is important that this man and his embodied principle was the one who killed Clifton only after Clifton plunged outside history, aligning himself with the Sambo rather than The Brotherhood. Ellison's narrator recounts,

> And I could see the cop bark a command and lunge forward, thrusting out his arm and missing, thrown off balance as suddenly Clifton spun on his toes like a *dancer* and swung his right arm over and around in a short, jolting arc, his torso carrying forward and to the left in a motion that sent the box strap free as his right foot traveled forward and his left arm followed through in a floating uppercut that sent the cop's cap sailing into the street and his feet flying, to drop him hard, rocking from left to right on the walk as Clifton kicked the box thudding aside and crouched, his left foot forward, his hands high, waiting. . . . And somewhere between the dull roar of traffic and the subway vibrating underground I heard rapid explosions and saw each pigeon diving wildly as though blackjacked by the sound,

and the cop sitting up straight now, and rising to his knees looking steadily at Clifton, and the pigeons plummeting swiftly into the trees, and Clifton still facing the cop and suddenly crumpling. (*Invisible Man*, 436)

The officer, "thrown off balance" by Clifton's spinning dance, unable to predict its spontaneous motion, the "jolting arc" of his torso, concave/convex, "carrying forward," could only respond as the totalizing project of reason and history to Clifton's quick counter, dropping him hard—with a rapid explosion and a large whipcracking sound. The choreographed response to improvisation is death. This was Clifton's plunge.

What we are witnessing is a ritualistic event—a singular and unrepeatable occurrence, which is somehow repeated, with only slight variations—one that has been scripted by "the discontinuity of social tradition and that sense of the past which clings to the mind" and is meant to bring the narrator back to himself but different.[40] What Ellison is reminding us is that black male vulnerability is this choreographed dance of death in which reason and history will either drag you under and consume you there or take your improvised resistance on the surface and shoot it down. What we are witnessing is a "conceptual/performative singularity . . . as a disorienting repetition of philosophical/improvisatory intensities," a "tension between the imperative to repeat antecedent structures and the necessity to do so in a way that expresses originality."[41] In other words, Clifton's death is the narrator's own: the repetition of difference would be the cause of the death—underground or in the street—set to an alternate rhythm. But this does not signify a dialectic; there is no unfolding of progression of knowing here, just disorder dressed as order or tradition enacted as authority and history and reason in the snuffing out of black male life. In the end, Clifton and the narrator as witness are brought to their "knees, like a man saying his prayers," but the prayer is not that of Abraham or the man of faith but that of Isaac, he of dissonance; his prayer is the prayer of blackness—the cry of a man in the wilderness. More will be said of this in the next section.

The questions inherent in the novel—Can a black man live outside history and reason? Can a black man challenge history and reason?—are swiftly answered with a sound ("rapid explosions") and a gesture (Clifton's body "suddenly crumpling"). It is in this moment when the narrator makes a direct connection between himself, Clifton, the dolls, and history. Clifton and he *are* the dolls.[42] Black men, then, are like these dolls, their strings pulled by history and reason; and without these narratives, they are thought to be lost and lifeless—or, more directly, they will have their lives taken from them. The dance that the dolls performed—"some mysterious mechanism was causing to move up and down in a loose-jointed, shoulder-shaking, infuriatingly sensuous motion, a dance that was completely detached from the black, mask-like face"—was the dance that the narrator was doing, and what

Clifton had refused, for history and reason. It is in this moment that the narrator, although he has tried throughout the novel to believe in history and reason and the "release" they would offer him, is forced to admit—not realize but admit to himself as his own realization—that history and reason are failed projects.

It is also in this moment that the narrator realizes that all of the dances end in death: Clifton's dance with the police, in physical death; Clifton's and the narrator's dance with the dolls, in ontological death; and Clifton's and the narrator's dance with reason and history, order and organization, predictability and control, in metaphysical death. And the narrator is left asking, What could be next, after physical, ontological, and metaphysical death? Instead of directly facing and answering this question, the narrator instead flees down into the subway, into the subterranean world where he finds his answer.[43]

But Ellison is again taking advantage of us. All the while, the narrator seems naïve, and all the while, the narrator seems as if he coming to terms with reality; but Ellison has nonetheless told us that "the end is in the beginning" (*Invisible Man*, 571). That is, what the narrator learns in the epilogue he already knows in prologue. And there is something valuable in this—for black men, it is not about understanding or learning about reality but about coming to terms with what one already knows. The distance between these is the distance between the performer who knows he is performing and the performer who does not want to admit he is performing, cuts the invisible chords hanging him from the ceiling, and attempts to actually fly! The scene with Clifton is the cutting of chords, and the subway station with the zoot suitors is where the narrator falls.

It is in the subway where the narrator finds his answer in those whom he refers to as the zoot suitors—boys who seem out of place in the contemporary time and space of modern U.S. life. But what strikes the narrator as especially strange about these boys is that they seem to exist in a parallel reality to that of the other, white passengers on the platform. It is as if they are not being recognized and do not attempt to be recognized. Why, the narrator wonders, if white techno-modernity is totalized in reason, would one not want to be recognized and find one's life within this totalized reason? Why would one want, as Clifton had, to throw oneself outside history and reason? The narrator wonders what it is about these boys that invisibility is not a problem for them. What can these boys know that he, Clifton, or The Brotherhood do not?

It is here, in this second moment with the zoot suitors, that the narrator recognizes another form of failure in the dialectic. As he watches the boys, walking, arms swinging together in unison, speaking a "jived up language only they could understand" (*Invisible Man*, 441), he realizes that there may be a reality outside the dialectic, outside recognition.

Again, Ellison revisits the theme of dance in describing the boys. He writes, "I stared as they seemed to move like *dancers* in some kind of funeral ceremony, swaying, going forward, their black faces secret, moving slowly down the subway platform, the heavy heel-plated shoes making a rhythmical tapping as they moved" (*Invisible Man*, 440; emphasis added). It is instructive to note that Ellison also situates the boys' dance in terms of death, but not the death of being consumed underground or shot in the street, like Clifton's, but a death that *they* announce, the death of something other than themselves. They were a funerary procession announcing transition from this life to the next life. But who or, more properly, what is to die? What or who did their presence suggest had, was going to, or needed to die? What sort of insights could be derived about life and death by those who were untouched by reason or history and did not need, did not believe in, or had never heard of The Brotherhood? (*Invisible Man*, 440). What could be gleaned from those who did not plunge outside history as Clifton had done but were "men out of time"? The narrator wonders, Could they be "the bearers of something precious? The stewards of something uncomfortable, burdensome"? (*Invisible Man*, 440). And, if so, what? This is the challenge that these boys carry within them and that causes the narrator to actively wonder, "What if history was a gambler, instead of a force in a laboratory experiment, and the boys his ace in the hole? What if history was not a reasonable citizen, but a madman full of paranoid guile and these boys his agents, his big surprise!" (*Invisible Man*, 441).

These boys constitute the joke of history—the evasion of its own chaotic roots constituted in reason, which itself would be comical if not for the fact that we are not all in on it, all implicated in it, having to face its consequences collectively. Instead, we are reminded of what is on the other side of reason and history and that this evasion carries within it cthulhic results, distorting the human form in a paradoxical set of relations: the progressive unfolding of techno-science in the hypercity is the same principle of chattel slavery, eugenics, and death camps. But, with this end, with this inversion, this evasion not only comes with the joke but the tragedy of historical and material consequences, making it at once tragic and comic: what Ellison terms, "tragicomic." This is what makes Ellison's juxtapositions so startling—that which heals is that which kills, or as Ellison reminds us, "Beware of those who speak of the *spiral* of history; they are preparing the boomerang, Keep a steel helmet handy." Those who speak of life are preparing death; those who speak of whiteness are really hiding their blackness and preparing, in their denial, to denigrate it and themselves. The joke of European and Anglo-American identity is that the very idea of teleology with regard to humanity, that is, the spiral of history, folds back on itself, finds itself in tension with itself, and because its own cultural tools demand unity, all it can do is attempt to unify difference or call for the end of itself. Ellison's warning, then, is a warning that the idea of Europe and the illusion of America collapse back on themselves or return, like a boomerang, unexpectedly and violently.

The joke of reality, then, is found in the performance—the fictional sawing of a woman is underscored by the actual violence. That is, what underlies the joke and makes it functionally real is the presence of a reality that violently and invisibly undergirds it. It is the tension between real, invisible violence and that of staged, fictional violence that constitutes reality and allows these tensions to dance together.

History becomes, for Ellison, not organized or structured but a kind of improvised disorderly disorganization, an inducement or incantation of sorts, rather than the organized composition. And Ellison's narrator, Clifton, and the zoot suitors become figures like "the bebop virtuoso who struggles to achieve an individual identity through the creation of a unique improvisational voice."[44] Taken together, this voice—that of Clifton, the narrator, and the boys—reflects the fact that history cannot be understood and controlled as the action of reason but is, indeed, irrational, mad, and chaotic. Yet, for Ellison, this did not mean that life was formless. An improvised virtuoso performance transforms the irrational, the madness, the chaotic into an expression of relation rather than one of sublation into absolute form. In other words, it allows the irrational to be irrational, the chaotic to be chaotic, and the mad to be mad but fuses them through setting them in a relation that is a cacophonous performance. The black male performer, like the theatrical up-close magician, must be able to bring disparate elements together in such a way that they *seem* congruous, all the while dancing atop an underlying incongruity that allows for instantaneous alteration.[45]

It would, though, be unsatisfactory to think that jazz improvisation and virtuoso performance function like something of a solution, in a different form. The tension is still there, the death is still there, the undercurrent of the theatrical magician's act is still there. What underscores the narrator's mock naiveté is still there. The performance of the zoot suitors, who refuse the performance, is still there. The tension, or what Ellison refers to as the "old Bad Air" is still there and must remain, "can't be thrown out, because it would have broken up the music and the *dance*" (*Invisible Man*, 581; emphasis mine).

It is here that we are brought to another realization: black life within Euromodernity is an unavoidable eschatological dilemma—one that has revealed that though history and reason have failed, they still functionally operate as if they are still pure. With the next address, we will analyze Ellison's overturning of Kierkegaard's notion of faith as the possible solution for this eschatological dilemma. In other words, it will address how, for Ellison, black men are to deal with this coordinated, choreographed dance with death, conceptually and materially.

Scene Three: Faith and *A Sickness unto Death*?

Søren Kierkegaard's *Fear and Trembling* and *Sickness unto Death* are texts that are both ultimately concerned with a trace: the trace of reason in faith;

the trace of history in revelation; the trace of the human world in the divine; and the trace of Absolute in inutterable isolation. It is in the biblical story of Abraham and Isaac that Kierkegaard locates and analyzes these traces. And yet this alone does not prepare us to discuss these traces or the story of Abraham and Isaac in relation to Ralph Ellison's stunning appeal in the form of a reversal of Kierkegaard—rather than the estrangement of the Spirit from itself, from the world leading to the sickness of the metaphysical, this estrangement leads to ontological upheaval of form in the spontaneity of creative expression in the blues. What makes this declaration stunning is how it becomes manifest within the structure of Kierkegaard's quotidian repetition and in Ellison's "paratheology."

Kierkegaard begins his investigation into the biblical narrative of Isaac and Abraham with his own biographical rendering:

> Once upon a time there was a man who as a child had heard the beautiful story about how God had tempted Abraham, and how he endured temptation, kept the faith, and a second time received again a son contrary to expectation. When the child became older he read the same story with even greater admiration, for life had separated what was united in the pious simplicity of the child. . . . His only wish was to be present at the time when Abraham lifted up his eyes and saw Mount Mariah afar off, at the time when he left the asses behind and went alone with Isaac up onto the mountain; for what his mind was intent upon was not the ingenious web of imagination but the shudder of thought.[46]

Kierkegaard's desire was simple: to understand "what was on [Abraham's] mind" when Abraham saw Mount Mariah and contemplated what he was there to do, what he *must*, in fact, do—and, implicitly, what he must become in this acknowledgment, this moment of lifting his eyes, this moment at the base, knowing his task, leaving the other men behind, and, in touching his son's shoulder, gently leading him up the mountain. It is at the base, in this contemplation before any possible action, that Kierkegaard pauses with Abraham and locates the trace in what Abraham is willing to do.

Kierkegaard theatrically remembers this reflection and this trace in his body as a shudder. But this shudder represented not so much the failure of thought to capture Abraham's internal dialogue in this moment but the trace that followed behind Abraham when he saw the mountain, knew what he must do, and touched his son. The incommensurability in these three moments is what caused Kierkegaard's somatic condition of his quaking flesh. In a sense, what made Kierkegaard quake was the fact that what existed in these three moments was completely private, in Abraham alone, yet could be witnessed—stopping at the base, the pause in motion, the touching of Isaac's shoulder—but could not be registered; there was something in this experience that outstrips the material order, that one could be unreachable, beyond empathy—alone, utterly alone even when, and especially when, among others. This moment could be repeated but was absolutely unique, for God spoke to Abraham and Abraham alone; Abraham listened to God and God alone; Abraham acted in the world but stood outside the world, his actions, and his own body at the base of the mountain, in the pause, when he lightly steered his son forward. This is all historical but does not—cannot—belong to history. These are all things that can be thought but do not—cannot—belong to reason. They must exist and surpass existence as a matter of their existence.

But there is still more. For Kierkegaard, the shudder exists in the quotidian—the ordinary turned extraordinary in those details that belie themselves, surpass themselves, and become, like the Eucharist, other to themselves. There are other quotidian details that sometimes go unseen than those above—the mountain, the man, and the boy. There is also the mother and the preparation for the journey. These quotidian details also bring us back to the world, in order to surpass it. Let us pause for moment on Exordia I, II, III, and IV and notice what dwells there, in the repeated phrases, each slightly different from the previous. Let us notice, in each subsequent detail of the day, the trace.

> Exordium I: "It was early in the morning when Abraham arose, had his asses saddled, and left his tent, taking Isaac with him, but Sarah watched them from the window as they went down the valley—until she could see them no longer."
>
> Exordium II: "It was early in the morning when Abraham arose: he embraced Sarah, the bride of his old age, and Sarah kissed Isaac, who took away her disgrace, Isaac her pride, her hope for all generations to come."
>
> Exordium III: "It was early in the morning when Abraham arose: he kissed Sarah, the young mother, and Sarah kissed Isaac, her delight, her joy forever."
>
> Exordium IV: "It was early in the morning and everything in Abraham's house was ready for the journey. He took leave of Sarah."[47]

Each morning Abraham rose. Each morning he was met by his wife. Each morning she and Abraham announced the day through each other—with Sarah first watching him at a distance, then embracing him, then kissing him, and then, finally, taking leave of him. And each morning, Sarah, too, embraced their son, who transformed her into herself, first from a disgrace, then as her pride, and then as her hope and delight. Why does Kierkegaard need four versions of this morning? Why the slight variations in the same story of waking, embracing, and leaving? This morning was like all mornings but different. These embraces were like all embraces but different. Kierkegaard is instructing us in how to read and hear the story, how to gain access to his own mind as he is writing about it. The evocation is not only in the ride to the mountain and up the mountain and to the altar but in the quotidian details that announced the beginning of this day—the day when everything normal was transubstantiated. The shudder, in addition to what Abraham will do and become, is the very idea that he will do what he will do and become what he will become under the guise of an ordinary occurrence—life will be the same, but it will be remarkably different.

We are to read and hear this story in the details of an ordinary life that has an extraordinary end. We are to feel the trace in these details. It in this trace that we find the horror of Abraham's faith. In addition to the Exordia details is this one last detail: each morning Abraham's wife, Sarah, who bore the child Isaac, wakes up with Abraham and Isaac, not knowing what the day will bring, and packs them a lunch—food to sustain their bodies for a trip in which Abraham is to slay Isaac's body. The food, in the moment, is transubstantiated from that which is to nourish the body into the body's unbinding.

This is Kierkegaard's meditation on himself, a lyric of his own consciousness trying to come to terms with absolute faith in this moment: of waking up, embracing one's wife, taking the son on a journey, all the while knowing what is to happen and knowing this silently, unable to speak its becoming, for no one other than yourself can hear you as anything but a monstrosity. It is in this that Abraham is invisible, utterly invisible, except to God—he is in absolute relation to the Absolute, yet his flesh touches the flesh of his wife and his son; and when it does, it is no longer as husband and father but as estranged faithful servant of God. This is the absolute of estrangement, from oneself or who one was in the world; the absolute of silence, internal and external; and the absolute dissolution of the quotidian, in which every detail becomes other than itself. Kierkegaard meditates on all of it: What is this kind of faith that substantiates by dissolution, bonds by outstripping, unifies by unbinding?

Kierkegaard tells us early that he "is by no means a philosopher. He has not understood the system, whether there is one, whether it is completed.... Even if someone were able to transpose the whole content of faith into conceptual form, it does not follow that he has comprehended faith, comprehended how he entered into it or how it entered into him."[48] In this moment, reason cannot take this absolute into itself as its own content. Here Kierkegaard is distancing himself from the Hegelian project of absolute knowing. He is instructing us on how to read, that is, hear, him. It is not as a philosophical system of thought but a lyric, as is announced in the title. We are to understand this as a deeply personal insight or meditation into the prelogical, evocative self, of the man who is remembering reading the story of Abraham and hearing Abraham's voice in the shudder of his own flesh.

It is true that we have heard that Abraham's real journey was not to the base, up the mountain, placing Isaac on the altar or taking out his knife but that the journey begins when his hand is fully raised above Isaac's head and begins its descent. "Who strengthened Abraham's arm, who braced up his right arm so that it did not sink down powerless! Anyone who looks upon this scene is paralyzed. Who strengthened Abraham's soul lest everything go *black* for him and he sees neither Isaac nor the ram! Anyone who looks upon this scene is blinded."[49] It is here, in the apex of this pause, in the unified disunification of unrepeatability, that Kierkegaard finds Abraham shrouded in darkness, that everything goes black, and that Abraham becomes irrevocably and invisibly black. But what can this mean for his faith? For himself?

We are to hear Kierkegaard, regard him, feel his shudder through Abraham, by contemplating the trace in Abraham's story, contemplating the darkness in which Abraham is shrouded and the utter blackness that threatens his soul. This is Kierkegaard's shudder for Abraham—for what he is to become. But what of Isaac? Is there a requiem for his dissemblance? For his invisibility? For what is to become of him because of Abraham's own becoming? Of the monstrosity that will befall him because of Abraham's monstrosity? Where is the Eucharist for this transformation? Why does *this* not make Kierkegaard shudder? Why does *this* not move in the casing of Kierkegaard's own flesh? How would *this* cause us to hear and read this story differently? What would it call on *us* to become?

In rendering Isaac through Ellison's address and redress of Kierkegaard's moment of paralysis and blindness, we come to understand, fully, Ellison's inversion of reason and history. We can hear this inversion in Ellison's declaration, "Before I lived in the darkness into which I was chased, but now *I* see. I've illuminated the blackness of my invisibility—and vice versa. . . . But I am an orator, a rabble rouser—Am? I was, and perhaps shall be again. Who knows? All sickness is not unto death, neither is invisibility" (*Invisible Man*, 14). If we are to hear Ellison in this moment, to feel what he is telling us in the quotidian turned extraordinary, we would see that darkness has become a form of light, a way to see, rather than a means of shrouding. We would see that what troubled Kierkegaard's soul—the absolute powerlessness, paralysis, and blindness of silence—has been transformed into the foundation of speech. Amazing grace has been inverted—the Absolute does not offer sight by removing blindness, by excavating the darkness for light; grace is in allowing one to see the lightness in blackness and blackness in lightness. We would see that blackness is not a curse but the revelation of being, of absolute being. And we would see that it is, in fact, Isaac and not Abraham who reveals this lesson. But why?

Ellison's reversal reveals Isaac as he is and was. It reveals that Isaac is the vessel for Abraham's becoming, that it was he, and not Abraham's faith, that allowed for Abraham's transubstantiation, for the alteration of the ordinary. That it was he and not Abraham's willingness to sacrifice him that was the Eucharist—he was key to it all: God's test, Abraham's faith, the absolute relation to the Absolute, the absolute silence, the absolute distance, the dismemberment, the disunity, and the reunification. In Isaac's flesh lay dormant the infinite finitude of his own blackness. It is the sublimity of this darkness, this blackness that makes Ellison shudder.

> In the beginning . . .
> . . . there was blackness . . .
> Black will make you . . .
> . . . or black will un-make you. (*Invisible Man*, 9–10)

In this rendering, Isaac cannot be thought of as Abraham's or Sarah's son or even God's child but that through which Abraham becomes both the outcast and the man of faith, for it is not in the act that Abraham is constituted but in his willingness to commit the act that he becomes at once the man who is willing to kill his son (community outcast) and the man who is willing to follow the command of God (man of faith). Isaac, though, is neither faithful nor transgressive; he is black, so irrevocably and absolutely black. It is in the density of his blackness that he is invisible to Kierkegaard and inaccessible, even to God, for being Abraham's son alone casts him both outside God and outside man, for neither offer him protection. He is alone, utterly alone in this moment.

Isaac is, in Ellison's terms, the mask through which Abraham jokes or plays at becoming both outcast and man of faith. But, as noted earlier, the joke is not one of mere caprice but what is at the center of identity, for in that great pause when the blade cracks brightly against the sky, right before its descent into Isaac's breastbone, Abraham's identity is cemented and the joke is revealed: faith and estrangement, unity and disunification are one, existence is irreconcilable, irreducible. And it is Isaac who reveals this—this is why he must remain silent and invisible in his blackness, why Kierkegaard cannot speak to him or through him only *about* him. There is nothing in this moment, in this pause, that can reconcile it—it is the black Saturday between Good Friday and Easter Sunday, where everything and nothing exists simultaneously, where the holy of holies dwells. This is the paratheological blackness of which J. Kameron Carter speaks, in which blackness challenges and dismantles Kierkegaard's theological rendering of the world.[50]

Yet in Isaac's blackness there is no illusion of avoidance, as with Abraham, who passed his blackness, the pressure of his own internal and eternal darkness, onto Isaac through his dissolution into the mask of faith of which Isaac was the icon. It was in Abraham's masking his blackness that Isaac became black, as, with America, it is the blackness of whiteness, or the darkness of the light, that is passed onto the Negro/nigger, making him black. And it is the illusion of faith that passes along this mask of blackness, for it was Abraham's inability or unwillingness to be the dark of holy Saturday that made him raise the blade and move toward its descent.[51] It is this darkness that brought Abraham to the bottom of the mountain and made him make the ascent. Abraham could not tarry with and become the darkness of God's command and man's law, and, as such, he passed this darkness to his son through his own actions, just as white Americans, through the ritual of the mask and the "darky act," pass along this darkness in their inability or unwillingness to tarry with what it has taken and continues to take to construct the hypercity, to construct a new nation out of the wilderness. It is this darkness that troubles and stays with Kierkegaard from his youth to his adult years; it is blackness itself that Kierkegaard is battling to understand.

What, though, do we do with this blackness that refuses both reason and history and even faith? How does one enter this or allow this to enter oneself? Is it, as Ellison suggested, to be unmade?

If one is willing to tarry with the darkness to become black, willing to become the nonaligned spirit, though it may lead to the despair of ambiguity, one will realize, as Ellison did, that this tarrying is not spiritual death but rather the opposite: it is the life of the spirit. It is only through ambiguity and the antinomic experience that one can actually become oneself and grasp reality itself as lived experience—in the estrangement of unified disunification without needing to pass it along to make another black, sublate it into reason or history, sidestep it in faith, be resigned to it, or demand that the world recognize you in it.

In other words, it would not be the source of silence or, more precisely, the inaudibility of voice but the source of a prelinguistic sound—the wail. It will become the aesthetic principle of the craft of prescient technique. In the overturning of Kierkegaard, Ellison is claiming that rather than leading to death, such a condition results in an aesthetic expression of the blues. The blues, Ellison writes, "is an *impulse* to keep the painful details and episodes of a brutal experience alive in one's aching consciousness, to finger its jagged grain, and to transcend it, not by consolation of philosophy but by squeezing from it a near-tragic, near-comic lyricism."[52]

Rather than resigning to the tension of contradiction in the everyday details of a consistently inconsistent estranging reality that refuses transcendence, the blues allows one to tarry with it in order to accept existence as what it is and to extract from it—by will alone—the principle of its emergent, paraconsistent reality. The blues is all of it—the black ram, bleating as it replaces Isaac on the altar; the voice of God, commanding obedience; Isaac strapped down on the altar and the look in his face imploring protection from his father; the crunching of the breastbone against the spiny denseness of the blade; the look on Sarah's face after Abraham has killed their only son; Abraham's arrest and detainment; the gathering crowd shouting in anger and horror over what he has done; his lack of language to tell them all that he is a man of faith; and God's silence on the matter. It is all there in that moment, all possible realities, all possible outcomes, all possible lives in that moment when Abraham takes his son up the mountain, ties him to the wooden altar, unsheathes his blade, and holds it over Isaac's head, and yet none of it is there. In this moment, there is nothing but the blues.

Neither Isaac nor Abraham can speak in that moment or after. There are no words to capture what either is tasked with becoming, no words to capture either pause, to capture these feelings, to explain how this blackness is there, between them, but does not need to be transferred from one to the other but could be a dwelling place for them both. This blackness that threatens them all, could release them all. This is what Ellison leaves us with:

> I feels bad. I tells them how it happened in a dream, but they scorns me. I gits plum out of the house then. I goes to see the preacher and even he don't believe me. He tells me to git out of his house, that I'm the most wicked man he's ever seen and that I better go confess my sin and make my peace with God. I leaves tryin' to pray, but I caint. I thinks and thinks, until I thinks my brain go'n bust, 'bout how I'm guilty and how I ain't guilty. I don't eat nothin' and I don't drink nothin' and caint sleep at night. Finally, one night, way early in the mornin', I looks up and sees the stars and I starts singin'. I don't mean to, I don't think 'bout it, just start singin'. I don't know what it was, some kinda church song, I guess. All I know is I *ends up* singin' the blues. I sings me some blues that night ain't never been sang before, and while I'm singin' them blues I makes up my mind that I ain't nobody but myself and ain't nothing I can do but let whatever is gonna happen, happen. (*Invisible Man*, 66)

In this moment, we can see how, caught between sinning by following God's command and sinning by ignoring God's command, between being guilty and not being guilty, and when he tries to pray, tries to dissolve himself into the Absolute in a leap of faith, he is not brought to God—there is no black ram to substitute for the absolute chaos of his blackened condition—but ends up "singin' the blues." In other words, rather than sublating or resolving or dissolving the Spirit, it becomes that which cannot be overcome. This is the moment of the Spirit's transcendence, not beyond his situation but deeper into it. It is in this moment that Ellison, through the blues, alters or distorts the meaning of transcendence from the erasure of subjectivity to an absolute obedience to one's own life without falling into despair. We can hear Ellison's narrator looking up at the stars, recognizing that "I ain't nobody but myself" and that if "whatever is gonna happen" is gonna happen, then the Spirit that asserts itself, asserts itself for itself, *as* itself, and can conclude, as Ellison's narrator does, "I'm shaking off the old skin and I'll leave it here in the hole. I'm coming out, no less invisible without it, but coming out nevertheless" (*Invisible Man*, 581).

Conclusion: Prestidigitation

> A second time they summoned the man who had been blind. "Give glory to God by telling the truth," they said. "We know this man is a sinner." He replied, "Whether he is a sinner or not, I don't know. One thing I do know. I was blind but now I see!" Then they asked him, "What did he do to you? How did he open your eyes?" He answered, "I have told you already and you do not listen."
>
> —John 9:24–27

Ellison invites us to rethink the unspeakable within Kierkegaard, to ascend the mountain, to sit there with Abraham and with Isaac, to watch Abraham tie Isaac to the altar, unsheathe the blade. He invites us to imagine that it does not matter whether Abraham explained to Isaac what was about to happen, if Isaac pleaded for his life, or if Abraham actually saw Isaac or the black ram. Ellison invites us not to explain any of it but to leave the irreducible ambiguity of the moment absolutely estranged, to leave unresolvable the tension inherent in this moment between life and death, being and becoming, to leave irremediable this invisibility. He invites us to remember his opening lines, "I am an invisible man," and to tarry with the nature of his invisibility—the refusal itself. And to think with him the unrequited possibility of resolution and to hear, in this moment, a lasting mode of inquiry—"I'm coming out, no less invisible without it, but coming out nevertheless"—and realize that this a burnt offering: the dance, the blues, the performance of improvised form, and still the invisibility and the unbinding and the sight to know that one is unbound but that being unbound is different from not existing.

Ellison leaves us with the narrator's grandfather, with Isaac himself in a state of disorientation, to remain, as it were, in a space where gravity, order, structure, time, and space remain foreign, estranged—the narrator must live with the unknown of his grandfather's advice as Isaac must live with the fact that his father intended him dead. This is a state of performance where no one will believe you when you tell them who you are or reveal to them who *they* are.

The narrator invites us to consider this space to see the light of darkness and the darkness of light, to see the joke of dismemberment in reason and history but also to see the blade raised in the bright sunlight of faith. We are invited, along with Ellison, to witness that "there is a death in the smell of spring," without succumbing to such death as darkness but only to realize that we must be neither for nor against reality but see and "see" in it the infinite possibilities of definition and form and structure and meaning. He invites us to tarry with him, to stay with him in his hole, where he begins the story and where he ends the story—to stay there, in his "warm hole," until we are prepared to act, prepared to accept what we have become and who we are, prepared to accept the mask and the joke and boys killed in the name of faith—in one's God, in one's country, in one's principles, in one's self. We are not prepared to act until we can carry this up the mountain and listen to the silence there and that which we have refused language and that which has refused to speak.

[*Stage direction*] The Negro stares out, straight ahead. He is pensive. The audience is still draped in black. The spotlight glows radiantly on the possibilities of his face. He cannot know if the audience is still present or if they have left, if they are angry, confused, or joyous, but he knows, still, that he must act. He loosens his tie and unfastens the top button of his shirt, takes a long, slow step backward, and recedes into the dark . . .

[*End of scene.*]

Interlude

Some Notes along the Way

> The bean is present and therefore means something. . . . The bean of course implies the seed which it both *is and contains*, being *what it is* and that *from which it comes*. It is its own birth, complete and whole, from the ground, the land and so, is complete as a picture itself, a landscape. This growth from the self while being the self is the ultimate action.
> —Percival Everett, *Erasure/fuck*

[*Stage direction*] The house lights (1,369, to be precise) abruptly come on. Blinding. The audience squints multiple shadowed figures onstage, moving chaotically to and fro. The lights, the movements: it is all electric. There is no intermission printed on the bill—this is more of an interlude, a literal break. The audience is pinned to their seats by the brightness. One of the lights blows, then another, and then another and another until the stage is once more dark: smoke and sounds fill the air.

What we have learned so far along the way is that within black male literary form, narratological structure is as much an element of the argument as is content itself. We have learned along the way that black male texts are as literal as they are metaphorical, which is significant for all literature but especially significant for black male authors, because what is at stake is not merely the aesthetic choice of form but the ontological condition of the expression itself. That is, we have learned along the way that when we are reading black male texts, we also reading black male lives. As such, what may be read as a literary device may also be read as disclosive of a living element. The lacuna of information, the narratological gaps and inconsistencies in storytelling, while they are but some of the literary devices in black male text, are also representations of black male lives, for as the text itself does not directly confront reality, black men, too, find themselves unable to directly confront their living realities; their literature, like their living encounters, must go underground, directly confronting reality by the flight of direct indirection.

We have learned along the way that in the black male novel, truth is always a moment of exchange between what is taken to be reality and what occurs as the subtext or undercurrent of reality. And much like a pea plant, which is both how it appears (as a total picture of development) and not how it appears (the seed underneath, hidden away as a moment in the development, not *the* development but critical to its understanding), the black male novel is that "which it both is and contains," that which "it is and that from which it comes" simultaneously. It is at once its form and its content, at once an argument and an ontology, at once a literal, metaphorical, and living experience. This is an important insight to remember as the reader moves forward. What, specifically, have we learned so far in this text?

* * *

Our man in the prologue imagines that he can, through sheer will and guile and being one step ahead and in knowing that he is performing, manipulate his image and thus shift the context of his existence. He believes, as our black existential hero, that if reality is fluid and meaningless, then it is, and must be, infinitely flexible to him, who will only utilize his ingenuity to create a vision for everyone else who believes in the sanctity of ontological facts.

Our man from the prologue, in traditional existential fashion, believes, *must* believe, that because reality is inherently meaningless, it is also a nothingness or no-thingness through which one can view it as infinitely open and on which one can situate oneself as this infinity by becoming nothingness or no-thingness itself in the performance of identity.

Ellison's narrator, who is also aware that he is performing, is supposed to learn that his knowledge of his performance, while it may not alter his immediate circumstance, will allow him, through tarrying with it and with learning to endure it, finally to act. We see this as the inherited insight from the narrator's grandfather in his deathbed reveal.

With Douglass, we see and "see" the construction of a narrative of both silence and presence. Douglass's voice is somewhere in between wanting to be seen and manipulating how he is seen; he is somewhere between *being* his constructed, projected image and *projecting* his own constructed image. But Douglass gives us the additional insight that the debate is not merely over the existential clarity of reality as a performative act. For Douglass, reality is really constituted by feeling. He reminds us that the image of the Negro is not merely a philosophical, a sociological, or even a historical debate but an emotive, phenomenological revelation.

* * *

We have learned along the way to be mindful of narrative silence and narrative gaps, of hiding and disclosing. We have learned that, at the heart of the evocative, phenomenal exchange with the viewing audience, each of the black male performers, whether he knows it or not, reveals to his readers the vulnerabilities inherent in black male hypervisible invisibility. As such, black male authors are never quite where they are expected to be, never quite how they are expected to appear. In other words, these authors reveal to us that they are and are not in their texts, are and are not in their words—they are both there and somewhere else.

This is where Colson Whitehead's *Apex Hides the Hurt* emerges for us. For Whitehead, our man from the prologue, Ellison's narrator, and Douglass himself may have been looking in the wrong place all along in trying to understand reality as the exchange between actors and actions. Reality is not in what takes place on the historical world stage; nor is it constituted in what is said or what is not said; there is something deeper to what constitutes reality. Reality is but the condition out of which the words themselves, naming itself, things themselves, history, consciousness itself emerge.

As we will see, Whitehead's novel seeks at once to locate the space and time of black manhood through a similar ironic literary device of having a nameless black man narrate himself, guide the reader as to the nature of his reality and the world itself. In doing so, Whitehead allows his nameless narrator to find—that is, create—the language to name things and, in doing so, to perhaps name himself. Whitehead places the reader as audience both within his narrator's language and also within the historically existing world of names and things. In other words, Whitehead attempts to reveal something to his reader about the space and time of the performance of narrativity and language as a way to analyze how the condition of a black man, himself the subject and object of language (and naming), situates both him and us as reader inside and outside the space and time of normative language and naming.

As we will see, Cecil Brown's *The Life and Loves of Mr. Jiveass Nigger* takes Whitehead's insights seriously and challenges them forthright. Brown's novel questions the very premise of Whitehead's novel—that naming or language can, by virtue of metaphysical speculation, articulate something about existence and capture the experience of black men. For Brown, though, it is in naming ourselves—the desire to be seen—that black men have lost something of their own existence to the logic of Western modernity. Rather than situating black male existence in terms of the language of Western modernity or that of black men, Brown posits that our approach should focus on feeling—not that of the phenomenological encounter, as Douglass notes, but that of jazz, the excess of improvised form.

With Whitehead, as with Brown, we must begin again, not at the beginning but synoptically in the middle: for Whitehead, with an examination of language and naming; and, for Brown, with the evocation of form. In doing so, we will begin to understand what has been and what is and imagine what will be, both bean and seed, "what contains and what is being contained," setting the ground for the "ultimate action" of listening and hearing that which has been silenced and that which has refused to speak.

Chapter 3

✦

Colson Whitehead's "Dark Matter" Prophecy

> He came up with names. They were good times. He came up with names and like any good parent he knocked them around to teach them life lessons. He bent them to see if they'd break, he dragged them behind cars by heavy metal chains, he exposed them to high temperatures for extended periods of time. Sometimes consonants broke off and left angry vowels on the laboratory table. How else was he to know if they were ready for what the world had in store for them?
> —Colson Whitehead, *Apex Hides the Hurt*

Scene One: In the Beginning . . .

[*Stage direction*] It is once again silent. It is still black. The dark envelopes the sound and the audience. The audience waits darkly. There is figureless noise on the blackened stage. Invisible sounds: footsteps, taps and shuffles. A single light appears and moves to the center of the stage. There is a figure. It is the Negro, again. He stands still, looking straight ahead. His gaze seems affixed to a point beyond the audience, to somewhere else. He, once again, opens his mouth, as if he is about to speak . . .

> We are born into a language; we are birthed through the form of the sign.
> Before the word, we are formless.
> *Before* the word, we are formless.
> Only the word has form.
>
> In the beginning is the word.
> And the world is given shape to test what is spoken
> And what is written
> Against itself.
> In the beginning was the testing of form
> And the battle over formlessness.

In the beginning is the self-expressed will
And what it manifests;
And how it will be tested.

"I am a negro! Yes, negro from "necro" meaning death
I overcame it, so they named me after it."[1]

"Art thou the prophet?"
And, he answered, "no."
Then they said to him, "Who art thou that we may give an answer to those who sent us? What can you tell us about yourself?"
And, he answered, "I am the voice of one crying in the wilderness."[2]

Scene Two: Of the World and Its Naming

I

They brainstormed, bullshitted, performed assorted chicanery, and then sometimes they hit one out of the park. Sometimes they broke through to the other side and came up with something so speculator and unexpected, so appropriate to the particular thing waiting, that the others could only stand in awe. You joined the hall of legends.

—Colson Whitehead, *Apex Hides the Hurt*

Colson Whitehead's novel *Apex Hides the Hurt* challenges us; it is a series of prosaic questions presented to us as a novel.[3] They are questions that demand answers, but they are also ones that cannot be answered within the realm of normative language. They are questions that must be answered in an *other* realm, in an *other* language. They are questions that, when asked, create the possibility for their answers, the possibility of an other realm, an other language. They are "dark matter" questions of and about the darkness out of which we come. They are questions that are formed out of our own formlessness. They are questions posed, ironically, within a language that seeks to shroud their annunciation. They are metaphysical remonstrations. *Apex Hides the Hurt* is written in this metaphysical realm, somewhere and sometime other; it is a metaphysical challenge to normative reality, normative experience, and to normative language. Somewhere and sometime an other voice speaks out from the wilderness, in the wilderness, as the wilderness to and through a language set to challenge the world we have been given and the language it has manifested.

Frederick Douglass posed "dark matter" questions: What is black liberation within the normative context of antiblack enslavement? Ralph Ellison, too, posed metaphysical questions: How can a black man assert his existence within this realm—that is, the normative space and time of social and political invisibility? What would an enslaved man asking questions of liberation do—materially and psychically—to the normative ideal of freedom? What would a black man asking questions of visibility and invisibility do—materially and psychically—to a social and political order predicated on these questions not being asked? These are thoughts, once formed, once uttered that, in their very constitution, actively disassemble the prevailing normative form. They are questions and utterances that once formed become formless, threaten with their formlessness, and reveal the arbitrary quality of modern Western material being. They are thoughts and utterances that bring forth an *other* world to challenge the prevailing world, the meaning of its prevailing and constituting words with *other* world life lessons, preparing, as it were, to make paths straight, preparing to undo and to make again.

Who is to hear these questions? Who can bear witness to the meaning of their being posed? Who can, in other words, provide an answer when and where the questions themselves, their annunciation itself, exists outside of the space and time in which they have been asked? Douglass and Ellison represent a kind of theatricality, an ironic staging of Western modernity, where what is spoken and what is unspoken both conflict and complement one another—where the question of freedom, liberty, recognition, and the like are uttered and negated simultaneously by the black male speaker. In other words, they represent Western modernity's active destabilization.

Douglass and Ellison, then, were not just writers; they were conjurers of sorts; they were metaphysicians of the spirit that brought within itself the preparatory way. They were metaphysicians of language. They analyzed sets of relations (social, psychic, somatic) annunciated in the meaning necessitated by modern Western words and concepts. They offered us an *other* world to test the words and concepts, to show to the normative world both itself and its possible alternatives. They challenged us, for example, to think about what framing ideas of freedom or visibility through the perspective of the enslaved or invisible might do, not only to our understanding of these words; but, what is more, what a reframing of these concepts might do to how we shape and reshape the material world constituted to justify, to reify their emergent meaning.

When they spoke, their call on and for black meaning tested white words, tested white language, tested the white world, but also tested the possibilities of black words, black language, to shape and reshape the meaning and structure of the material world—in addition to challenging Western modernity, they also challenged black writers themselves, black men themselves to question whether freedom or visibility should be the goals of their emergent words and worlds. In the process, they instructed us on how to see, read, and hear that which is formless, the formlessness of that which has taken itself to be formed, and to see, as possible the formless forms of stable contradiction (an heroic slave, an invisible man) both for those who are willing and those who are unwilling or cannot make manifest the clearing for this path. In the words of Colson Whitehead, both Douglass and Ellison "knocked around" words themselves to teach them these critical "life lessons."

One of these lessons, critical for understanding Whitehead's novel, is presented by philosopher Charles Mills as the reality of dueling metaphysical substructures. Douglass's and Ellison's work underscores the fact that our social and political institutions are themselves moral and aesthetic intuitions, ones that are manifest or material expressions of metaphysical substructures. They reveal to us that these institutions are constructed and maintained by the words and meaning we breathe into them. What is also revealed is that we speakers of language, breathers of form, are also created as subjects of and for these institutions. For Mills, the landscape of Western modernity, its substructure and the words used to reify its existence, are racial. That is to say, words such as "freedom" and "equality," "liberation" and "recognition," the makers of Western modernity and the markers of the world as white, are contrary to black lives and are themselves deniers of a black world.[4] The distance between black and white worlds is constituted not only in the meaning we give to words but to the material world made manifest in and through this meaning, that is to say, how these words are taken up in the materiality of one's life. For Mills, it is not, then, merely a theoretical difference that marks these worlds but a difference that goes to the root of the conceptual and material order of and for each world. It is not so much "a question of minor deviations, which, with a bit of bending and twisting here and there, can be accommodated within the framework"; rather, "an enlightening metaphor might be the notion of a parallel universe that partially overlaps."[5]

Whitehead's novel is a theatrical staging of this partial overlap: it is an interrogation of the conflict between the linguistic and material order when these parallel universes are made to intersect in a meaningful way, that is, when the words themselves are tested, not just by white normative life but by both intersecting and contrary lives—*What happens to our words then? What happens to language then? What happens to form then? What happens to formlessness then? What happens to us then?*

> Some are teethed on a silver spoon,
> With stars strung for a rattle;
> I cut my teeth as a black raccoon—
> For implements of battle.[6]

II

Part of the theatricality of Whitehead's novel is its setting. Rather than staging "dark matter" questions, those posed in the wilderness, from the wilderness, as the wilderness in an other realm, like that of science fiction—that is, the future, reimagined present, an other historical or temporal sequence, or an other planet—Whitehead places or sets these questions within a generic midwestern American town. Whitehead immediately places us in the challenge, and in doing so, creates a discordant experience for the reader—everything is like it ordinarily appears, but something is slightly off. Like most generic midwestern towns, it has a history: at one point, years ago, it was relatively thriving, but as technology changed and the economy shifted, the town found itself on hard times. The town's leadership surmised that the best way to jump-start the town was to do away with a past that no longer exists and to rename the town into and as its future condition. Initially, this story line is an ordinary post-Industrial narrative of identity and time, but what is slightly off-kilter about the novel is its usage of an unnamed black man to navigate this transition.

What is also slightly off about the novel is the fact that the "dark matter" questions are not those that immediately present themselves to the reader, like they do with Douglass and Ellison. Though the plot line runs through the issue of the town name, the reader comes to realize that it is not so much the name of the town that is under investigation, for it is not really the town that is being named; rather, what is really being discussed is the question of how a name can create the conditions of reality and how language shapes how we live our worlds—what is really being named are the people themselves. Whitehead accomplishes this in, perhaps, one of the most extreme of ways, staging the discussion—of the naming of the town, the naming of the people, and the naming of history—through the deployment of a black man, who literally names things in the world, as a narrator for the novel. In doing so—the naming and the selection of narrator—Whitehead instructs us as to how we are to relate to things and how we are to live within the world and within the connections underlying words, ourselves, and the things named.

Locating the analysis in a black man, Whitehead is testing not only the names against black maleness in Western modernity but also the naming process itself. Can a black man, once having been named by the American context, by the nation itself, by the very techno-economic-theocratic institution of chattel slavery itself, become a namer of things? Can a black man become the naming expert and create the context through which the world and the things in the world come to have an identity? Is meaning altered by the historicity of his body, or *any* body? In other words, does the historicity of the body underlie meaning and the structuring of the world through which, out of which we come to name things and ourselves—and, if so, what are the consequences of having a black man as nomenclature specialist?

Whitehead intensifies the reader's already discordant experience. This black man, though nameless, is situated as the best naming specialist for an American PR firm, whose task is the self-assigned capitalist venture of naming products so as to transform individual persons into consumers who will come to identify with and be in need of things. Our nameless black man, once property central to modern capital expansion, is now steering the ship of postmodern capital expansion. The question remains: is he, though, like Douglass's heroic slave, creating an other context, of and for freedom (an other reality); is he, like Ellison's invisible man, charting an other course for recognition, for himself in this land; or, perhaps, is he working to construct an other land of an other space and time?

What is unique about Whitehead's novel is that his irony functions bidirectionally, referencing itself—in the performative irony of a black male nomenclature specialist—but also history, historical peoples and relationality, and the logic of reality. In this way, language itself, naming itself, is the specific analytic strategy, and the black male as specialist is Whitehead's unique deployment of this strategy. Throughout the novel, Whitehead seems to taunt his reader with this possible misdirection, having the black male naming specialist go through various schemes of naming of various commercial products, some more successfully than others, might alert readers to the significance of naming but may also serve as a distraction from *what* is really being named and by whom. For Whitehead, the commercial products are themselves metaphors or, more precisely, are the specific ways that the narrator deploys himself and marks his own vulnerability as the unnamed, invisible source of this constructed world.

There is one commercial product in particular that is the crux of the narrator's metaphorical deployment, the product for which the book is titled: Apex, for which the marketing slogan "Hides the Hurt" was the narrator's greatest naming achievement. Toward the end of the novel, Whitehead gives us a glimpse of the narrator's metaphorical deployment. In an evocative scene revealing the narrator as that which is named and consumed rather than the named product, Whitehead flashes back to a conversation in which the specialist is told by a colleague, "Wise up—you *are* the product," after which his colleague "paused to let this apparently obvious concept settle in" (*Apex*,146; emphasis in original). If we think of the naming of commercial products as the narrator's own deployment, then the narrator being told that he *is* the product alerts readers that the narrator, in effect, is marketing and selling himself as a commercial product. In the context of the time and space of Western modernity, this suggests the commercialization of black male bodies but also suggests something further: it begs the question if a black man can liberate himself from these conditions by achieving the heights of these conditions for himself.

The title of the novel, *Apex Hides the Hurt*, also suggests that the narrator's performative deployment as specialist is akin to Ellison's opening line, "I am an invisible man," in which Whitehead's narrator, by asserting expertise and control, is really enacting a self-assertively self-negating *lack* of control. The title of the novel, along with this suggestive self-negation, brings the mind back to our initial discussion in this chapter: How can a black man constitute himself within a linguistic space that negates his existence? In other words, can a black man become captain of industry in the space and time in which his own body has been and continues to be commodified and sold as a commercial product?

Whitehead's novel leaves us in a quandary: What is he telling us? If the title references the narrator, we are left to puzzle out, what is the Apex, and what hurt does it hide? Why does the highest point not only fail to solve but exacerbate the hurt by hiding it? Is the highest point the highest precisely because it hides the hurt? And from whom is this hurt being hidden—from himself or from all others? Before we uncover more of the title, we first have to learn more about the town and its history and how this man came to this town to rename it.

III

> It was the kind of business where there were a lot of Eureka stories. Much of the work went on in the subconscious level. He was making connections between things without thinking and then, *bam* on the subway scratching a nose, or *bam bam* while stubbing a toe on the curb. Floating in neon before him was the name.
> —Colson Whitehead, *Apex Hides the Hurt*

To recap, with more detail: our nameless black specialist is chosen by a midwestern town to settle a historic dispute. The dispute: a town is at a crossroads; the city council is trying to decide on a name. The council is choosing, ostensibly, between two names: the current name, Winthrop, and the original name, Freedom. They are deadlocked, for there are only two members on the council—the descendant of the original settlers who named the town Freedom and the descendant of the man for whom it is currently named Winthrop. They have called a consulting firm for help. As the company's best namer of things, our narrator is tasked, almost poetically but certainly ironically, with mediating a naming dispute between the descendant of a wealthy white land entrepreneur and capitalist expansionist, Winthrop, and the descendant of the dispossessed but self-possessed, newly "freed" runaway enslaved, Goode and Field. Our narrator is told that Goode and Field had agreed, in "basically a business deal," to rename the town after Winthrop.

> Winthrop comes along and falls in love with the area—that river traffic, at any rate—and so they [Goode and Field] decided to make it [the name change] legal. I think it was hard to argue with the kind of access Winthrop'd provide to the outside world—having a white guy

up front—so they got together to incorporate the town. . . . At that point you needed a certain number of citizens in order to incorporate and be officially recognized by the state. There was a whole community already here to pump up the numbers. Both sides got something out of it. (*Apex*, 95–96)

Just like that, a business arrangement settled the name of the town, at least historically. The matter, for them, seemed to have been settled, but this is not how history actually works—though the matter may have been settled in the past, we do not engage the past really; we engage ourselves in the present representing the past to ourselves. As such, history is, and remains, for the descendants, still an open arrangement. The town history, like the name itself, is something that must be lived with, must be negotiated by each subsequent generation, to see what we have done with the words, with language, and if the language and the meaning inherent in its living condition is still adequate given what we have made of the world: Does Freedom still mean for us what it did for Goode and Field? Would we still make the same arrangement as had Goode and Field for the access Winthrop originally provided? Are the sets of relations between the descendants the same as they were for Goode and Field and Winthrop?

To complicate matters, the town has fallen on financial hard times, and it is decided that it requires a new direction. The name, it is decided, needs to be rethought—perhaps the old name merely rebranded. In comes a business man, Lucky Aberdeen. Aberdeen, though not of this history, seeks to weigh in on this open arrangement of history and naming, introducing the new name possibility New Prospera, to reflect, as it were, the new prosperity that he promises to bring. And, as Winthrop had done in the past, Aberdeen can provide access to wealth and opportunity for the town, all at the cost of its name; history is ironic in that the fate of capitalist expansionism, which had visited Goode and Field, was now visiting Winthrop and carrying with it the same edict: the reconstitution of reality in exchange for access to the outside world. Industrialization meets post-Industrialization.

To settle this dispute between an original black town, turned from Freedom to Industrial white town of Winthrop and now from an Industrial town to, potentially, a post-Industrial town of New Prospera, is a black man, as specialist, who will navigate the pre-Industrial past of enslavement, the Industrial present, and the post-Industrial future. We are, it seems, always "tarrying for the Lord," always reconciling ourselves with ourselves—always preparing to make the path straight. How, though, does our naming specialist navigate such a divide?

First, the two descendants have to agree to our consultant's terms, "simple, albeit a tad unusual. If the clients were going to hire him, they had to let the name stand for a minimum of one year. . . . His intention was that it would force them to consider the process—his process—with the appropriate gravity" (*Apex*, 31). Whitehead is alerting the reader to the fact that there is gravity in living the consequences of our decisions—that is, there is a certain denseness to names that can only be understood by existing in the world that they construct for us. But in this particular case, there is the additional density of consciously giving shape to an other logic, not just the descendants deciding their fates but the presence of an external voice emerging to artificially construct, from outside this history, an other logic of the past or the present enacted in a name. Historicity, especially that which is consciously constructed, is for Whitehead very much a metaphysical proposition.

Whitehead is also alerting readers as to the difficulty of reading a novel such as *Apex*. Whitehead's novel does not merely analyze language and its relationship to reality. It is also a novel of an other time and space, an other historical trajectory that somehow appears in the contemporary time and space to offer itself as a challenge. And although the story is about a town that physically exists within the novel's contemporary universe, it is also about a novel whose temporal reality is no longer in the past, the present, or the future of its own universe. The novel's temporality seems to be in conflict with its spatiality. The narrator is, thus, both here (in this town, with its descendants) telling the story and not here (somewhere else other than the town renaming the town) in projecting the possible future of the town; both there in words and names and simultaneously not there in creating a new context of and for the meaning the town. This both/and quality of the novel gives it a sense of history and ahistoricality, a logic that disrupts its own logic. It is, in this way, both artifact and archive, an atonal cacophonous rendering of a space and time when parallel worlds partially overlap.

Some are teethed on a silver spoon

Our narrator is confronted with this cacophonous rendering of conflicting historicalities by the town inhabitants. Throughout the novel, the narrator is confronted by different inhabitants who attempt to sway his decision about the town's name and the generation of its future. There are two such conversations that stand out in the novel, ones that represent divergent renderings of the town's past and the meaning of its past names.

The first instruction that the narrator receives of the town's logic and history is from the town's white librarian. She tells the narrator,

> The Winthrops made their fortune in barbed wire, not too bad a gig at the end of the nineteenth century. Land grants, land grabs, you needed something cheap to keep everything in, and keep everything out. "With the zeal of a true American entrepreneur, Sterling

> Winthrop found customers among the region's farmers and homesteaders, who delighted in the inexpensive alternative to costly timber. Even the railroad enlisted the aid of Winthrop's fine wire to keep its lines free and clear."
>
> . . .
>
> "Where others saw untamed wilderness . . . Sterling saw endless bounty and prime opportunities." Underdeveloped land in the modern jive: a lowly parking lot where high-rises deserved to tower. The river provided a way to move the goods. *And the place was empty. Mostly.* "After winning over the area's main inhabitants—a loose band of colored settlers—Winthrop opened up his factory and started producing his famous W-shaped barb, which can still be seen all over the county. Grateful for the fresh start, they passed a law and named the town Winthrop, after the man who had the courage to dream." (*Apex*, 60–61; emphasis added)

From the town's white librarian, the keeper of the town's authorized knowledge, our narrator learns that the town's history is one of enclosure, that the town's logic is one of creating boundaries. But our narrator also learns that the town's history is one of erasure: in the creation of boundaries and enclosure, the town also created a sense of dispossession and the dispossessed captured in the phrase "the place was empty. Mostly." That is, the only way to grab land and enclose it is to imagine it to be empty, untamed, wild. As such, the name "Winthrop" articulated in the "W-shaped barb" carried within the material reality of said enclosure and erasure.

Additionally, our narrator is told that the inhabitants were "grateful for the fresh start" that enclosure and erasure brought to them, and they named the town after the man "who had the courage to dream" of the idea of exclusive ownership, of wilderness, and the creation of such boundaries. Winthrop gave the town not only a direction, a logic of organization, but also a calling, one that marked time and space—enclosure, which was a material reality, was also the conceptual strata through which the land as well as the individuals occupying the land could understand themselves. The newly minted Winthrop, like many midwestern American cities, was created by the context that perpetuates its existence: "where others saw untamed wilderness . . . Sterling [Winthrop] saw endless bounty and prime opportunities." Winthrop, as it were, found itself amid the milieu of land grabs and American western expansionism and replicated these in itself.

With stars strung for a rattle

From the town's local black bartender, our narrator learns a different history and a different logic of and for the town:

> "This was a colored town once," he said. "Founded by free black men and women, did you know that?"
>
> "No . . . I read something about barbed wire," he said.
>
> "*Barbed wire*. That was later. No. This here was founded by free black men. They came from Georgia and set up and built themselves a new life. It was after that Old Man Winthrop came here with his factory and put it on the map. He came here after." (*Apex*, 25)

Our narrator learns from the black bartender, a descendant of the original settlement, that the town's original logical structure and organization was not that of enclosure or boundaries, not even that of erasure, but a counterstatement of sorts. Founded by "free black men and women" who "came from Georgia, and set up and built themselves a new life," this town was a statement against enslavement, a statement against enclosure and boundaries; it was a statement of self-discovery. Our narrator learns that the original inhabitants were not "a loose band of colored settlers" in need of a "fresh start," which would mean that they did not simply elect to change the name because they were grateful but did so for some other reason. If the original inhabitants named the town after their own self-discovery in Freedom, why would they change the name to a name signaling "land grants, land grabs," and cheap ways "to keep everything in, and keep everything out"?

I cut my teeth as a black raccoon—

Our narrator is thrown into theatrical staging. He hears two competing views of the foundation of the town, of its logic and its history, and must read between these two narratives to understand what has happened, what is happening, and its significance for how the town has emerged in this moment in which they have called him. Theatrical moments can be and usually are serious matters about serious matters—as we witnessed in our discussion of the theatricality of invisibility in chapter 2 and as witnessed in Douglass's heroic slave in chapter 1. Whitehead's theatrical moments are staged confrontations of naming as the deployment of a discursive strategy that underlies and is reified in our living conditions—Freedom, Winthrop, and whatever name will follow—and the narrator himself.

Whitehead here is instructing readers through the enactment of the town as to the phenomenological exchange of unresolved dualities, placing readers in the midst of the discernment of living history. On the one hand, there is the formally recognized and educated librarian and what is written in the publicly recognized texts; on the other hand, there is the formally unrecognized and uneducated bartender and what is not written but stated in folkloric texts. The phenomenological encounter between the statement of authorized historical force is met with the counterstatement of folk cultural historical memory; the synoptic American expansionist image of Winthrop, about whom we assume we always already know plenty—he is the sort of man for whom building and streets are named—is met with the conjured image of enslaved men and women, about whom little is known, except within the oral historical record.

And in the name, we see a further exchange of history and logic: in Winthrop, the merits and "zeal of true American" liberty and freedom in enterprise and industry. Winthrop, though named for a man, is more of the principle of understanding of modern Western materialism in enclosure and boundary making. In Winthrop the larger argument is over reasoned control over the environment, of the status and victory of civilization over nature. In Freedom, the condition of men and women, recently objects of Western materialism, thought to be wild and untamed like the land itself, in need of enclosure, like the land itself, having freed themselves in the form of marronage, found their freedom in the untameness of the land and in their own untameness. In Freedom, untameness was a resistance to Western modernity and a counterstatement—by not enclosing the land and refusing enclosure in their own life, they had founded a town and themselves with their freedom.

For implements of battle

We see a battle, then, not only of and for history—the telling or narrating of the past—but also of and for the logic of cognitive and spatial organization and meaning for how reality is to be understood and lived within a name, within language, how the town is to be defined, either by the self-liberating act of marronage or by the specific act of encircling the land with the technology of modernity and capitalism. The theatrical element, for our narrator, is that the town is both of these competing histories; the town is a both/and ambiguity that reveals Goode and Field and Winthrop as mirrored reversals of one another, in the same way that in the American context, blackness and antiblackness or whiteness are mirrored reversals.

It is here, then, at the level of the name, at the level of language, that we must discover how our narrator will explore this conflict and, in the end, how he will handle the future. To do so, we must ask how language functions, specifically, how names function and how they relate, reveal, or conceal reality. In other words, we must discover the relationship between names and things, names and reality, naming and the meaning and logic of the world. Whitehead offers us what can be surmised as nine theses or suggestions as to how language may function, how naming may function, and how it may structure the logic or the inner life of reality. The next section is an exploration of these theses, navigating Whitehead's analytic strategy—in the inherent ironic deployment of a black nomenclature specialist—and how in this post-Industrial landscape we can both situate and understand the American context of past, present, and future. Through an analysis of Whitehead's theses, we can come to understand, at last, the name that the specialist decides to give the town.

Scene Three: Selected Theses under Consideration

Thesis One: Things Evoke Their Names (and Vice Versa)

The relationship between naming, names, namers, and things or experiences named and the process of their emergence is serious business. If the relationship is not adequately and/or strictly followed and things or experiences are misnamed, the thing, experience, and/or namer recedes beneath the incorrect category. The name can conceal the thing, experience, or namer underneath a pseudonym that promises clarity and disclosure. The name can reveal, but it can also conceal; and the thing, experience, or namer, as it is hidden beneath a visage, may actually hide itself beneath this misapplied adequation.

The process is imprecise and relies on trial and error. Sometimes the name comes first, waiting on the thing et al. to appear. Sometimes the thing et al. is just there, dangling, waiting to be named, to make its entrance into the world. Without its proper name, the thing et al. still exists but not for us, not to us. Rather, it remains out there, just beyond our reach, having its affects but unknown in terms of what it is. That is to say, we cannot really know a thing et al. without having its proper name. That is to say, we cannot experience reality properly if it is misnamed. If we could know the proper names of things, then we could really know what they are and know how to engage them in the past, present, and future—and possibly know their destiny. This is why naming is serious business—the fate of reality itself is at stake. Whitehead instructs us as to the narrator's consciousness and process of naming. He writes, "Sometimes he [the narrator] came up with a name that didn't fit the client but would one day be perfect for something else, and these he kept away from the world, reassuring them over the long years. . . . A good name did not dry up and get old. It waited for its intended" (*Apex*, 4).

Our narrator suggests that we not waste names on things et al. that are not directly related to the thing. The irony here is that in a hypercapitalist or late modern capital world, efficiency is more important than effectiveness, which is captured in the very fact that the town would outsource its name—its future, its destiny—to a company that has no knowledge of its history, of its people, or of the significance of the past and the current name. In this hypercapital moment, our narrator still values the process and the name itself, for even though in this moment, the name or its capacity to be bought and sold seems to determine its value, our narrator resists the capital encroachment onto the metaphysical plane. But if it happens to actually be the right name, well, then, it would be one of those "Eureka stories," where the name would be "floating in neon before him" (*Apex*, 4).

This is the difficulty of this town—to find its proper name, not one that is agreed upon but one that actually captures the living element of the town itself, both literally and metaphorically. The narrator's task is to thread the needle of metaphysical insight and commercial success—that which is both economically viable for profit but also captures something about the inner structure and logic of a thing et al. But what, exactly, *is* the meaning of a town that begins as Freedom and ends with Winthrop, that is, begins as the extension of individual will (marronage) and ends in capture?

What does the original name of the town, Freedom, still say about the town, about its inhabitants and their inner relationship? Does it still capture this metaphysical or essential quality of living relation? If so, what would this mean about who the descendants were, are, and will be? Have they been concealed under a false name, Winthrop? What was, is, and will be their freedom? Will it be the same as or different from Goode and Field's?

What about the name Winthrop? What does it still say about the town, about its inhabitants and their inner relationship? Does it still capture this metaphysical or essential quality of living relation? Is this name an ongoing business transaction between historical parties and now their descendants? If so, does this mean that the townspeople became and still are homo economicus similar to or, perhaps, different from what Goode and Field and Winthrop were? Or have they been living under a false name?

And, what of New Prospera? Is this a serious contender for the essential workings of this town and its set of metaphysical relations? Are the sets of relation somehow new? If so, how? What of the old has changed? Does prosperity mark the change from old to new? Was the old set of relations not prosperous? Is this name literal or metaphorical or neither? Is it aspirational, directing us to who we should become? Can and should we name things et al. after who or what we are or what we need to or desire to become?

In threading this needle, the narrator must also ask about the relationship the ancestors had with and to themselves and to their outside world. How and by what process can the narrator judge if he has threaded the needle just right, if he has gotten the name just right, if he has captured the thing et al. and not further hidden it and ourselves from itself and ourselves?

Thesis Two: Things Become Their Names

If a name evokes a thing et al. (and vice versa), then a name can, in a sense, create the conditions for the possibility of an experience. Does this mean, then, that things et al. are or become the names we give them? Did we get it wrong in the first thesis? Things et al. do not evoke their names but are captured in a name that states their metaphysical condition? And in their evocation, they become themselves (in the realm of appearance) through their names? We name things et al. and then, once having captured them, continue to evoke their essence in the name? As such, the name is more essential than the thing? Can we, then, vanquish the thing et al. and keep only the name, existing on a metaphysical plane of the real or reality? Does the thing et al. only exist to point (literally and metaphorically) to that which is beyond itself, its own metaphysical condition revealed through the name it has been given? And once we have captured this, the thing et al. no longer has a function? Is the process of naming, then, not to understand how to relate to things et al. but how to circumscribe ourselves within our living essence discovered in things, to not metaphysically be adrift at sea of "blooming, buzzing confusion"?[7]

If this is so, then, does a thing et al. become absorbed by its name, the way a twin sometimes absorbs its sibling in utero, syphoning the resources of life? Does a name act as a sort of vanishing thing syndrome? In this case the thing et al. named does not exist below or beneath the visage of its name but becomes the name. And this is the seriousness of naming—getting the metaphysical constitution that is to direct our living condition just right? Is this why our narrator is willing to wait for the right name for the thing et al.?

What, then, of the material world? If the name consumes the thing et al., where does the material thing exist? How does it exist? If it is still physically present but metaphysically absent, how is this negotiated with the experience of reality? And what of the namer—what of the namer is consumed in this process? If we are concerned with our pure experience and our pure knowledge of reality, what becomes of reality that is not constituted by us? Or do we, have we, consumed ourselves by consuming things et al. with a name? Whitehead gives a literal and metaphorical answer:

> He [the narrator] drifted off reminiscing about the tools of the trade. He drifted off thinking of kickers. Somewhere in the night he had a nightmare. Rats bubbled out of the sewers, poured out of gutters and abandoned buildings. Making little rat noises. They were everywhere, and he knew that even though they wore the skin of rats, they were in fact phonemes, bits of words with sharp teeth and tails. Latin roots, syllables to be added or subtracted to achieve an effect, kickers in their excellent variety, odd fricatives, and they chased him down. They finally cornered him in an old warehouse and he woke as they started nibbling on his vanishing toe. (*Apex*, 52–53)

Do these rats, the elements of words, individually gnawing our narrator piece by piece, come together to form words, names to eat things et al. whole? Do names consume the thing et al. to reveal the lineal root genus of reality? Did the name Freedom originally come into existence to consume what that false state of human affairs had wrought in consciousness and in the nation itself, in which men could own other men? And did the name Winthrop come into existence, encroaching on the wildness of the land with the logic of barbed wire and boundary making, to remind us of our continual failure—to remind us that just because we had amended the Constitution, we had not yet achieved the Freedom of Goode and Field but had traded their Freedom for the more nefarious concept of freedom in the capital expansion of Winthrop? Did Winthrop remind us of what could happen when things et al. are consumed within a false metaphysical reality? Or did Winthrop come into existence to remind us that human freedom was but a dream and that, all along, throughout human history, all that has ever existed is conquering, enclosure, and enslavement? And what of New Prospera? What new metaphysical reality emerges out of prosperity, and what current or past set of false relations was being consumed for us to live within in this new metaphysical frontier? Is this name to remind us that "nobody lasts because there's always somebody else" and that, perhaps, if names always consume and wait for a new set of metaphysical relations to emerge with a new name, perhaps it is naming itself "that was their undoing. They should have kept the place nameless"? (*Apex*, 188). Perhaps, this is the lesson of New Prospera or what we are to learn from Freedom and Winthrop—the liberation from metaphysics altogether. But what then? Can names ever liberate a thing et al. in itself, or do all names reveal things et al. in order to erase them and us?

Thesis Three: Names Are Impositions

If the thing et al. disappears, is consumed within a name, and, through this process, the name names a deeper, metaphysical condition of the thing et al., then the thing et al/ disappears or is consumed within its own metaphysical condition. That is, the thing et al. itself is only one, superfluous mode of its expression, and the essential nature of things et al. are not in their material expression but in the literal and metaphorical expression. *The name of the thing subsumes it as its condition for being named.* But the matter is not yet settled: Where do these names come from? Are they divined by consciousness or created by consciousness in relationship or interaction with the thing et al.? Either way, it does not solve the dilemma inherent in interpretation. In other words, if names are divined by consciousness, the question remains, Is there a proper way or method of understanding of such divination? Or if names are but the creation of consciousness in relation to things et al., what, then, is the real metaphysical essence of consciousness itself? Are things et al. but the manner and mode of consciousness coming to know itself through naming its reality?

How, though, does consciousness relate to itself in the mode of others? Who decides on the essential structure of reality inherent in a name? Is this essential structure open to all consciousness in the same way? Does it elicit the same meaning, the same interpretive structure? For example, is the freedom of Goode and Field, metaphysically enacted in marronage, the same as the Winthrop's notion of freedom enacted materially through taming the land to metaphysically reveal to it (and to consciousness) its untapped potential?

This seems to be a critical moment of relationality and in naming, between evoking and becoming, interpreted by different persons, who then decide the meaning and mode of discovery and consciousness itself. Who, between Goode and Field and Winthrop, decides on the proper metaphysical structure for the town, for themselves? And given that so much is on the line, where does our narrator come in?

Whitehead alerts us to this trouble: "You call something by a name, you fix it in place. A thing or a person, it didn't matter—the name you gave it allowed you to draw a bead, take aim, shoot. But there was a flip side of calling something by the name you gave it—and that was *wanting to be called by the name that you gave yourself*. What is the name that will give me the dignity and respect that is my right? The key that will unlock the world" (*Apex*, 192). For Whitehead, the name locks and unlocks reality—that is, gives us a more direct and insightful way of knowing and engaging reality. Whitehead here seems to be suggesting something further—that social and historical power dynamics create names for things et al., and in doing so, things et al. neither evoke nor become but have their names imposed. Is this really what consciousness is doing—imposing order onto reality?

For, as Whitehead instructs, there are moments when these things et al. respond, refuse to be consumed, to be banished, to be named, and announce themselves in their own name to consciousness, to reality, to the world itself. What happens then? Is *this* what Freedom constituted—a refusal to be named and to name oneself? But, as Whitehead reminds us, someone was on the land and had already named it before Goode and Field arrived and named it Freedom. Freedom marked their existence but not necessarily that of the land. What is the name of the land? Can a name ever really evoke the land itself? After a parade of names, of "conquests and false hopes," one is left asking of the possibility of a shared world—one of evocation or becoming without imposition? (*Apex*, 188).

Can things et al., then, ever be liberated in this process, from this process, from having their fundamental condition named? And if names are not eternal and the relations are always shifting, then names can never really capture the essence of things et al. in perpetuity, then, it seems, names and the naming process are bound to fail, bounded by failure—bound to, as it were, wear out and be overcome. How, though, do we know when a thing et al. has outgrown its name? Is it when the people themselves have changed? Are there warning signs? Or is the warning sign the revolution itself—the revolution of things et al. against their names and against their namers? Is this what the narrator has stepped into—the cyclical revolution of the town against its name? Is the narrator's task to discover a name that will not cause a revolt, or is he just putting a Band-Aid on the problem until the next revolution? In other words, how can one choose a name that can capture essence without imposing this essence onto reality as its condition of being?

Thesis Four: Names Are Functional

Suppose that this discussion of metaphysical structures and essential natures of things et al. is just the imposition of consciousness onto a reality that does not actually exist. What if this reality is either indifferent to or unaware of consciousness's imposition—of our names, of our perceptions, of our desire to control, to understand it as the basis for our truth?

Suppose one cannot be a good or a bad namer of things et al., for things et al. have no relation to their names—metaphysical or impositional?

Would names just name the condition under which they are brought about? Would names become but the logic or understanding and interpretation of a particular context, in which they are but functional representatives of consciousness? Would names merely be the functional operation of consciousness within a world that it has created to reify itself and understand its existence?

Would Freedom be just the actions of men and women who no longer wanted to live in bondage but not itself a discourse on the merits or lack thereof of bondage itself? Is there no actual freedom, just our actions in a particular set of circumstances?

Would Winthrop just be the representative name given for the condition of our desire to control the land we have placed in opposition to consciousness?

Would New Prospera be the opportunity to start over, new and fresh, without having to deal with the past?

Whitehead suggests that names are just the set of expectations given to reality and how reality will appear to consciousness. He writes, "Some might say a rose by any other name but he [the narrator] didn't believe that crap. That was crazy talk. Bad for business, bad for morale. A rose by any other name would wilt fast, smell like bitter almonds" (*Apex*, 5). In other words, a rose by another name might trigger different expectations on what the experience of the rose will be. But that says nothing about the name or the thing, only ourselves, our expectations of what a name signifies about a thing et al. But a name is just that: an expectation set in the world as to the meaning of a thing et al.

In the case of the town, it is not the name that matters; the name merely triggers our expectation of what our experience of the town will be. The town itself is just the organization of space as the material expression of consciousness. There is no particular way that matter must be organized or that it be organized at all. It is a choice, it is *all* a choice; and one can choose for, against, or neither for nor against a set of relational and organizational principles.

And though we can sometimes lose or get lost in the function of a name and take the name to be metaphysical, history will remind us of its inherent variability. This could be what the narrator is stepping into, a reminder from history that the name itself is a function of who we want to be or become, what we are trying to remove ourselves from, how we are trying to shape the expectations of ourselves and potential others. In other words, names are the business of thought. The narrator, as an expert of names, as an expert of thoughts, is hired to control, constrain, create, and manage expectations and, thus, must discover exactly how the town has functioned, how it continues to function, and what the parties themselves really desire of and for themselves.

Thesis Five: A Name Is Earned

Nothing or no-thing has a name. A name cannot be discovered, nor can it be imposed. A name cannot consume the thing et al. A name is not merely the functional representation of our intentional consciousness, just as history is not merely the record of our names and the expectations articulated through them. A name is something real but not metaphysically so. It is something manifested through the material world; it is just not what we have thought it was so far—it is not in consciousness, in the material world, or in between. Rather, a name emerges out of or through its experiences, through the conflicts and revolutions over it. A name is not something that can be divined or simply given. A name is something that exists only after it has been fought for, only after it has died to itself and been reborn, only after it has been earned. Whitehead writes, "Warning: The Name Remains the Same, But Contents May Have Changed Over Time. A warning sticker equally at home on people as much as things, he thought. There were plenty of people walking around wearing their old names, even though their old names had been gutted. Happened all the time" (*Apex*, 159).

The fullness of the narrator's contractual condition—"they had to let the name stand for a minimum of one year"—is now understood with the fullest weight. The name needs time to settle into the world, be properly vetted by experience itself, vetted by history itself, in order for the town to become its name. This is the historicity of a thing et al., in this case, the town.

We are once again visited by the "dark matter" questions that began this chapter. Is this what these questions were meant to signify, that names had to be tested by the world to see if they would stick, to see if the world would reject them, to see if there would be a revolution, to see what they had to offer to us, not to things but to us who, having suffered and having been alienated in the world, by the world, are to come to know ourselves in our fullest measure?

The original name, Freedom, was something that Goode and Field had achieved in their conflict with enslavement. The town earned this name through what it took for Goode and Field to achieve their own reality. The difficulty, then, would be that this name would eventually have to be overcome—that is, the experiences of the town itself and people themselves would surpass this meaning, for future conflicts would elicit other names. *Names must give way to other names.*

Winthrop represented the beginning of a new historical cycle of a modernized economy away from slave labor and toward mechanization and wage labor. The conflict was new and needed a new name to capture this new historical condition. The town had surpassed Freedom and was now Winthrop.

The difficulty of New Prospera, as with the postmodern condition in general, is that it represents the intuition that our names and the naming process itself do not, cannot, specify the organic development and changes within consciousness. What postmodernism offers and is offered in "New Prospera" is an intuition of another possibility: the possibility of substantive; internal change is undercut with a lacuna of knowing on the part of an equally unknowable subject. New Prospera represents a new, different battle over possibility: the possibility of a future cut against the presence of the moment. But, what is more, in fighting for possibility, it, like the postmodern condition, also settles itself on the idea that there is no independent reality, that all naming and things et al. in their various meanings are capricious. *Names did not need to be earned; they were just there, to be picked up, put on and arranged and rearranged.* The real was a desert filled with mirages.

While New Prospera signified something old, perhaps "Spanish or Italian," the history of how this cultural ethos developed, how the language developed, how one could hear in it the history of conquests and losses, this was all wiped clean. New denied and defined the historicity of Prospera, came to define it as it saw fit: "what it meant in those languages, that was unimportant, what was important was how it resonated here. . . . *Prospera* left no fingerprints on its gleaming surface" (*Apex*, 52.) In short, New Prospera, like its postmodern condition, was an attempt to shortcut the process of becoming and emerge already fully formed in a world deconstructed of meaning, with a history it could not possibly fully understand.

As such, the long arc of human consciousness that produced Freedom and Winthrop and came to know itself in these names was to be replaced by New Prospera, a name that represented the denial of consciousness's history and historical becoming. Rather, the name signified, "New, new, new money, new media, new economy. New order, New Prospera" (*Apex*, 52). It represented a break or an ontological rupture—a break from the past, a break in and a break from the baggage of historical consciousness, a break from the weight of coming to know yourself as a historical being unfolding within history.

But the difficulty of naming a thing et al. after what could not be earned or after what is earned through historical becoming is that, in either case, it is not the thing that revolts against the name but ourselves who revolt against ourselves, against the names we have given ourselves; and in the course of revolution, we give ourselves new names after new names. Does the naming ever end? Does consciousness ever come to terms with itself, with its experience as the formative completion of its task in full self-recognizing knowledge? Or is it ever continually searching? Can one ever name this ontological upheaval and end the war? Name this "*content* to be the *Self's* own *act*"?[8] Would naming the condition of consciousness release consciousness from itself? Is this task of the narrator to offer a name that would be the accomplishment of self-reflective consciousness?

*from the chalice of this realm of spirits
foams forth for Him his own infinitude?*[9]

Thesis Six: Names Are the Work of Science

Suppose a name does not name or arise from the history of consciousness's internal conflict. Suppose that what a name names is not the historicity of subjective knowledge or its historical becoming but the relationship between stimuli and response? Suppose that historical consciousness or self-reflective consciousness is but expectation generated from this relationship? What sort of approach would be needed to name this name? What sort of specialist or professional would be necessary to name epiphenomenal, epigenetic expectation? Would our narrator need to be a scientist of sorts to understand that history is just stimuli and historicity or historical becoming just the response? And suppose that what we call "knowledge" and "experience" or "consciousness" coming to know itself are but epigenetic, epiphenomenal expectation? What sort of scientist could name expectation?

> Consider a simple organism—say a planarian or an amoeba—moving non-randomly across the bottom of a laboratory dish, always heading to the nutrient-rich end of the dish, or away from the toxic end. This organism is seeking the good, or shunning the bad—its own good and bad. . . . Seeking one's own good is a fundamental feature of any rational agent, but are these simple organisms seeking or just "seeking"?[10]

> Nature has placed mankind under the governance of two sovereign masters, pain and pleasure. It is for them alone to point out what we ought to do, as well as to determine what we shall do.[11]

> The world often begins to practice a thing long before it begins to speculate about it.[12]

Suppose that the phenomenal world is a laboratory dish and that we are moving across the dish, either toward or away from certain experiences. Those experiences we move toward we find tasteful or pleasurable; and those experiences we move away from we find distasteful or painful. And suppose we name those experiences and in naming them constitute a relationship between the word and our body or consciousness.

Names, then, would name the history of the body—the history of pleasure and the history of pain and the history of connectors of good or bad registered in the body and expressed linguistically, would name the history of receptors that are activated or triggered in some particular way. Freedom would mark the experience of the pain of enslavement or the physical bondage of the flesh, and marronage, or moving away from bondage, would then mark the response. Yet this experience of pain preceded any name, just as the act of marronage preceded the name Freedom. The name Freedom, which marked this moving away and moving toward, was both reminder and trigger of and for pleasure and pain. And Winthrop was but the experience of a protracted and controlled body moving away from pain—controlled and protracted by another set of circumstances, not enslavement but the bondage of cultural and religious tradition—and toward what was experienced as pleasurable: the control and boundary making of the material world. Winthrop, too, like Freedom, came only after the expression of a principle—in the case of Winthrop, that of creating boundaries, the barbed wire but a material expression of this principle. And New Prospera—what is being moved away from and toward in this name? What is being remembered and triggered here? Would it just be the postmodern condition of alienation from nature, of techno-scientific organization of space and time? What pains does this elicit? What pleasures does it promise?

To understand the town, the townspeople, to properly name it and them, the narrator would have the task, then, of a scientist—of understanding pain and pleasure, of knowing what is being moved away from and what is being moved toward, and of naming that. To do this, he would have to sift through the expectation—that is, the history of engagement or exchange between consciousness, the body, and the material world—at the level of pleasures and pains. This would be more than the work of scientific hypothesis; it would be the science of historicity. That is, it would set out to discover the epiphenomenal and epigenetics of pleasure and pleasure and expectation—those set into the world through names and in naming. This is the only condition under which he would be able to really name the town.

But Whitehead's narrator is not a scientist of any sort and certainly not of the epigenetic and epiphenomenal sort of theorizing pains and pleasures or the naming of that which has already happened and is not yet named. He is a commercial nomenclature specialist whose job it is to create consumers, not name their underlying condition. Whitehead tells us, "I name things like new detergents and medicines and stuff like that so that they sound catchy. . . . You have some kind of pill to put people to sleep or make them less depressed *so they can accept the world.* Well you need a reassuring name that will make them believe in the pill. . . . So I think up good names for things" (*Apex*, 22).

The narrator tells us that part of his task, part of *the* task of commercialization itself, is to reassure people, to allow them to accept the world as it is constructed and constituted for them rather than by them. The significance of the town charging a commercial firm with this task rather than allowing the name to reveal itself in the already existing conditions tells us something about the post-*post*-moment inherent in Whitehead's novel. Perhaps the people themselves can no longer endure their historical knowledges and require an expert to give them a name, not to change the world but to allow them to accept the world. Perhaps the pains of having to face pains and the pleasure in evasion or outsourcing the task *is* what is being remembered and triggered here with the invitation? Perhaps this is the task of commercialization; and, what, perhaps, marks commercialization as the new science—not of pains and pleasures or expectations, but acceptance? In either case, the task of our narrator, then, appears not to be that of a prophet or a traditional scientist but that of a marketer, a brander whose epigenetic and epiphenomenal task is that of allowing people to accept the historical knowledges already existing (*Apex*, 117). And perhaps this is the central aspect of a nomenclature specialist and perhaps what is most troubling about Whitehead's novel: it is not really an engagement with pleasure and pains, not a response to stimuli, but a structured evasion of phenomenal experience. What happens if we take the "dynamic force of a name" and distill it in digestible pill form? (*Apex*, 137).

What happens if we were to approach the town as a scientist turned industrial psychologist turned market capitalist, who in marking the history of pleasure and pains, in knowing this history, rather than revealing it to itself and to us as stimuli and response, turns it into an opportunity to create new desires, to create an altered context, in a sense to alter the neural connectors and turn the town itself into a kind of commercial enterprise—one that does not mark pleasure and pains but marks commercially produced desire?

Thesis Seven: Names Are the Work of Our Inner World

If the narrator, as nomenclature specialist, is tasked with helping the town's council members accept the reality, he still must know the history of stimuli and response that got the town and the townspeople into their difficulty to begin with. How, though, does he gain this knowledge? Even if he is not engaging in "dark matter" questions of metaphysics, he is, nonetheless, engaging in a sort of metaphysics in the science of historicity, or the historicality of desire. In this particular situation, Whitehead's narrator is tasked with trying to understand the historicity that emerges out of and accounts for that stimuli and response preceding and captured by Freedom and Winthrop—or the historicity of enslavement, Reconstruction, the Industrial Revolution, and post-Industrialization that constitutes what we call "America," situated in this midwestern town. He must divine the neural chemical receptor relations between pleasures and pains situated in those variously bodied who engage and experience the phenomenal world variously—Goode and Field and Winthrop and their descendants. Is he, in his attempt to have them accept reality, also attempting to have them accept the historicality of their epiphenomenal, epigenetic becoming? If so, for what purpose? Is it only because he is being paid?

> The Negro is a sort of seventh son, born with a veil [caul], and gifted with second-sight in this American world.[13]

Is he a diviner of the affective feeling of stimuli and response within the material world, historical becoming? Does he understand how affective states are transubstantiated through phonemes into words, sounds uttered that would and did cause one to remember, to recall a past buried within the memory of the body? Would he, as a naming specialist not of this history, without the recall of embodied consciousness, then, serve as a bridge—perhaps more accurately a tunnel—between historicality and epiphenomenal, epigenetic being?

Whether he is a diviner or a nomenclature specialist, Whitehead still has to account for where he gets his names. Where do the words, his words, come from? Given that the narrator is outside this town's historical becoming, this particular shift from one mode of existence to another (from chattel slavery, liberation in Freedom to the early capital expansionism, boundary making in Winthrop), his words do not emerge from his historical memory of pain or pleasure or even that of evasion. Whitehead seems to suggest that the narrator not being of this historicity—or, really, of any historicity given that he drops down from nowhere, without a name, without a tangible past—actually reveals that language is deeper than just stimuli and response, deeper than pains and pleasure, deeper than neurochemical relations of words and desire. He seems to suggest that language is somehow deep down in us, as our own private worlds, worlds that we climb over and through to get to one another—and that language is a remembrance of this world. *The meta of meta*—before names metaphysically calling forth things, before names being imposed onto things, before names naming us as the source of their construction, before names being what is earned in the history of consciousness coming to know itself, before names being the expression of stimuli and response set epiphenomenally and epigenetically in the body, there are our inner worlds that we, then, come to share with one another. Our narrator tells us,

> But the names. After two weeks of listening he was full of them. Every day the door cracked another half inch and he could see beyond the tiny rooms he had stumbled around in his whole life. He pictured it like this: The door opened up on a magnificent and secret landscape. *His interior.* He clambered over rocks and mountain ranges composed of odd and alien minerals, he stepped around strange flora, saplings that curtsied eccentrically, low shrubs that extended bizarre fronds. This unreckoned land of his possessed color he had never seen before. *Flowers burst petals in arrangements never considered by the natural world,* summoned out of dirt like stained glass. These beautiful hidden things scrolled to the horizon and he walked among them. He could wander through them, stooping, collecting, acquainting himself with

them until the day he died and he would never know them all. *He had a territory within himself* and he would bring back specimens to the old world. These most excellent dispatches. His names. (*Apex*, 34–35)

This world, *his* world, was beyond the natural world but contained elements of the natural world—flowers, like those of nature but transformed into stained glass sprouting out the soil, out of *his* soil. The world of names into which he was born had made him unaccustomed to his own world, and he had to acquaint himself with this world. From this world, he would collect specimens and bring them back to the shared world. His specialty, then, was himself—he was a nomenclature specialist, and his names were him.

Did the name Freedom swing open the door to the interior of Goode and Field and the historical moment of America, conjuring an internal world once held at bay by enslavement? Did Goode and Field climb over the "rocks and mountain ranges composed of odd and alien minerals" of a dying world, giving rise to a new historical reality through their act of marronage? Were Goode and Field conjurers from their inner world into our world? What "was the word that came to their lips? What was the only thing they can think of when they see this place they have chosen? The word on their lips?" (*Apex*, 117).

And Winthrop—did it swing open that door to "strange flora, saplings that curtsied eccentrically, low shrubs that extended bizarre fronds," marking the possibility of infinite self-expansion in the world? Was the town the outgrowth of this internal impulse toward growth, toward manifesting the inner world into the shared world, as the shared world? Was the problem with Winthrop the singular belief that one's inner world could be utilized to dominate the shared world as its singular meaning, as a weed would grow around a tree and suck out nutrients?

And New Prospera—what was its inner life? Was its inner life marked by "not-yet": "the red brick bordering the park was recently laid, . . . and there were holes in the ground surrounded by plastic orange fencing where they were adding the new improvements" (*Apex*, 9). Was the not-yet but camouflage for the fact that "new" is shorthand for the erasure of the past, the turning to the interior and setting it on fire? That is, is it "dressed . . . in rustic sincerity," while adhering to "the rapacious philosophy of the multinational" (*Apex*, 39). What, in other words, is the historicity of subterfuge that is not the marronage of Freedom or the expansionism of Winthrop but that which exists to erase? Is the historicity of principled life grounded in the negation of what was?

Our narrator is tasked with the transformation and transubstantiation of the epiphenomenal and epigenetic desire into a name, tasked with navigating the historicality of consciousness set in the material world. But his task is also dimensional—that is, he must transport between his own inner world, the shared world, and the apperceived inner worlds of others, of Goode and Field and Winthrop and the contemporary townspeople. How does one interdimensionally travel? Whitehead gives us a hint. He tells us that he discovered the possibility of interdimensional transport when traveling in Europe, watching television commercials in a foreign language; and though he did not understand the language, we are told that he somehow knew, somehow understood:

> He [the narrator] had traveled abroad. In European hotels he watched European TV and on it European commercials. Be a tourist, walk the narrow streets, see one old church you've seen them all, but the commercials. *It didn't matter if you didn't understand the language, a good name cuts through.* Does it sound like candy, does it sound like perfume, does it sound like a fancy car you would like to be seen in. These things cut across cultures. In European hotels he could get five countries' programming in five different languages but it felt like home because he understood the names.
> . . . He was in foreign territory but the television brought him back, reassuring his ears with the common roots of their languages. (*Apex*, 32)

Interdimensionally, the words are no longer phonemes suggestive of meaning; they are what things et al. sound like, what the movement of air vibrationally evokes in us and for us—this, he argues, "cuts across cultures." We are told that this is the root of all languages. And in this we get a hint as to how the narrator will travel interdimensionally and speak across all inner worlds to eventually find a name for the town that will not so much name the historicity or the historicality of consciousness and/or desire but sound like the town and the townspeople.

Thesis Eight: The Science of the Word

Here is where things get complicated. What the narrator seems to be in search of is not just a name or the hidden metaphysical condition of a name or the stimuli and response a name can register, can cause, but the lineal root genus of naming itself that underlies all of these and unites them, connecting the inner life of the town's council members to the inner life of the past, present, and future of the town. He is in search of what is transdimensional rather than interdimensional. The common root of their inner language, though, cannot be language at all, at least as we commonly think of it, but something that cuts across language, some hidden realm both familiar and unfamiliar.

What the narrator is in search of is metaphysical but not in any of the ways that we have discovered so far. Our narrator must discover that which undergirds response to stimuli—that which determines pleasure and pain. The difficulty of his task is that he must go inside names, reveal that which is beyond naming, but he still must come up with a name. He must reveal that which is beyond being yet still manifests itself into and as the material landscape of the town.

In revealing the lineal root genus of our epiphenomenality and epigenetics of language, the town and the townspeople, the narrator will also reveal something about America, race, and what really ties Goode and Field and Winthrop together in this town. What will be revealed will be more than liberation from enslavement or access to the river needed for capital expansion. What will be discovered will be an overriding logic, one that draws all these elements together as the creative life force or living element of America, one that will not and cannot let Goode and Field and Winthrop ever remain too far apart or isolated from one another but keeps them dancing in creative tension, necessitating the town council's contemporary dilemma and our narrator's presence.

Sylvia Wynter gives us a possible direction as to what is at stake, what is really being discussed, and what the narrator's task really is. She argues, through Aimé Césaire and Negritude poetry, that language as a life force is never stable but is ever changing, ever adapting, and along with it, we (or what we constitute as ourselves) change with it. For Wynter, language, like identity, appears meta-stable, but this appearance is undermined in the exploration of meaning: once we attempt to discover the metaphysical root of meta-stability, we discover that, in a circular fashion, identity and language have this appearance because we have given it this appearance. Specifically, she notes, "Such a science would be defined by the fact that the study of the Word would now determine the study of nature. The implication is this: the study of nature, in this context, will now be specifically a study of the *implementing bios* agency of the human brain. Here the 'first set of instructions' (genetic codes) and the 'second set of instructions' (nongenetic codes) emerge."[14] The science of the Word, then, would be a metaphysical examination into the metaphysics of language to reveal that the inner workings of language are akin to the inner workings of our own identity. Critical to this reification of truth for Wynter is the additional element of political power—or the determination of acceptable or normal persons and unacceptable or abnormal persons enforced through the institution of life and death deemed as the natural process that accompanies relative political power or disempowerment. As such, the investigation into the metaphysical roots of language is also an investigation into communities and the relative positions of the citizen and the noncitizen foreigner, categories that for Wynter are "the 'imagined communities' of our respective ethno-class nation-states." That is, "the genre-specific subjects of each such nation-state are enabled to subjectively experience themselves/ourselves in fictively eusocialized terms . . . as inter-altruistic kin-recognizing member subjects of the same *referent-we* and its imagined community. As such, kin-recognizing member subjects law-likely and perfomatively enact themselves/ourselves as 'good men and women' of their/our *kind*."[15]

The literal and metaphorical foundation of naming suggested in theses one through seven finds its "sea legs" here with Wynter. Wynter suggests that what constitutes reality is humans' engagement with the material world and with one another. What we think of as the genetic or natural or biological elements of this relationships are but the set of mythos or narratives that we tell ourselves to instruct ourselves as to the meta-stability of our social order, no matter how unequal or death laden. We, then, inscribe ourselves within these narratives and within this social order as the foundation of our biological or natural selves: "man is a rational animal," "man is a political animal," and so on. Society, then, is the reification of this prescribed natural order through a set of mythologically based narratives we tell ourselves about the natural order to make sense of it.

For example, there is a naturally occurring abhorrence to enslavement, which manifests itself in revolution, in the declaration of freedom or liberation and in marronage. Yet there also seems to be a naturally occurring demand to dominate another, which manifests itself in enslavement (of other beings or of the land, the earth). The narrative we tell ourselves of the human will and the inherent dignity and freedom of the person is how we have decided to make sense of this very natural ordering of being. Yet this is also what draws these two sets of relations together—drawing Goode and Field and Winthrop in creative tension. Similarly, the narratives we have told ourselves about the natural state of the enslaved, the natural element of racial difference, has allowed for the institution to continue without a rupture in the relationship between space and time, the material order and generational knowledges or epistemic orders. This is what separates Goode and Field and Winthrop, but it will not let them stray into isolationism, for their different *bio-mythoi* of what constituted what they experienced as reality inherently involved one another.

As such, the social structure of abolitionism and the social structuring of enslavement are mythological narratives reifying the bio-markers of survival—for both those who require slaves and those who resist enslavement and for those who can and have achieved rank of citizen, man or woman, and those who we imagine deserve life and those who we imagine deserve death. Society, then, as the functioning element of this *bio-mythoi* creates and reinscribes those who will fit into these categories and regulates their behaviors, along the way creating general categories of morality to situate and guide our actions within this particular circumstance, deciding who should live and who should die—or, in this case, who should be enslaved and who should be free. Freedom, then, as Winthrop, is a mythologically based bio-marker of survival set to and against a larger social order erected to constitute the mythological to be experienced as reality. This is why Goode and Field and Winthrop cannot simply walk away or why their ancestors cannot simply walk away or why our narrator cannot simply solve the problem by making up *any* name. Goode and Field and Winthrop and their ancestors were inscribed within this framework underlying each of the *bio-mythoi*, underlying the markers of race as that which is both familiar and unfamiliar. The name of the town has never really been the issue, but that connective tissue between expectation, will, desire, materiality, and consciousness—very strictly speaking, life and death—has been what has constituted lived experience and the knowledges accrued therein. What is at stake and what the narrator is tasked with is, as Wynters notes, word and the world "alchemically *made flesh*."[16]

Taken slowly and in parts: there is no there out there, outside of us. But there is also no us to us. Rather, what *is* is in between the there and the us. In this constitution, the world or reality emerges as already present and given, solid with meaning. And it is from this meaning that we constitute all our fields of study without knowing their *bio-mythoi* foundations—from the human to natural sciences. And it is in these fields that we search for the answers, when the problems are not, exactly, in the disciplines but elsewhere.

For example, the name Freedom is not merely a linguistic change from "slave," nor is it merely a declaration of the will against historical circumstance. Freedom cannot be understood within the fields of study that produce these logics. Rather, Freedom can only be understood in terms of the transition, in the being or becoming of a living condition reified in the particularities of an identifying name—Goode and Field were not free because they named their town Freedom. They were not free even because they left their condition of enslavement. Goode and Field were men who left a set of historical conditions and generational knowledge and through their enactment of marronage altered the space and time of their condition, introduced into it new and different possibilities. It was out of this that the "kin-recognizing . . . *referent-we*" shifted and the "origin-mythically chartered symbolically encoded and semantically enacted set of symbolic life/death instructions" were recoded. They were free because they redefined their existence and in doing so created a new category of being—the free black subject.

This, it seems, is where we have failed, where the descendants of Goode and Field and Winthrop have failed. We and they have attempted to locate the ontology of reality within the linguistic world and/or within the disciplines erected around those linguistic worlds. And in doing so, we and they have imagined that this inner world and, thus, the meaning of space and time—of our social circumstance and our historical knowledge—can be changed by changing the names of things et al. And when the circumstance does not change and the name has failed, we and they find a new name, and it continues like this, ad infinitum, putting a conveyor belt of names before ourselves, hoping that one of them will solve the dilemma, will fix the problem. An infinity of names.

Our narrator captures this dilemma, noting the continual failure of words and our continued effort to erect new words:

> Colored.
> The sliver of himself still in tune with marketing shivered each time Gertrude used the word *colored*. He kept stubbing his toe on it. As it were. Colored, Negro, Afro-American, African-American. She was a few iterations behind the times. Not that you could keep up, anyway. Every couple of years someone came up with something that got us an inch closer to the truth. Bit by bit we crept along. As if that thing we believed to be approaching actually existed. (*Apex*, 192–93)

It is as if we and they believed that there is something beneath the name and that, once stripped down, we can finally find and locate ourselves in the human and fix the problem. But with each name change, each shift from Freedom to Winthrop, colored, Negro, Afro-American, African American, we are not drawing closer, for there is nothing and no-thing to draw ourselves closer to other than a lineal root condition of existence in which things et al. evade naming yet demand their existence, which cannot be known but demands to be seen. Our narrator puzzles, "What is the name for that which is always beyond our grasp? What do you call *that which escapes*?" (*Apex*, 183; emphasis in original).

If the eusocialization of race and history and identity and the material reality of existence tell us that there is something there, something real, enduring, something structuring, foundational, critical, and even if we have progressed not to believe this to be metaphysical but social and political and economic, we still have not gotten to the root, for our narrator reminds us, "Before colored, slave. Before slave, free. And always somewhere, nigger" (*Apex*, 192). It is not the name or even the material condition at hand but what conditions our experience with the material world as such—with reality—and how that manifests itself in a set of logical relations we deem rational, if not natural, that gives us the names we call things et al. that populate this world. Beneath the words and names themselves, Whitehead is telling us that in America, there is race or, more precisely, "somewhere, nigger." "Nigger," then, becomes not a marker of an individual or a negation of individuality and/or personhood but that *bio-mythoi* marker of life and death reified in the material world. As readers sift through iterations from theses one through eight, hoping to find something to solve what may be termed the linguistic dilemma, they should ask themselves if they have been looking in the wrong place, without knowing it, and not only evading things et al. and ourselves but also those constitutive elements that are our world.

Thesis Nine: Names Bring Us Back to Ourselves

While we cannot definitely say that there is not a biofeedback auto-institution of meaning in the structure of how we represent and experience reality at the level of life and death, we may be able to state that if there is, there may be no way of accessing that plane of existence to rewire ourselves and reconstitute reality. The question remains: if we were eusocialized, how can we step outside ourselves and our reality to measure the meaning of our eusocialization? In a sense, we are on the road to both skepticism and cultural criticism, wherein all that we can know and thus critique is where we are but not really how we got to where we are or where we are going. For example, if where we are is a combination of generational knowledge and the materiality of our living existence, then we cannot know what we are doing or who we have become until we reflect on it. In the moment, we are merely existing what they had endured—Goode and Field could not have known where they were heading, but once they arrived and named it, then it was who and what they in fact were. Similarly, the town council members can analyze the different town names and what they mean for them but not what they meant for Goode and Field and Winthrop, for their worlds are no longer. Additionally, the town council members cannot give themselves a new name until they have endured their own material existence and the historical knowledges passed down to them. It seems that the town is at a standstill—ontologically, epistemically—until they have endured and discovered themselves and their names.

The folly of history and historical thinking is that we can understand the past as the people in the past experienced it, that we can offer new, different insights into the failure in the thinking and actions of the people in the past. The folly is that we can become objective enough to distance ourselves and think critically about the past. As such, we imagine that the past remains open to us, for us, not in the sense of its influence but in the realm of criticism and understanding. But perhaps the past is closed. Its meaning is closed. The relation of things et al. is closed. Its inner life is closed. Its world is closed. Closed, not dead—inaccessible.

Perhaps all that is left is ourselves, and we are brought back to ourselves, who are constituted in our historical, generational knowledge and in our material existential conditions but who cannot, because of our eusocialized reality, *really* access either. Nevertheless, we are brought back to ourselves, those eusocialized selves, influenced by but unable to capture the meaning of our present reality. Can we, though, be brought back to our early selves, the selves that initially experience reality, before we are told what things et al. are, before we learn their names? Can we ever escape to these selves that lived, freely, in one's inner world without contradiction or shame within the shared world? Our narrator laments the past, laments the eusocialization of this proto-, prelogical self: "Isn't it great when you're a kid and the whole world is full of anonymous things? . . . Everything is bright and mysterious until you know what it is called and then all the light goes out of it. All those flying gliding things are just *birds*. And etc. Once we knew the name of it, how could we ever come to love it? He told himself: What he had given to all those things had been the right name, but never the true name. For things had true natures, and they hid behind false names, beneath the skin we gave them" (*Apex*, 182–83). It seems here that what Whitehead is talking about is not metaphysical reality of things in relationship to the false names we give them, force them to live under. After having gone through the other theses, it becomes clear that what Whitehead is discussing is immediacy—our immediate relationality to ourselves and to things et al. that is calcified the moment we try to capture any of it within a totalizing scope of a concept or a name. What Whitehead seems to be instructing us on is the fact that there is a certain kind of endurance at work here. Rather than the name being earned, a name emerges through what we have endured—having lived through our own eusocialization, our estrangement from ourselves, and having to locate within this estrangement moments of the familiar and unfamiliar to remind us that reality is indeed constructed and that what we are is not given but made from the stories we tell ourselves about ourselves.

Perhaps Freedom was an attempt to reify what we originally feel within a place, and Winthrop was created as that out-of-control reaction to losing control of one's own inner life, creating physical boundaries to hold out everything that may influence what exists within; and perhaps New Prospera was the attempt to get it back by removing the past, making a new way in the name itself. The task of the narrator, then, is seemingly compossible, in that he is tasked with at once slapping "a bandage on it to keep the pus in" and naming that which is "beyond our grasp," that which evades (*Apex*, 183; emphasis in original).

Perhaps they and we had it wrong all along—words and names do not consume things, they don't replace them, they are not metaphysical entities, and they do not capture the inner working of an immortal soul or rational consciousness coming to know itself. Perhaps their role is not to stop time or halt it in a moment to be understood, exemplified, and analyzed. Perhaps they prolong time, keep it open, keep it going. Perhaps they hold open that window of impressionability, of experience, and we find ourselves dangling between what was, is, and will be, and in this openness we find ourselves, learn who we are, and exist. Perhaps, we only stop existing when we rest on a name and rest on a settled reality. Perhaps this is what the town's council had forgotten and what the narrator was really set on reminding them: they were fighting over a name as if names are ever supposed to stay the same, as if the town was not changed by the sheer fact of the debate itself. Perhaps what continued to draw them together was something that could not be solved, only endured. Whitehead's narrator leaves this for the reader, in his name that he has chosen for the town: Struggle.

The struggle of existence is between being and becoming. That which *is* is always challenged by that which is to come, by the changing element at the heart of existence. Historical consciousness and the material world are trapped between these two conflicts. And a name complicates matters even more, for we imagine that a thing et al. is stable if we can name it, but names themselves are dynamic; they capture historical becoming rather than fixed being. This is the town's name, for this is what endures.

And in the American context, the enduring struggle of existence in being and becoming, permanence against change, takes place on the plane of race, which both defines and strips away definition, grounds and denies grounding, demanding at once both Freedom and Winthrop, both statement and counterstatement, losing itself in every moment in an attempt to find itself. Whitehead leaves us with this final remark: "As he fell asleep, he heard the conversation they will have. Ones that will get to the heart of this mess. The sick swollen heart of this land. They will say: I was born in Struggle. I live in Struggle and come from Struggle. I work in Struggle. We crossed the border into Struggle. Before I came to Struggle. We found ourselves in Struggle. I will never leave Struggle. I will die in Struggle" (*Apex*, 211).

Scene Four: The Specter of Excess

What we are to learn from the various theses, what we are to gather from a novel that is ostensibly about meaning and language and naming but that ends ambiguously with a name that refuses finality, refuses order, is something about the deceptive nature of language—rather than revealing some ethereal metaphysical order or bringing structure to our living condition, language is no better, no more metaphysically rich, than those who construct it. In other words, the narrator, in naming the town Struggle, offers this last lesson—we cannot simply rebrand ourselves with a new name and, in it, undo history. This belief—to wish away the past through a gesture of changing names without changing the material order itself—is the "Apex" that hides the hurt. This is what Western modernity has attempted to do with its past and with the presence of difference within its material order without recognizing that the estrangement it placed in the world, between itself and things et al., was an estrangement that began inside and was left to rot and fester.

Whitehead situates his narrator as the constructor of the ultimate marketing strategy for Western modernity—the brand of bandage adhesives named Apex with the slogan "Hides the Hurt"—as an implicit and explicit reminder of this fact of language and of Western modernity. For within the narrator's own living black male body is the residual fact of this truth—he outstrips history in both its linguistic and material forms, reminding us that we cannot simply change our nation's past, present, or future by the declaration of a name change; enslaved living property cannot become brother-in-arm-citizen with the mark of the pen, with an amendment, if the living material conditions remain the same. Name changes like this only hide the hurt; they do not change the conditions of it. Whitehead reminds us of this fact when, at the very end of his novel, he writes, "Before colored, slave. Before slave, free. And always somewhere, nigger" (*Apex*, 192). Always somewhere, the condition of the "nigger" remains and is the ubiquity of Americana, in its quotidian detail, no matter the name change.

The hiring of a specialist to resolve what are, in fact, ontological problems tells us something about the kind of living we have already enacted in ourselves, for ourselves, and as ourselves. The narrator, as specialist and black male, who set out to solve but also reveal the ontological problems of naming and history, is no prophet; he is merely the one sent to make clear the way—for the townspeople to consciously live the reality they had already been living, to face the world they had constructed and inhabited. Hence, the narrator names the town Struggle to reveal to the town its already existing name—not Freedom or Winthrop but that internal conflict between the past and the present—and to offer the town one last instruction. In the words of James Baldwin, "people are trapped in history, and history is trapped in them."[17] Any new name—New Prospera or the like—that did not deal with this internal conflict would only offer a bandage to the problem, would only ever cover the hurt, rather than change the underlying metaphysical reality of what is.

Whitehead seems to suggest that the only way for the town and the townspeople to really deal with this internal conflict is to live out the consequences of the choices that they have made—to be forced, as Baldwin notes, to "pay for what they do, and still more for what they have allowed themselves to become, . . . very simply: by the lives they lead"—and this is precisely what the narrator tasks them with.[18] As part of their contract for his services, the townspeople had to agree to live with the name for one year, regardless of what they felt about it. They had already been in Struggle, had been born in, lived in, would probably die in Struggle; and now they would have to consciously exist in Struggle.

But this work does not make the narrator any more visible than he was at the beginning of the novel. And though it may help to resolve the dilemma of the town, our narrator still has to face his own internal estrangement. He still must be a black man tasked with saving another town, another reality, from itself for direct financial compensation but without social, historical, or linguistic compensation. The town now has a name and thus has regained the possibility of its past and its possible future. He still has no name—no past, present, or future. He is still a voice crying in the wilderness; he is still trapped in the overlap between his own constructed world and that of Western modernity.

Perhaps what we are to learn from Whitehead's novel has nothing to do with "dark matter" questions as they relate to language. Perhaps the questions were themselves a ruse, a bit of misdirection, for what is unknowable is not the world itself or things themselves but black maleness in pre- or post-Western modernity. Perhaps, we are to learn that living at the intersection of his world and the other world, he cannot be anything but a whisper, a call in the wilderness, from the wilderness to those who might not be able or willing to hear its pronouncements. Perhaps we are to learn that he is no more than a haunt. The philosopher Lewis Gordon argues that those who are alienated within this specific space and time frame—Ellison's invisible narrator, Douglass's heroic slave, Whitehead's nomenclature specialist—constitute no more than a ghost. As Gordon notes, "what the Euromodern world has done in its concept of modern . . . is to say there's a future, and in the future and in that future some people belong to it. . . . If some people belong to the future and some people don't, in the present you have no future, what is the status of your present? . . . We tend to use the language of a haunting, . . . the language of ghosts" to describe this kind of existence.[19] Are black men but the ghost of Western modernity, their "dark matter" questions the haunt of their embodied existence? Read in this way, the deployment of a black male nomenclature specialist is the deployment of excess, a deployment of what cannot be held within a given form—linguistic or material. In existing between two worlds, only appearing in those moments when the worlds overlap, they both vanish and appear; sometimes they can be seen as a glimpse, sometimes in full body, but often they can only be heard like the whisper of wind. For what else is a ghost but the excess of being cast out of form?

But is this the task of black maleness? Is that all we can, should, or would be, the subconscious of Western modernity?

> *'Twas in another lifetime, one of toil and blood*
> *When blackness was a virtue, the road was full of mud*
> *I came in from the wilderness, a creature void of form.*
> *Come in . . . I'll give ya shelter from the storm.*[20]

Conclusion: By Way of Transition/al Phrase

Whitehead's novel *Apex Hides the Hurt* is aptly titled: it is at once a haunt, a warning, and a tongue-in-cheek ironic undertaking of the possibility of impossibility—writing, as it were, from an other space and time to our contemporary space and time. But it is more than that. Whitehead's novel deploys a black male naming specialist to discuss, in addition to the metaphysics of naming, the relationship between our nation and black male hypervisible invisibility, leaving us with the question of whether a black man can ever really exist within Western modernity as anything but a whisper, a gesture, a glance, a ghost of a voice speaking from sometime and somewhere else. If so, at what cost? But are these the questions that ought to be asked, that ought to animate our reading of black male texts at all? Are these the central concerns of black male existential identity? Is this unknowability of form within Western modernity the task of black maleness—the accumulation of specialization . . . all for the sake of freedom? What freedom? Whose freedom? When freedom? Where freedom? What, really, is at the heart of the novel?

That is to say, as mesmerizing as the "dark matter" questions are, the reader, perhaps the black male reader, is left a bit unsettled. Like at the end of Ellison's *Invisible Man*, which is marked by the narrator's persistent invisibility—and after 587 pages!—the reader is left at the end of Whitehead's novel with a similar dissatisfaction. For after the specialist has named the town and helped it to discover itself, he is still nameless. And afterward, he is still left with a perceptible limp.

Whitehead's novel ends as it began, with a limp that haunts the novel and the narrator. Much like the limp's role in the development of the plot, it begins imperceptibly but becomes manifest as an outright presence at the end. Like Struggle, the limp comes to be named at the end as an ambiguous, indelible marker of that which could neither be brought under the auspice of a word nor shaken loose from language. It is that which does not actually name a thing but points to a condition. And like a specter or ghost that is both present and absent, present in its absence, the narrator's limp marks the failure—the failure of Western modernity, that is, the failure of the logic of capture and containment to actually capture and contain that which is named. For it is only in the desire to capture and contain that we have excess—it is the marker of the failure of containment. As Struggle marked the failure of the town in its desire to capture and to contain itself in the present, black men mark the failure of Western modernity to capture and contain the human within a specific form.[21]

But this is not the only failure. The narrator's limp also marks his own failure to contain himself within a Western modernity that he himself had adopted. The narrator's limp also marks the excess in black men themselves and their inability to capture their own existence because of an overriding desire to exist within the normative framework of Western modernity. The narrator's limp, both figurative and literal, was a result of not so much the narrator's failure to be heard but the absolute neglect of himself in his desire to be heard to begin with. Is Ellison's narrator invisible because he is hypervisible, or is he invisible because he wants to be seen? Is Douglass's heroic slave enslaved because he wants to be a free man—because he wants to exist in a way that was never meant for him to be—like those men of 1776? Does the narrator equally haunt Western modernity as he haunts himself?

Whitehead tells us that his narrator had been stubbing his toe throughout the novel, but it was not until the end of the novel that he discovers how bad the injury was. He explains to the doctor that "he hadn't even known anything was amiss down there, apart from the pain from the constant stubbing, which truth be told, he had accepted as his lot" (*Apex*, 200). Because, in fact, the Apex had been hiding the reality of the hurt—apart from the pain, which he had accustomed himself to—he did not, could not really understand the extent of the damage. But he is told that he should have known better: "a guy like you should know better" (*Apex*, 200). It was as much what the narrator did not want to know, what he did not want to be aware of, what he wanted to cover up so that he could continue limping through his life that was the cause of injury itself.

More specifically, it was the narrator's inability to recognize the signs for the injury—to acknowledge the deformation that was going on just beneath the surface—that was the problem. And this constituted, for Whitehead, the fundamental neglect. Even though "the real culprit was infection," a collection of "microscopic creatures," the injury was self-inflicted given his failure to see, to really understand himself (*Apex*, 199). When he is told that he should have known better, what is meant is that he should have known far before he was "discovered, delirious and muttering, sprawled out on a street corner," far before the "ghastly shock waiting underneath the adhesive bandage" was discovered, what was festering beneath the surface (*Apex*, 198). But instead of sensing a problem, all the narrator saw, *could* see, was "those were good times. In the office they greeted each other with *Hey* and *Hey, man* and slapped each other on the back a lot," without understanding that "the amputation of his putrefying toe" would be the eventual outcome (*Apex*, 3, 99) of his intellectual, emotional, and spiritual gentrification. In other words, the narrator should have known that even as a specialist—*because* he understood himself as a specialist—his existence was only ever partial, would only ever be partial, a partial acceptance, partial visibility, partial being, and that no matter how much he tried, all others would be able to do, no matter "how well dressed" or professional he appeared, is to look at him, no matter how earnestly, and say, "Can you hear me in there?" Why could he not see that his specialization would never save him from his invisibility, from his own namelessness until it was too late (*Apex*, 198), until the "Advanced State of Necrosis" had set in? (*Apex*, 200).

And what is more, because the narrator did not see it coming, did not predict his own amputation, he could not attend to the real problem, even at the end of the novel, where he says to himself, "There had been a moment . . . when he thought he might be cured. Rid of that persistent mind-body problem. That if he did something, took action, the hex might come off. The badness come undone. He thought, plainly speaking, that he'd lose his limp. . . . As the weeks went on and he settled into his new life, he had to admit that actually, his foot hurt more than ever" (*Apex*, 212). Still, he believed that it was because of not enough action, not enough movement, not enough explanation, rather than too much of each, and not enough introspection that, at in the end, after all he had done, "his foot still hurt more than ever."

One can read from this that the real culprit of the deformation and the material manifestation was not anything material but the very structure under which the material world gained its structure. It was not the eventual infection but that he allowed the infection to spread—he allowed his professional success to convince him of the possibility of his humanity within Western modernity. This, much like the town itself in its refusal to recognize its fundamental problem, is an attempt to evade ambiguity, instead choosing to cover the "invisible wound," which led to the deformation of his literal and figurative body.[22] The limp thus was neither physiological nor psychological but something else, something more fundamental (*Apex*, 139).

Jesse S. Cohn argues that there is a kind of impotency at the heart of Whitehead's novel.[23] That is, Cohn argues that what adds to the narratological mystery of the novel is a hesitation "between desire and consummation." At the heart of the novel is a kind of doubling—that is, between that which is and that which is hoped for. The desire to exist within Western modernity and its denial of black male existence create a kind of desire that can never be consummated, which, according to Cohn, creates a "pervasive atmosphere of sexual tension."[24] Adjoining the narrator's own incapacity to name himself and the townspeople's incapacity to name their town, Whitehead seems to suggest that the relationship between history and meaning, specifically in the American context, is one of perpetual incompletion of a task. If Cohn is correct, then this impotency—this inability to consummate desire—has as much to do with the inability to act as it does with that on which one is to act, in this case, impotency manifested in the hesitation of Struggle and the narrator's limp because of what is desired.

If Struggle is the metaphor for black male identity, and those "dark matter" questions are the specific deployment of black maleness within Western modernity, does this mean that black men are impotent to the extent that they desire to exist within Western modernity?

These questions, implied throughout, are explicitly suggested at the end of Whitehead's novel and make way for the revelation of Cecil Brown's *The Life and Loves of Mr. Jiveass Nigger*, which is concerned with black male potency and its relation to black male existential existence. At the heart of Brown's novel are the questions, What would happen if black men sought ambiguity rather than an evasion of it? Could a black man will ambiguity itself? That is to say, can a black man manifestly will his invisibility in order to manipulate existence and perform his liberation subtextually? Would this mean that black men would no longer seek to affect or even speak of their existence and experience subtextually or by indirection but directly, accepting that it may never be heard as it is spoken—or that there may be, in fact, nothing metaphysically pure or existentially true that is spoken but only that which is expressed, only that which is lived? What would this voice sound like? How would it be written? Would it be merely a challenge, a violent confrontation elicited by the phrase "black power" and reinterpreted in the contemporary moment as black male "toxicity"? Or would it sound and read as other to what we have heretofore understood about black male hypervisible invisible vulnerability?

The transition from Colson Whitehead's *Apex Hides the Hurt* to Cecil Brown's *The Life and Loves of Mr. Jiveass Nigger* is not just in terms of writing style but in terms of an overture, of what is offered on the grounds of address—on the grounds of speaking. In other words, the transition between the novels is in terms of translation. Rather than approximating experience into something other than itself—of trying to translate itself into an other language, logic, and/or form—Brown's novel rejects the idea of knowledge, truth, meaning, and/or value, even the value of words or language, rejects the metaphysical relation of what we speak to how we live. Instead Brown's novel attempts to elicit a feeling. It attempts to argue through feeling that what exists are the actions we take, rather than the language we use. Brown's novel, in this way, can be seen as distancing itself from and a critique of Douglass, Ellison, and Whitehead to the extent that it issues a warning of the tragedy of trying to cover over experience with the history of racialization, as approximated within the specialization of the knowledge of Western modernity. Brown's novel simply refuses this gesture. Rather than trying to explain experience with something other than itself, it attacks experience with itself.

In rejecting theory as specialization, Brown's novel turns the question of ambiguity that is central to "dark matter" questions into the feeling of vivacity, the evocation of life itself—what will be termed the "jazz of life." In this, Whitehead's metaphysical haunt is transformed into Brown's jazz vernacular statement of spunk or the essence of excess—of that which cannot be contained.[25] As part of Brown's translation, the excess of what language cannot capture, rather than leading to impotency, becomes the heart of potency—the literal and metaphorical expulsion of excess into improvised form. In other words, if reality is unknowable and unreachable by language, thought, or definite form, then it can be the ground on which we play, where form and structure and truth and force become adventures and usher in with them a creative capacity to show that our living is but the multiplicity of inchoate variegated forms. The jazz of life and the life of jazz, then, are a statement of perpetual making and remaking; rather than active doing or acting according to principle, jazz wrests from knowability and form the unknowable infinity in the very possibility of form.

The trouble that Brown points out is, in fact, an error of translation and can be attended to in the realm of reorienting desire. While Whitehead's translation only yielded him Struggle and a limp, Brown's novel tells us that there can be so much more. Brown's novel gives us jazz, gives us jiving, gives us a jiveass Nigger, gives us a life of infinite excess—the creative expulsion of endless form.

And, with this, we can finally, *really* begin . . .

[*End of scene.*]

[*Stage direction*] The stage once again returns to darkness. There is silence but not the absence of sound. There is a sort of buzzing, like around a beehive or a hornet's nest: the sort of silence that forebodes something that is to come—something that, perhaps, has already started making its way.

[*Close curtain.*]

Chapter 4

Cecil Brown

The Functional Negro and the Rise of "Jiveass Nigger"

> He knew he'd have to think up some lie to tell then, knew he had to play some phony role, which finally would not be phony at all since it would get him what he wanted. He was Mr. Jiveass Nigger himself, and knew that there was nothing under the sun that was really phony if it was functional.
> —Cecil Brown, *The Life and Love of Mr. Jiveass Nigger*

Scene One: Introductory Remarks

The publisher Farrar, Straus and Giroux describes Cecil Brown's 1969 novel *The Life and Loves of Mr. Jiveass Nigger* as a "funky, shocking, often wildly comic novel." It argues that it is principally about discovering why the lead character, George Washington, is "such a jive artist, why he constantly weaves elaborate tales and lies that impress others and delude himself." To do this, though, it argues that George Washington must "leave America and come to Europe," Copenhagen to be exact. Throughout his travel and his adventures, George Washington, the publisher argues, only discovers that "the life of the black stud amounts to pandering to the white world rather than an attack on it."[1] All these elements that the publisher notes are certainly present in Brown's novel, but they need to be further or better explained and more deeply engaged. Yes, an American black man moves abroad to Copenhagen. His experiences in Europe are framed by the lies he tells everyone about himself—his name, his past, his occupation. And, yes, he sleeps with many, many white women (and a few black women); he loathes white male elites; and he befriends other black male American expats seemingly doing and feeling the same. And his name *is* George Washington. All of these elements, taken together on their face, amount to what the publisher describes as a "funky, shocking, . . . wildly comic novel," but it is about much more than this.

What the publisher does not ask is, Why does George Washington imagine that jiving, that is, deceiving, is a suitable alternative to linear truth telling? Why would his jiving lead to his playing the role of a "black stud"? What does this specific mode of deception have to do with the fact that George Washington is an American black male? Why must George Washington leave America in order to discover for himself why he jives, why he deceives, its meaning for his life, and why he believes the idea of the "stud" is a suitable mode of jiving? Can we think of jiving, of lying, not in terms of morality but in terms of improvising and argue that "Life begins at improvisation. Life is a sustained improvisational interaction"?[2] And, lastly, why does Brown name his central character George Washington? Does this name have anything to do with being American and a specifically American way of life: locating your identity abroad, jiving as a mode of existence, and playing the role of stud as the specific mode of jiving? But, more, the publisher does not ask how these elements constitute the novel's complex narratological structure and how they, when taken together, amount to "a theory and a concept."[3]

What makes Brown's novel unique is not only that he poses these questions—for similar questions have been posed by the other authors discussed in this text—but also the manner in which he attempts to answer them. Though ironic in nature—for example, naming his central black male character, a jive American stud, George Washington—Brown's novel does not conform to much of the central black male literary mode of direct indirection. Rather, like Richard Wright, he directly attacks without subtext. What Wright noted about the famous American author Ernest Hemingway, that he "makes a great impression on the reader's mind not for establishing perspective but for creating style," could be, from Brown's perspective, said of Ellison and Douglass especially and Whitehead to a lesser degree.[4] In other words, Brown did not stylize black male hypervisible invisible vulnerability—that is, the vulnerability inherent in black male lives contingent on the very idea of black male hyperpresence as physically and sexually powerful and violent, what the publisher understood as simply the "black stud"—through elaborate technical avenues inherent in the history of letters and that of craftsmanship (a submerged narratorial voice, inchoate sentence, and argumentative structure, etc.); rather, he structured the conceptual framework of his novel and its narrative arc in terms of this vulnerability.

Published in the shifting intellectual and political climate beginning in the early and mid-1960s, marked by authors such as James Baldwin, Chester Himes, Claude Brown, and John Williams (among others), and highlighted by the 1967 publication of Harold Cruses's *The Crisis of the Negro Intellectual*, Brown's novel was a product of its time but also reached backward to discuss other times and forward to foreshadow more recent literature, for example, Marlon James's *Book of Night Women* (2009), Darius James's *Negrophobia* (1993), Percival Everett's *Erasure/fuck* (2001), and Dany LaFerriere's *How to Make Love to a Negro without Getting Tired* (2010). Enacting the sagely wisdom of Amiri Baraka, another black male writer of this same generational turn, who in critique of black art wrote in his 1964 play *The Dutchman*, "Some kind of bastard literature . . . all it needs is a simple knife thrust. . . . If Bessie Smith had killed some white people she wouldn't have needed that music. She could have talked straight and plain about the world. No metaphors. No grunts. No wiggles in the dark of her soul."[5] Baraka here is not arguing that all black literature must have the same form or the same content of social and political commentary or protest. Nor should it be inferred that all black literature must be written in a realistic or naturalistic way any more than it does that black literature must be surrealistic about black male existence. This would be the subject of Kenneth Warren's provocative claims in his essays, "Does African American Literature Exist?,"[6] "What Was African American Literature?"[7] and later in his book, *What Was African American Literature?*,[8] where he argues throughout that, "the need is here to make it clear why this literature, like all literatures, was an historical phenomenon, and, further, why this literature, unlike perhaps for most, the possibility of its demise was built into its very reason for being."[9] Warren goes on to defend his position, clarifying that because "African American literature emerged in response to the disenfranchisement of blacks in the south, which set the stage for the consolidation of Jim Crow segregation," and, "With the end of Jim Crow and southern disenfranchisement African American literature has likewise come to an end."[10]

Taking Warren's point seriously leaves us, not dismissing his claims on historical grounds, but taking them up on aesthetic grounds—that is, in terms of an aesthetic argument of craft, style, and content in literary production. The question that has animated *The Buck* is an aesthetic one—how does the experience of black men in the United States come to shape a literary genre? That is, "how does one write about black maleness—how has it been done and how can it continue to be done—in the aesthetic of narrative form that captures and *becomes* that hypervisible invisibility that is black maleness?"[11] Engaging Warren's ideas on aesthetic grounds, transforms his suggestion—that black literature was a response to historical circumstance—into an ontological concern about how one transforms an external condition into a subjective form of knowledge. As such, though the conditions of creation might "have come to an end" (and this is debatable), the aesthetic issues of craft remain as that around which we can and should construct a genre or canon. It is in this aesthetic concern over transformation that resists historicism, or the idea that once the historic conditions are over, the art itself also ceases to be.

Returning to Baraka's words and reflecting on Brown's novel in light of an aesthetic critique of Warren, we come to the conclusion that style and content should not be separated; rather, the relationship between style and content should be explored to see how they are mutually informing. Style can be used in conjunction with content to elevate art to political significance—but even saying this is too much, for the content *is* the style as much as style is an argument, formally or informally. What Brown's novel invites us to query is an argument and a content that tarries with, rather than evades, what is circumspect (invisibly hypervisible) about black male existence.

But style can and often does recede behind the shadow of content and, at the same time, can be and often is used as a garnish to hide the actual content of a text from some particular (i.e., white) audience. The both/and aspect of style or the technical aspect of craftsmanship can at once be used to make radical and potentially controversial content palatable; but style can also make the content invisible or can itself be made invisible by the content that it has helped to conceal or illuminate. This, ironically, like the black male writers themselves, makes their work, like themselves and the content of their work, invisible, yet hypervisible. Brown's novel, though, refuses this particular form of invisibilizing/invisibilization of style and plays both with and within the tension inherent in black male literature between speaking the truth and appeasing a (white) audience, that is, the tension of his hypervisible invisibility. Brown's novel acts as a sort of metareflection on Douglass's essay "Why Is the Negro Lynched?," in which Douglass notes that the dubious charge of rape allowed for mob justice disguised as social justice; Ralph Ellison's *Invisible Man*, in particular, the "Battle Royal" scene where Ellison paints the evocative image of the U.S. flag tattooed on the pelvic region of a white woman; and Colson Whitehead's *Apex Hides the Hurt*, where the ever-present limp in his nameless narrator is a metaphor for an ontological and metaphysical scar of history. Brown's novel makes the mutual exchange of form and style, argument and content, central to the narratological structure of his novel rather than fodder for narratological insight into a generalized theme—which for Douglass was the theme of freedom; for Ellison, the theme of radical authenticity; and for Whitehead, the poststructuralist theme of the diminishing meaning and value in and of language.

The question that Brown's novel raises, and what is inherent in Baraka's quotation, is less the concern over the relationship between black art and politics that is germane to much criticism of black aesthetic theory and more the metaquestion of the generation of aesthetic form. It is a referendum on the structure and style of black writing and how to construct the aesthetic form of the discipline itself, in terms not just of the human experience or the general racialized experience but the specific experience and mode of being black men.

Brown's novel asks, when we speak of "the human condition" and when we write about that condition, what language do we use, whose voice is it in, and is it possible to write *the* human condition outside the framework of influence of culture and history? It is difficult to read Brown's novel and not hear a serious meditation on past form and Wright's observation that "in many cases it is good for a Negro writer to get out on his own, and get stuff first hand rather get it through the regular educational channels."[12] That is, it is equally a question of influence as it is a perspective on how one generates one's view and approach to reality. In short, Brown's novel asks the question of why so much of black male literature is subtextual—that is, utilizes style as a mode of concealing and revealing content—and if this needs to change.

The question of narratological form and structure is gestured toward by Charles Johnson in *Being and Fiction* but is not fully developed toward a black narratological form. Citing Henri Bergson's comment that "doing philosophy authentically would consist in *creating* the framework of the problem and creating the solution," Johnson argues that black literature needs to establish its own aesthetic grounds for analysis and critique—what, for him, constitutes a phenomenological perspective of storytelling.[13] Following the phenomenological tradition, Johnson argues that what constitutes the perspective of philosophical or literary theory and construction are the details chosen to represent an experience and/or its reality. For Johnson, "this [creating the framework of the problem and the solution] is what black literary practice must do, for it still tends to rest on shaky esthetic grounds" because it fails to select the details of an experience beyond the sociology—or racialization—of the very idea of blackness. Similarly, Brown's novel challenges the sociology of literary construction and analysis wherein the truth of narrative has more to do with an exploration of a set of scientific conceptions of a general population (i.e., black people) or the refutation of them more than the specific experience of a life—which can be and often is discordant and fragmented. Constituting what Hortense Spillers terms the "*auto-biosgraphe*" of a "black creative intellectual" project, Brown's work can be seen as "the perspective of historical time and agency."[14]

Brown's novel situates the imaginative unfolding of a specific man, George Washington, as the Archimedean point of departure to discuss the larger sociohistorical context in which his (Brown's and George Washington's) consciousness is formed, but his novel resists sociology, for it resists the coherent structure of theory—that is, it resists explanation and the ordered logic from which explanation emerges. Rather, it insists, using a jazz theory of improvisational organization, on the excess of improvised form. What Vijay Iyer wrote of jazz improvisation applies well to Brown's novel, namely, that it "dwells not just in one solo at a time, but also in a single note, and equally in an entire lifetime of improvisations. In short, the story is revealed not as a simple linear narrative, but as a fractured, exploded one."[15] It is the story of one man (a single note); it is through dwelling in and on this single man or note that we reveal, and evocatively so, not ordered logic as the foundation of what we are to hear or read in the text but something else.

As a novel understood in the tone of jazz improvisation, it situates itself incoherently: it lies as a way of telling a larger truth, it is improvised from beginning to end, but it also plays alongside an already scripted or compositional form—the nigger, as scripted or compositional form, becomes a kind of "architecture: the construction of spaces that frame, enable, and contextualize human action," the foundation from which Brown's George Washington plays, riffs, bullshits, and creates. Brown's Washington becomes, as it were, "an architect of environments, a contriver of situations" grounding the possibility of infinite form.[16] And this is what both Ellison and Douglass also realized and feared: the absolute malleability of form and the absolute formlessness of existence as the precondition for social living and personal freedom. The nigger is the architect—an archive, as it were—of both what it is and what it is not, both itself and its own otherness—the nigger is what Fred Moten terms, "a kind of lyricism of the surplus,"[17] the excess of form and also its infinite possibility.

Something critical, though, is revealed within this archive of surplus or excess. As formless form—or that which resists and rejects the ordered structure of scripts or compositions, the nigger, as improvisational actually works to undo history and historical memory through the embellishment of fact, in the distortion of itself and its history through memory, not in terms of critical reflection (that is, negating negative stereotypes, etc.), but in the active creation of living truth by the imagination. It is critical, then, to read Brown's novel in the tradition of black folklore, which, instead of responding to history, as Warren claims of African-American literature, utilizes the imagination to improvise on a given form (historical narrative as archive) to create an other, a counter archive that rather than relying on "empirical data"[18] to generate its narrative structure—what, in other words, makes us believe anything that is said about George Washington, or what he even says about himself—Brown's novel utilizes the method of "antiphonal structure and improvisational form" inherent in the "music itself"[19] to produce a novel that is less concerned with facts and more "with the way it registers 'the very changes wrought by memory.'"[20] Brown's George Washington gives us a "*different* credibility,"[21] one that is invested in "imagination, symbolism, and desire."[22] Yet, this is not to say that it is the form itself that overcomes or overruns the content in Brown's novel, as can be said of Douglass and Ellison and Whitehead; rather, it is *the content that generates the form*. The formlessness of black male life creates the formlessness of jazz structure of Brown's novel. The "*formal* effects"[23] of jazz, the "shifts in chronology or narrative sequence,"[24] appear in Brown's novel in terms of the lies that Washington tells, or the jiving he does throughout. In reading Brown's novel we, then, need to "consider the resonance of the ways it departs from fact,"[25] rather than seeing it as "funky, shocking, . . . wildly comic novel," *because* it departs from facts.

But, the expulsive elements of jazz itself must also not be forgotten—that is, the ways in which the music as metaphor and as method are refusals of tradition, and, as a music finding itself through its own performance of itself, is both a critique of normative life and a self-expression of an alternate life. Ran through George Washington, as both an individual and as an exemplar of black men in the modern Western landscape, this expulsive element, its "symbolic, psychological, and formal"[26] realities, read through his hypervisible invisible vulnerability—that is, through his body, through his flesh, and the meaning of it—come to be interpreted as sexuality and sexual threat, hence the publisher's remarks that in his novel, George Washington is a "stud." A jazz novel about a black man, then, appears to be a novel about sex, about fucking, about the literal expulsion of the self—in which jazz comes to have a literal definition as *jasm* or *jism*—into the selves of others through manipulation, lies, riffs, bullshitting, evasion, inversion, creation, and the infinite possibilities of the "cock."[27] But, this interpretation only appears within a given framework of Western modernity in which black men are understood in this way. A traditional rendering of George Washington—and black men generally—his body, its meaning (symbolically, psychologically, and formally)[28] become obscured when read through his own narrative telling, the meaning of his flesh, of his body and its meaning are "warped, blurred, or refracted" once we realize that he, like Brown's novel "is a lost thing finding itself"[29] within a context that refuses his existence, and within his own narrative scope that collects the materiality of this existence, but instead of correcting or contradicting these ideas, refuses to distinguish truth from lie, exaggeration and manipulation from confusion and misremembering. This leaves us, amid all the stories, all the details, all the datum to puzzle out, just who is George Washington—just who are black men? Are they what is said of them, the generated historical, empirical facts? Or, are they what belies the rumors—are they the self-generated alternate framework of "unsourced and underground fragments"[30] that depart from said facts? If the latter, how do we understand a framework that is a self-telling narrative of who George Washington thinks he is and what he has made of himself—and, in general who black men think they are? How do we read such a text?

It seems that we cannot understand him within an already existing totalizing, choreographed and scripted narrative of what he is taken to be. Rather, it seems, if we are to understand him in his own voice, one which refuses narrative totalization and is guided only by "what was outside"[31] of it, we need some other framework, one that can "annotate its own progress."[32] This is where reading Brown's novel in terms of Johnson's phenomenological concern of creating the framework for the problem and for the solution comes in. This is where reading Brown's novel in terms of jazz form comes in. In both, we are given this critical insight: "when a legend travels through time and across media—when it is taken as a template, a founding model, a guiding orientation—what is misremembered or misconstrued can be the source of formal innovation."[33]

In addressing this dilemma of form and memory of black men themselves, and social and historical accounting of who black men are, Brown's novel asks, in brute terms, what it would mean if a black man became—that is, consciously lived—this infinite possibility, this formal innovation of form. What if a black man was excessive, could not be contained within the manifold of a changing, shifting logic, and became all things to all people? Could he summon the internal strength to withstand the (choreographed, composed) stereotype and create another world of infinite possibility within the stereotype, below the stereotype that he only knew, that was his own: a world of jiving jazz improvised form of excessive, surplus black maleness? Could he survive the descent into the idea of "the black male" in order to give rise, in the material world and within himself, to another form of living freedom?

Could he, in other words, turn his hypervisible invisible vulnerability into his strength, not by evading it or trying to solve it, but becoming it, fully, to see what might be on the other side? To do this, he would need to become, fully, a jiveass nigger—a creature of being, a creature of becoming, a creature of pure creation: a nigger who in becoming a nigger would become something other than a nigger, something perhaps greater than a nigger, a jiveass creator, a monstrous form of becoming in which one becomes what one is not to become what one is.[34] Why can't a jiveass nigger be the source of all willful, creative imaginations and the foundation of his own existence?

Yet this is not to say that Brown's novel invites a trickster reading. Brown's novel is not as concerned with representing "unreconciled opposites, living in harmony," or to be read in the way that Henry Louis Gates Jr. and others have described.[35] Rather, Brown's novel invites us to query into the various possibilities of form and the shapes of reality—physical and psychic—available when the ultimate truth of reality is abandoned for an ever increasing and changing reality navigated through the hypervisible invisible vulnerability of black maleness.

> *Night Music Slanted*
> *Light strike the cave of sleep. I alone*
> *tread the red circle*
> *and twist the space with speech*
>
> *Come now . . . don't*
> *be a savior; take your words and scrape*
> *the sky, shake the rain*
> *. . .*
>
> *can there anything*
> *good come out of*
> *prison*[36]

Can a black man, understanding that his very existence as the speculative projection of white people's imagination, then, through his own individual consciousness and imagination will himself to exist within and possibly control this projection? Can, in other words, a black man, once realizing that he is the projected thought of white Western logos, then reorient reality by steering into this logos, creating something altered, something new? Can one produce the unthinkable: instead of avoiding the black hole of blackness—one that sucks all life, all sound, all color, all light into its own crushing gravity—actually lean into it, assume responsibility for all its gravity, all its weight, and come out the other side into an altered reality with altered forms? Would we ever be able to identify this man? Can one have this level of imaginative self-belief to enact reality and the self as the infinite possibility of form and not just the speculative gesture or the raving from one's own selected isolation?

This is where Brown's novel begins, with a question: What must a black man become in order to survive this descent?

I want to wear
your smile on my sleeve
& break
your heart like a horse
or its leg. Weeks of being
bucked off, then
all at once, you're mine—
. . .

                            Loneliness is a science—
                     consider the taxidermist's
                                 tender hands
                    trying to keep from losing
                         skin, the bobcat grin
                             of the living.[37]

Scene Two: The Set-Up, in Three-Part Harmony

I. George Washington and the "Borne" Condition of the Nigger

His name was George Washington, which meant or could be inferred that someone, his parents—namely, his mother and presumably his father—had offered him to the world as George Washington. They wanted him to share in the name of the first president of United States of America—the man who crossed the Delaware and, in doing so, guided this young, newly born nation toward freedom and prosperity. They wanted their son to share in this autonomy and this self-fashioning. His parents gave him the name and thus a share in the tradition of the man charged with birthing into the nation the spirit that was born and manifested itself in the Declaration of Independence, a document sealed with a message announcing a new world order. His parents, too, were charged, like the original Washington, with birthing into one George Washington, their son, the namesake, this same spirit of independence, of autonomy and self-fashioning to declare a new world order. Their charge, then, like Washington's own, was to look after this newly born developing thing. How would this George Washington, the black George Washington, enact this principle, enact his liberty, his own declaration of autonomy, his own declaration of freedom onto the world? Would it, could it, be like the original? Would he, could he, like the original, become a statesman or a general or, less ambitiously, a lawyer or a doctor?

No. This George Washington, the namesake, the son, their son, named to share in the condition of self-fashioning autonomy, was black and interpreted self-fashioning autonomy not as the manifestation of will in a document of norms and laws but as its opposite. This George Washington did not exercise the principle of freedom and prosperity in terms of the new world democratic order, but discovering that because he was black these principles could never quite live up to the "kind of versatility . . . humming in his head" or humming in the world itself (*Life and Loves*, 8), he, out of necessity, inverted them. That is, the principled document of seeming order—rights, law, will, consent, justice, enlightened rationality, and so on—that established this nation was revealed, to this George Washington, the black George Washington, as document of *dis*order. As such, when he attempted to enact these principles for himself, he experienced their opposite—lawlessness, injustice, arationality, and so on; they exploded, erupted from internal contradiction, and revealed to him the discordance underlying the surface of narrative tranquility. They revealed to him the jiveness of reality, the jiveness at the heart of America and the original George Washington, not as the classical composer of "scripted, sculpted, premeditated,"[38] and rational form but as an improviser, as a jazz player who feared his own sound.

For this George Washington, the black George Washington for whom these principles revealed discordance, utilized this discordance to enact in and for himself the principle of jiveness, that is, the principle of acknowledged improvisation, of jazz. That is, rather than believing or pretending to believe in principles of rational order, as the original had, this George Washington became "a poet without the appropriate metaphor," a "hustler, . . . a jazz player," a jiveass (*Life and Loves*, 8). And this is how Cecil Brown's novel *The Life and Loves of Mr. Jiveass Nigger* begins—with the inversion of the basic principles of American constitutionalism for the principles of change, of becoming, of versatility of black male living in America.

Again, this George Washington shared in the name of George Washington, the man who steered the nation into its documented and principled freedom and, with it, liberty from the tyranny of absolute law, and he did it, the original, through disavowal and the act of grand marronage from his mother country. Thus, George Washington, the original, had thrust the nation into chaos to create order. But in the process, this nation, newly developing in its freedom and liberty, fashioned their order by thrusting other men and women into the chaos of bondage. And this George Washington, born out of this chaos, was also fashioned within the bondage necessary to extoll the modern Western virtues of freedom and liberty—for it was, in a large sense, the wealth generated from enslavement and the taxation of this wealth that spurred the original desire for freedom and liberty among the colonies, the autonomy in the act of grand marronage, and the establishment of the Declaration of Independence. It seems, then, that the difference between the black George Washington and the original was that the black one grounded his declaration of freedom and liberty in the chaos or the principle of becoming and change, that is, jiving, while the original sought, through his and the nation's own mythological becoming—a nation built on enslavement that had proposed equality and liberation from the enslavement of taxation without representation—to ground himself and itself in a new, transcendent order and cover over its own chaotic disorder or jiveness.

Though it may appear that the two George Washingtons have little to nothing in common, they can be understood as mutually necessary ends of the same articulation of reality—one born black through the violent condition of enslavement, the other born white through the violent condition of enslaving. Their strange birth—one articulating reality through the normativity of law, the other interpreting the normativity of law as jive—actually unites them. Both George Washingtons find themselves strangely born into a blackness of the both/and fluid condition of America. The violence and pillaging that offered the white George Washington liberty from England and equality and freedom at home was also the same condition that created the black George Washington with, seemingly, none of these attributes. Yet both George Washingtons are tied, not only in the liberation that is America but also in the simultaneous contradiction of the condition itself—that which affirms, by its nature, also negates; that which situates also decenters; that which reveals also conceals, both black and antiblack.

Ralph Ellison reminds us of the "ironic facet of the old American problem of identity. . . . For the ex-colonials the declaration of an American identity meant the assumption of a mask, and it imposed not only the discipline of national self-consciousness, but gave Americans an ironic awareness of the joke that always lies between appearance and reality, between the discontinuity of social tradition and that sense of the past which clings to the mind."[39] In naming their black son George Washington, his parents imbued within him an affirmative negation, a past that engulfs the present, not like the image of Sankofa, a bird with its body facing forward but head turned to backward, eating an egg on its back, signaling the significance of the past in guiding the future, but like that of Ernest Hemmingway's hyena—the "self-eating devourer of the dead, trailer of calving cows, . . . potential biter-off of your face at night while you slept"—unaware that he has been "shot at a great distance, in the heat shimmer of the plain," circling madly, "snapping and tearing at himself until he pulled out his own intestines out . . . and eating them with relish."[40] The nation had imbued in him a past that it (the Nation) cannot announce as its own foundation and thus ensuring his jiveness as well as its own. His parents ensured that he must face the foundation of the nation, and the negation of his existence, in his own name.

In this condition of George Washington's emergence, blackness at once could be understood as a "certain triumph of the spirit, speaking to us of those who rallied, reassembled and transformed themselves and who under dismembering pressures refused to die," and that which attempted to kill it off yet needed it not to die as a precondition for its own existence.[41] It is in this doubling—that which insists on both the death and existence of blackness—that each of the George Washingtons discovered this jive principle of America. So when James Baldwin declaratively stated in a 1963 interview, "Well, you know this, anyone's who's tried to live knows this: That what you say about anyone else . . . reveals you. . . . In America, we have the nigger. I didn't invent him. White people invented him. . . . So I give you your problem back. You're the nigger, baby, it isn't me,"[42] he may have been wrong in the sense that the "nigger" names not blackness but the jive condition into which the nation as a whole has been thrown in its acts of freedom and liberty through grand marronage. And it is this that we are all called to perform, more or less. The task, then, it seems is to see and "see" the blackness of whiteness or, formally, the "ad nigram"—the condition of the nigger, the formative causal agent for American self-fashioning subjectivity. As Brown will instruct, the difficulty of the condition and its fundamental jiveness is the inherent desire to evade the condition and its consequences by locating all of it in the black body.

But both George Washingtons were born into this condition of the nigger. Both were borne of this chaos of life and death, of desire and revulsion at the heart of America's nigger. Both were borne of this chaos, emerged from this chaos, and tried through their own will to deal with this chaos—the original through the mythology of his and the nation's existence in transcendental principles, the namesake by refusing the sanctity of principles.

Interlude: Swallowing the Nigger Whole

Fanon once recounted a story of himself riding on a train. He is seen by white passengers but is spotted by a particular passenger, a white child. The child initially remarks on Fanon's body, "Look, a Negro." The child remarks about the spectacle of Fanon's blackness three times, before a last remark: "Mama, see the Negro! I'm frightened." At each of the intervals, the child was not merely repeating the phrase "Look a Negro" and then merely ending with fear. The fear was being called forward with each of the repetitions: it was a dialectical progression of calling on and calling forward something already present, something already there. "Look, a Negro" is an incantation, a meditation, a conjuring spell. Like the child, Fanon, too, went through a dialectical progression of the Negro. He was initially amused to have been spotted and smiled. But as the spotting continued, the child was no longer pointing out Fanon's blackness but speaking to what it meant, to its historicity. So, after the third recalling, Fanon knew the nigger had been conjured; the nigger was now on the train and sat next to him, behind him, on him, and in him. He knew "he could no longer laugh, because [he] already knew that there were legends, stories, history, and above all *historicity*."[43]

This is where analysis of the story usually stops, veering off into the facticity or living existence of blackness in the Negro or as the Negro. But as with all tarrying, it is good to move both forward and backward simultaneously. Returning to the white child's conjuring of the nigger, the last iteration of acknowledgment came with fear but also came with a specific phrase: "the little white boy throws himself into his mother's arms: Mama, the *nigger's* going to eat me up."[44] It is this last iteration, the call on the Negro three times, that results in the appearance of the nigger, and when the nigger appears, he is going to consume you. Yet it was the white child who pointed out Fanon, the white child who conjured the nigger, and also the white child who feared being consumed by his own conjured image. What Fanon is trying to tell us is that the nigger is a conjured image that consumes everyone involved—it consumes blackness in the whiteness of conjuring, and it consumes whiteness within its own conjured image.

This is the condition of the nigger; this is the condition of both George Washingtons. It is this condition that causes the original George Washington to fabricate and constitute mythology as the founding element of America. It is this conjured image and self-negation that causes the extreme violence of colonial oppression. It is this condition that frightens all black men, for they know what it means; they know what is coming next—their own consumption! And in Brown's novel, it is this that causes the black George Washington to always lie, to jive, to become a self-acknowledged jazz artist to try to ride the wave of chaos into another kind of order—not that of the original but his own constructed truth. But as we will see, the question that Brown's Washington really is asking, Is it possible to know that one will be swallowed whole, allow it to happen, and survive? This is the descent that we described earlier in the chapter.

II. The Formal Construction of the Self in the Condition of the Nigger

George Washington, the original, in attempting to disguise this borne and emergent chaos as reasonable in documents, norms, and laws (as the principled manifestation of will), revealed the lineal root genus of the American tragic-comedy—by attempting to avoid blackness and the nigger in these documents, norms, and laws, he actually imbued these documents, norms, and laws with this blackness, with the condition of the nigger itself. They became both black and antiblack, and with them, concepts like freedom, liberty, justice, reason, manifest destiny, and democracy also became both black and antiblack—whenever anyone speaks these concepts, one is also saying "nigger" and conjuring him forward. In other words, the attempt to mask this doubling as reasonable and principled, as the intentional construction of an epistemic, ontological, historical, and metaphysical order, revealed it all as merely functional and, thus, jive.

Early in Brown's novel, George Washington, the namesake, fears the condition of disorder, of absolute negation, of the absolute outsider. He fears that this condition will find him and consume him. And it is this fear that, initially, drives him to jiving, in an attempt to create an alternate identity of absolute possibility, for, he thought, it is only absolute possibility that can hold at bay absolute negation. And so is the creation of "Paul Wintrop, Jr., . . . the most well-read Princetonian to walk the campus in many years, especially knowledgeable on English literature of the period 1590–1690," and his career of making up names, identities, history, for if he became anything at all, fundamentally, it would mean constructing an ideal, like the original George Washington, that could be and would be negated at any moment.

But, more precisely, he jives because he ultimately fears becoming his own father, who did not so much jive reality but cursed it. His father, in accepting the ambiguity of the principle, was able to curse all of it—spiritually and materially—and, in doing so, had placed himself beyond it but also beyond the recognition and comprehension of the people around him. He had placed himself beyond both man's law and God's law and thus could not be understood by either. He had, in a sense, fully embraced the chaos and had become the absolute density of blackness and that which everyone thought to be the absolute epitome of everything gone wrong in the world—the encroachment of the wild elements of existence onto the plain of civilization.

This George Washington spent his young life running from this fate, attempting to evade the fact "'something' done gone wrong deep down inside" (*Life and Loves*, 4), evading in jiving reality rather than cussin' it. But if he was borne into the condition of the nigger, how could he jive it and avoid it? Could he lie enough to hold back the haunt of his own father, who his own mother called "the cussinges' man ever born"? Could he avoid or evade what had been handed down by the nation itself, by his parents in naming him after the nation's own emergence in the falsehood delusion of self-fashioning? Could he evade the condition of his father—spiritual (the original George Washington) and biological (his own father)? Could he avoid or evade the chaotic contradiction of national documents, national monuments, and national behavior? How could he not cuss this condition? How could he avoid or evade his own inheritance from his father of "cussing when he came into this world"? Cussin' this history? Cussin' this emergence? Cussin' the internal contradiction of himself, of his name, and being given this contradiction by his parents? How could he *not* cuss the internal irony of the name itself: the original George Washington's foundational myth in which he "cannot tell a lie," contrasted with this George Washington's foundational myth that he is "black head to toe, a clear proof that what he said was stupid"?[45] How could he *not* curse this condition?

Brown also alerts that there may be more to cussin' than George Washington has been told or may have initially thought. There may be something that is inherently evocative of and related to the both/and ambiguity of the nation and the conjuring and consumptive elements of the nigger. Brown seems to suggest that the very condition of the nigger as affirmation and negation is both a rupture and a rapture—it is both that which cracks the fabric of ordinary space and time and, announced in this rupture, the end of an old world and the emergence of a new modern world.[46] In doing so, this condition has taken us out of the old world as a condition to ground us in a new world. And, in doing so, it takes us away to another world, another reality, another possibility of infinite forms.

* * *

Recalling Fanon's earlier example, the nigger is a conjured image. Similarly, as Brown reminds us, the nigger is a condition, one that is both created and evocative, and one through which we find our identity. It is both built and undergirds building. As such, this condition is much like a religious experience—a feeling that is at once a formative structure of the real. The condition of the nigger is sacred in that it invigorates the disorderly material world with metaphysical meaning. As a condition, it is that through which the material order has been organized and that which we continuously come back to for renewal. Mircea Eliade reminds us, "it is clear to what a degree the discovery—that is, the revelation—of a sacred space possesses existential value for religious man; for nothing can begin, nothing can be *done*, without a previous orientation—and any orientation implied acquiring a fixed point."[47]

On the train, when the boy begins to call the Negro, time stops and is displaced by a conjuring moment that breaks ordinary constructions of linear time, and like the crossing of the threshold of the church, it becomes like a sacred space from which the nigger emerges. Calling the name "Negro" is, in a sense, *not* speaking; it is a gesture that cannot be theorized or captured in the organization of air and sound that is beyond—*conjuring* is the calling forth of that which cannot be named.

As Nahum Chandler informs us, "in the face of incommensurability, ... in the face of such, we cannot *speak*, as in depart from or arrive at truth."[48] He further instructs us, "There must have been an explosion, an irruption somewhere, from the beginning of time, as time, and thus yet beyond time, neither in time nor not time, indeed displacing time," which for Chandler is constituted in W. E. B. Du Bois's opening of *Souls of Black Folk*—"Between me and the other there is ever an unasked question"—and continues forward to speak to a "fragment, an opening" to ask a question of *being*.[49] The nigger is but the manifestation of the condition—of which Fanon is reminded when the recall of "Negro" summons forth the nigger, and he is no longer able to laugh; he has to recall that at each of the formative stages of their exchange on the train, the nigger was always there structuring their relation on the train, structuring the space of the train itself, and the time on that train. When the nigger finally appeared and the child was finally afraid, time no longer existed, and space had become invaded with a presence already present but unaccounted for. The nigger is thus an "explosion, an irruption somewhere" in time as it is experienced; but it reveals that which structures time. As such, when it appears, the ordinary world disappears, and something else registers: a "fragment, an opening" in being. The white child on the train called and recalled and recalled the Negro, and when the nigger appeared, the child was no longer able to speak but could register a nonsensical phrase—"the nigger's going to eat me up"—akin to that of a wail in church or catching the Holy Spirit speaking in tongues.

But this has little to do with the one who finds himself evoked in the nigger himself. We have an image of Fanon on the train, the only black passenger. He is facing the white child, and the child points and says, "Look, a Negro!" over and again and eventually finds his way to "it's a nigger." We imagine Fanon facing a sea of white faces, the child, his mother, all the other white passengers, and the very idea of whiteness calling itself forward, as the congregation conjures him; and we imagine that Fanon is trapped, is *had* as an object of their projected world. But is there more to this story? Can more be said of Fanon himself, of he who, in the midst of the conjuring of form, also finds himself in a moment of rupture and rapture in the condition of the nigger and manifestation of the nigger? How is he raptured and ruptured in this moment, in this evocative occurrence? As the physical instantiation and marker of this transcendent moment of religious excitation? What Brown's Washington may have missed early in the novel is that maybe his father's cussin' *was* his response to the evocative presence of the nigger. Maybe he cussed all of reality, not in nihilism or defeat but as a way of introducing a new set of realities into existence. Maybe he cussed as a way to instantiate a new "interior of the church" as a "solution of continuity."[50] Could it be possible that his father was not cussin' to curse reality or even God, but maybe his "cussin' is his way of testifying"? (*Life and Loves*, 7).

Brown leaves open the possibility that Washington's father cussed the ordinary experiences of religious excitation, revelation, rupture, and rapture through which and in which the nigger and America are borne as a refusal to enact himself in this world; in his cussin' he was simply refusing to participate. Cussin', then, becomes an activity of the nigger, one that rejects and affirms—rejects humanity, reason, form, and thought that undergird the formal structures of identity and affirms in their place *nothing*. His father's signification of nothing and rejection of everything is what was, perhaps, most troubling early on for George Washington and why he refused to even consider its possibility. Perhaps, when Eliade tells us that "whatever degree he may have desacralized the world, the man who has made his choice in favor of a profane life never succeeds in completely doing away with religious behavior," he is only half right, because he only has half of George Washington's father's story.[51] Perhaps if Eliade had understood the rupture and rapture inherent in blackness and expressive of the nigger as the condition for modern Western existence, he would have understood that one *can* affirm nothing, one *can* reject and have in this rejection a kind of negative affirmation, that is, itself vibrant and alive. Perhaps one *can* instantiate that which is unreachable, not as profane disorder but as a recognition that "in the face of incommensurability, . . . in the face of such, we cannot *speak*, as in depart from or arrive at truth." Perhaps the cuss signifies just this—another divine order but one without mythology, without sacred space, without truth, and without a "threshold [to] separate the two spaces [and] indicate the distance between two modes of being."[52]

Early on, this George Washington could not stare into traditional spiritual and material order and cuss, could not throw himself into the abyss of what is beyond. Early on, this George Washington was unable to transform the meaning of "faith"—both spiritual and material—in an act of heresy, could not withstand the idea of actual chaos, of actual unknowability, in which one refuses the identity of norms or documents for the sake of jiving, which is but a playing with forms, rather than the formative denial of form itself.

Early on, this George Washington, the namesake, was afraid to place himself above and outside the law—man's or God's, the historical, spiritual, or material—in a new actualized order of negativity, so he placed himself at odds with his father, with the condition of the nigger; and in jiving, he created illusions to keep at bay the nation itself, the inverted status of his blackness and the presence of the nigger. He held it all back, he thought, through constantly shifting the grounding of his own existence. He attempted to hold it back by becoming Mr. Jiveass Nigger himself.

III. Something Wicked This Way Comes

Brown tells us that as part of his evasion of his father and the condition of nigger, George Washington tried not to curse at all, tried not to conjure this form, attempted not to let in any of this condition, to jive the condition, but he nevertheless cursed. On many occasions, he found himself accused of cussin', just like his own father, and what dismayed him was the fact that he was not aware that he done so. "But no! he had not cursed, it was his father speaking through him, speaking through him unconsciously. He began to hate his father who was buried deep inside of him and who was a nigger and cursed all the time. He began to hate the unconscious part of himself" (*Life and Loves*, 7–8).

The condition of the nigger, Brown seems to be telling us, is not so much a conscious, willed expression of existence as we seem to think is inherent in the self-fashioning of autonomous will; nor is it an act of faith, as the equally chosen affective belief in a principle. Rather, it is something that visits upon you, plants itself deep inside and stays; and every once and a while, it announces itself, surfaces where and when it likes. And it is this that seems to be our national inheritance, the given fact of our existence—in the namesake's cussin'; in the drunken groping of the black male cock, as discussed by Baldwin in the introduction; in each and every lie that the original George Washington told about himself and the nation. The body, it seems, is not just somatic—that is, a site for chemical, neurological, and electrical stimuli and responses; the body also actively relates to the construction of conscious and unconscious norms that guide its behaviors and actions in the world. Even when we try to consciously silence this body, its memories, and its knowledge by way of principled declarations of American hegemony—most famously, the hope of creating reality contrary to lived experience—the body returns, as it were, seemingly against our will and out of nowhere.

Here Brown echoes Ralph Ellison's protagonist in *Invisible Man*, who attempts to banish not his father but his grandfather, who had revealed himself to be a nigger and whose own advice, much like that of cussin' existence, was vibrantly negative: "live with your head in the lion's mouth, . . . overcomin' with yeses, agree 'em to death and destruction."[53] And similar to Brown's Washington, Ellison's narrator imagines he has succeeded in banishing not only his grandfather but also the condition and appearance of the nigger himself. But like Brown's Washington, the nigger nevertheless reemerges, against his conscious will, unsolicited, and unconsciously. In the pivotal opening scene, Ellison's narrator gives a self-avowed integrationist speech but ends up cussin':

"What's that word you say, boy?"
"Social responsibility," I said.
"What?"
"Social . . ."
"Louder."
". . . responsibility."
"More!"
"Respon—"
"Repeat!"
"—sibility."

The room filled with the uproar of laughter until, no doubt, distracted by having to gulp down my own blood, I *made the mistake* and yelled a phrase I had often seen denounced in newspaper editorials, heard debated in private.

"Social . . ."
"What?" they yelled.
". . . equality—" . . .
"You weren't being smart, were you boy?" he said, not unkindly.

"No, sir."
"You sure that about 'equality' was a mistake?"
"Oh, yes, sir," I said. "I was swallowing blood."
"Well, you had better speak more slowly so we can understand. We mean to do right by you, but you've got to know your place at all times. All right, now, go on with your speech."[54]

Ellison's narrator offers the phrase "social responsibility" and is made to repeat it three times. Like the white child on the train in Fanon's example, the repetition of the phrase three times is a kind of incantation, a kind of summoning forward, but what *came*, what emerged, was not the Booker T. Washington type of accommodationism but the nigger. What is evocative here is the fact that the incantation of respectability and normality actually conjured the nigger. In this moment, Ellison seems to be telling his audience that they are one and the same—that there is never any safe distance, for everything we do and say as formative truth is itself tied to the nigger, and even if we do not wish to call him forward, as the white child on the train had, he still may emerge.

But what is also instructive in Ellison's example is the phrase "gulping down my own blood." It is after this phrase that the nigger appears. But why? What is it about gulping down the rupture of one's own body that brings forth affirmative negativity? His grandfather's treachery was always right there at the back of the throat, hanging onto the word "responsibility," for this word and what it meant also invisibly signifies its opposite—he who would not or could not be responsible, for his existence negated the possibility of social responsibility. Rather, his existence was the inversion of responsibility, for "responsibility" implies rationality and civility.

But the placement of this phrase also points to the fact that the narrator's gulping down his own blood is the precondition for civil, normalized existence and exchange; and yet this is also the moment—of civil existence and exchange—when the nigger returns, disrupting the order and normality that it preconditions, and with its return reinstates chaos. The rupture of his own flesh brings forward the rapture of its meaning—social responsibility necessitates the very possibility of its vibrantly negative affirmation, "social equality," and with it not the ordinary sacred space of black flesh but the rupture of this space with alteration, a space that refuses boundary, border, or meaning—the unthinkability and incommensurability of black equality.

The slow emergence of ". . . equality" from the narrator's black male body challenges and silences the "uproar" of white laughter, calling attention to his black male body as always already potentially unruly and threatening, making it clear the always already presence of chaos and danger undergirding order and necessitating the swift and potentially violent reprisal for disorder. But it also signifies the inherent unknowability and uncontrollable nature of the black male body—more precisely, the possibility of the nigger himself to appear even when he is not conjured by the white congregation.

Thus, the "mistake" that Ellison's narrator admits acts as a medium of exchangeability between the world of illusory order and the chaotic possibility of the nigger, who cusses existence itself. Brown's George Washington, like Ellison's narrator, is straddled between the domesticated black male body and the unruly possibility of the nigger. The "mistake," then, being manifested is the incapacity of black men and boys to hold back the nigger, to suck back down the blood, to keep at bay one's own ancestry and lineage, all for the sake of knowing one's place. But what Brown and Ellison seem to be suggesting is that this cannot be held back, for it is not *in* them but *of* the condition in which they are made to appear. If the appearance of the nigger subverts reality by asserting the always already known inversion of expectation, Washington's father and Ellison's grandfather suggest that rather than trying to negotiate the divide, they could testify to another reality altogether, one in which they cuss both the condition of the nigger and the reality that emanates from it.

Interlude: In the Break

Ralph Ellison's narrator tells himself that his grandfather had slipped into the break between the crowd's expectation and his gulping down blood, slipped in between as a mistake; Brown's George Washington attempts to convince himself that his own father had slipped through between his conscious and unconscious selves—that his mistake was that he was not vigilant enough. Like Ellison's narrator, Brown's Washington did not believe that this was really a part of him but somehow his own father speaking through him. This slippage, this inability to hold back the nigger from emerging between expectation and action, to keep the illusory world safe from unruly disorder, alerts the reader that perhaps the nigger is not deep inside but somewhere in between, waiting, refusing to leave until it is heard.

This is also the moment when we recognize that George Washington's and Ellison's narrator's black bodies (and black men generally) house within them both the capacity for seeming domestication and also the capacity to, at any moment, break order and rebel. And this is the aspect of their bodies that both black and white Americans attempt to control, through the control of their speech and their actions, but that ultimately fails because the nigger is not in a body but in a condition that has been cast into a body, like the spirit into flesh. Yet, unlike the spirit trapped in flesh, the black male body is trapped in the condition (rather than vice versa). Similarly, Brown's George Washington, in his attempt to discipline himself through disciplining his speech, like Ellison's narrator, finds his own black male body betraying his sentiments and attempts at civility and order. And, like Ellison's narrator, the onlooking world is shocked, disappointed, and angered at this unruly, undisciplined body that even black men themselves cannot control until they realize that their blackness is not in their bodies but somewhere in between.

The question of the unconscious and conscious parts of oneself may result in a theory of the psychoanalytic subject to explain the presence of this upsurge in between, but it does not properly or fully explain the nature of Ellison's narrator's or Brown's namesake's mistake and what they were mistaken about. At the center of the mistake is neither the narrator's grandfather nor Washington's father but what is hidden—that is, what has been hidden and what one has hidden from oneself or resisted in oneself. When Brown tells us that "George tried not to curse" and Ellison tells us of his narrator, "whenever things went well for me I remembered my grandfather and felt guilty and uncomfortable. It was as though I was carrying out his advice in spite of myself," we are returned to the idea of domestication in thought and action of black maleness, rather than the realm of the conscious or unconscious reality, for the subject to which one may ascribe such reality does not exist within the context of the nigger. The address that we find in both Ellison and in Brown, then, is not psychoanalytic revelation, but the revelation that what is haunting and abiding, conditioning reality cannot be ignored and must be accepted: namely, black maleness is—by definitions of normality, civility, and order—unruly, uncivil, and undisciplined. This insight is that what is revealed (civility, order, normality) is also what is concealed (the need to violently domesticate and civilize the black male body in the material and conceptual order) and that black men must acknowledge that even if they accept this disciplinary boundary, their embodiment alone will continue to challenge the boundaries, even if against their will. And this insight of the condition of the nigger is what generates the cussin' and also what instructs us as to what the condition does to us if we refuse it, reject it—it buries itself somewhere down deep below tradition, normalization, civility and emerges to dismantle who we imagine we have become to show us what we, in fact, are.

And after this three-part setup, we can now begin our descent.

Scene Four: The Jiveass Nigger, a Three-Penny Opera

I. In the Crossing: A Hessian Condition

If George Washington could not banish his father completely, the key to the rest of Brown's novel is how he is to make his father (he who arrives in the condition of the nigger) useful in his own constructed image, such that when he does return, he will have already predicted its chaos and placed it in the service of his own imagistic self-project/ion. For as we are learn from this George Washington, "there was nothing under the sun that was really phony if it was functional. . . . Being whatever the shit you found yourself being. All that could be functional. Could be useful. *Depending on your spirit. Depending on your Energy, Imagination*" (*Life and Loves*, 22; emphasis added). The nigger could play an equally functional role in any of the projected identities that

George Washington would construct for himself—the Princetonian student, the homeless student abroad, the ex-patriot poet, whatever—each construct factoring itself into the total imaginative landscape of George Washington's projection. All that was required was the realization that behind it all, the pretext of civility, normality, and law behind the chaos, behind straddling in between the Negro and the nigger, was this haunting specter of possibility—and it is this possibility, George Washington calculates, that allows these two contraries to hold together. And this, George Washington thinks, is his novel contribution: the creation in oneself, as oneself, the space and time of absolute emptiness and plenitude, and that density of gravity and centrifugal force to keep us on the surface our worlds.

That is, George Washington believes that if he is skilled enough, precise enough at jiving, he could create a reality—a world with its own set of physical laws, its own atmospheric conditions, its own temporal frame in and for others to dwell—and when the nigger does return, his worldly inhabitants will not notice or will be incapable of thinking or acting without his guidance.

This George Washington, like the original, began the revolution, crossing the Delaware under the cover of dark, the ice in the river cracking around the ship for a surprise attack against the Hessian forces on the other side. This George Washington, like the original, discovered that it is not so much the fact of crossing the Delaware or staging the attack or even revolution itself that matters. It is merely the idea that it *could* have happened and what this says about him, as the man that *would* have risked it all, if the situation demanded it.

And this George Washington also discovers that it does not matter whether there actually was a Delaware to cross or a Hessian army waiting on the other side; it is enough that if there was a Delaware and if there was an awaiting army, he would have crossed it, and he would have confronted them, so he did confront them. He became he who would have, so he became he who did. And the secret is that there is no distinction between being and doing, praxis and theory, when you are the one that constitutes the world and its rules.

But, more than that, this secret also suggests that it is not so much in the crossing to the other side that provides the context for the action, for the creation of a world within its own laws, its own rules, its own structure. Rather, it is merely leaving the old world behind, which the original did when he left the edge of the Delaware and before he reached the other side. He discovered that the reality of the world was not in landing on either side—being neither the man who did not leave the shores nor the man who arrived on the other side but being the man who was in the crossing, in which case one could be both of these men and offer an infinitely variable form of becoming rather than the static form of being. The reality of the world, then, would be in the crossing, in the in between.

This George Washington faced his own Hessian condition, crossing his own Delaware of no longer and not yet—the Negro and the nigger—in a surprise ambush of the totalizing and occupying force on the other side: his white audience, his white congregation who conjures and attempts to control the condition of the nigger. This George Washington discovers that the task is not in actually crossing from one side to the other but in his *willingness* to become both the Negro and the nigger depending on the circumstance—in his willingness to be formless, no longer the man they thought he was, not yet the man they think he will be. This Washington concludes that if he exists in the crossing, he can, instead of being conjured, conjure from himself, for himself, a special relativity for his own world founded on the condition of the nigger but reinvented for his own usage. It would be a world similar enough to the other existing world, wherein each one of his terrestrial inhabitants—all the congregations and their visitors—would not resist its form, but he could control the content through his black male performance.

II. In the Crossing: The Compossibility of His "Sex"

Like the original George Washington, this George Washington thinks it is enough to create a narrative, a regulative ideal, a mythology of himself, from nothing to that which is beyond. This George Washington becomes an existential Negro. He creates, fashions for himself and for others, an image of man to capture all passersby—an image sophisticated and erudite enough to, seemingly, hold back the beast while weaving a wonderfully elaborate web that dances invisibly in the air around the edges of the nigger.

It is in this performance that this George Washington, the existentialist Negro, becomes all possibilities as the precondition to be the present and future of himself and stretches himself infinitely in between, in the crossing of the compossibilities of his latent and ever-present self. In doing so, he becomes neither what is expected of him nor what he imagines for himself: rather, he simply is in all of infinite varieties and gives to himself an alternate reality that he and he alone would inhabit.

He becomes a high-leverage, tightrope walker straddling across the divide, straddling himself across the two possibilities. George Washington, though, knows that once the performance begins and the congregation circles around below, he cannot actually finish his performance but has to remain on the tightrope for all time, night and day, and has to be ready to perform to keep the crowd there. This is central to his performance—the congregation could never know or suspect the performance.

* * *

> Man is a rope, tied between beast and ubermensch—a rope over an abyss. A dangerous across, a dangerous on-the-way, a dangerous looking-back, a dangerous shuddering and stopping.
> What is great in man is that he is a bridge and not an end.[55]

* * *

This insight is his functional self; his constructed illusion generates its own gravity, its own sense of time and space, its own reality, its own special relativity. But he also knows that if anyone else finds out, catches on to the performance—ever sees him climb the stairs of the tower, walk out of the door onto the rope, or even suspects there is a tower, a door or a rope, he would be lost and plunge to his death. Critical to his performance is the seduction of his performance. He discovers that in order to generate and keep a congregation, to generate and keep going his own terrestrial and orbital gravity, he has to seduce reality, seduce the physical laws of the universe and the psychic laws of consciousness—the laws of expectation—into appearing as he would have them.

But, to do this, he has to learn the difference between taking and giving. He has to learn the expectations of others and rather than being trapped by them—like Fanon on the train with the white child—he would have to use them as leverage to trap his congregation and control his audience. For if he could not, the condition of the nigger would trap him in a cycle of giving, of having others always take from him—take his being, take his essence, to, as it were, hold his soul in their hands—and they would get to his soul through his body. He would have to learn, then, to take and give the appearance that what he had taken was actually given; he would have to blur the lines between taking and giving so that no one other than he would know the difference. Critical to his performance, to his straddling between, to his existing in the crossing is offering himself as a way of seducing but also as a way of preventing himself from being taken. Central to this exchange—the seduction, the lies, existing in the crossing—is his body. As such, this is what he would have to use to gain and maintain control over his world—his body, his black male body. "[He] took the nigger's privates in his hand, one hand, still smiling, as though he were weighing them. In the cradle of the one white hand, the nigger's privates seemed as remote as meat being weighed in the scales; but seemed much heavier, too."[56]

"*Much* heavier, too": this line in Baldwin's novel is critical; it is not just that the testicles (the possibility of another social and political order) and the phallus (the instrument of the deployment of this other world) are meat, but in a Western patriarchal social, political, economic, and psychic order, the testicles and the phallus are literally and metaphorically those through which production and reproduction occur at the personal, state, and national level. It is this fact, historical and contemporary, that gives the "privates" more weight and makes Brown's Washington's attempt at creating and controlling a world, a congregation, of creating new laws of the physical and psychic universe, so dangerous, makes it a tightrope walk in the crossing.

That is to say, inherent in the black male body is the very idea of sex or the threat of sexual potency. It is this threat—the very idea of this potency—that establishes the sides of the Delaware: on one side, the Negro, erudite, reserved, respectful, impotent; on the other side, the nigger, unruly, uncivilized, exploitative, uncontrolled, and potent. In existing in the crossing, between the Negro and the nigger, Brown's Washington needs to know how to conjure which image at what time, enough to create a sense of reality but never enough to terrify the audience to tear him into pieces or worry that he will eat them. Brown's Washington would attempt to weaponize his hypervisible invisible vulnerability—its ambiguity, its fundamental unknowability, acting as his weapon to create inchoate principles from dehiscence.

And this is the challenge. Vital to his appearance is his body—the vehicle and object of his identification and his sexualization, his sexualization as his identification. As black male tightrope walker, he is straddling between these two poles—the Negro and the nigger—with his body itself as the rope. He would have to negotiate both the erudition and sophistication of the Negro eunuch with the brutality and animality of the nigger and to so with such flourish and fluidity that his audience would cheer rather than gather to lynch and castrate him.

The grounding of his compossible performance of iteration and act was the infinite idea of possibility inherent in his black male body and the ideas surrounding his black male body—it is, in fact, these ideas surrounding the black male body that allow for the infinite possibilities within itself and in relation to the other. And in his refusal to cross to one side or the other, refusing to become one thing (a Negro) over another (the nigger), he refuses being with becoming, and with it, he imagines that, as existing in the crossing, he could ultimately sex his sex.

That is to say, George Washington, knowing the hypervisibility of his flesh and the invisibility of his conscious life, uses the divide as a Lagrange point, as a point in space in which, because of the refraction of light and the gravitational force between two or more bodies, one can hide, undetected. For Washington, what was his vulnerability becomes his moment of liberation—he can shield himself from his black maleness using his black maleness as a performance.[57]

As noted earlier, it is not so much his body or the compossible performance of it that will draw and maintain the crowds but the lies he tells about and through it that matter. It is his lies that he tells from in the crossing that will hold as constant a chaotic and unpredictable existence; like a gravity stabilizer on a ship hurling through space, the task of his lies, the pretense of a regulative ideal—the possibility of order in the disorderly black male body—is to make those within it forget about the instability outside it. It is to make them forget what has been constructed and for whom and only to remember the world as it is and was.[58]

Such regulation is only possible when the regulative ideal is adequately seductive; the lie itself, of normalization, binds together expectation with the promise of its fulfillment. This George Washington, though, understands that his lies are unstable and have to constantly shift, and this, he thinks, is his strength, for he knows—unlike those existing in his reality—that his lies are lies—that is, he knows that his regulative ideal is jive. And because of this, his lies could not be scripted but have to be improvised to keep the threatening unstable world stable. As his procreative capacity, his lies, binding the conceptual and material worlds into a stable reality, seducing each into a constant, enfleshed order, are like jazz, "like a Charlie Parker riff, . . . more convincing when he did them *a l'improviste*" (*Life and Loves*, 23).

His lies move across an economy of truths, knowing that underneath it "everything is a lie. Life is a lie," as Charlie Parker had recognized that there are no notes, only sounds to be manipulated, seduced into various forms, and that in the crossing between notes was more improvisation, a *life of improvisation*. Washington's life of jazz is an existence in the crossing from one sound to the next, one moment, one lie, one appearance, one experience to the next. This George Washington knows, has discovered, that underneath truth and lies is chaos and, under that, more chaos, and so on and so forth, and that to bring these together requires dexterity, concentration, courage, whimsy, and above all a kind of dedication to the possibility of impossibility. Like his father, who cussed to testify, this George Washington undertakes his jiving as a kind of cleansing.

> There is never any end. There are always new sounds to imagine; new feelings to get at. And always, there is the need to keep purifying these feelings and sounds so that we can really see what we've discovered in its pure state. So that we can see more and more clearly what we are. In that way, we can give to those who listen the essence, the best of what we are. But to do that at each stage, we have to keep on cleaning the mirror.[59]

What Coltrane seems to be telling us here is that jazz as interpretation carries within it a kind of purity and a kind of impurity. Like George Washington's lies, the improvisation that depends on interpreting sound, interpreting notes, as it were, has to have a kind of impurity with respect to being—to adhering to music as it is written and expected to be played by the composer—but also a kind of purity with respect to becoming; for if the performer does not offer something that feels real, then his audience will not believe the performance. As such, there *is* something real in the performance, in Washington's lies, in jiving, but the reality itself is one of a shifting landscape and an exploded narrative form.

And in Washington's improvised reality, in his improvised lies, he would step between the notes and between reality—their laws, their conventions—and he would step over from one to the next, while maintaining his balance and without losing the rhythm. And he would do so with his body, through his body. He would use his black male body and its sex—its flaccid phallus and its erection—to constitute "the minute laborious acts that make up musical activity."[60] He would literally use his embodied lies as his jazz performance to ground reality, "inseminating its soul with 'life.'"[61]

His lies both reveal and conceal the in between of being and becoming, of taking and giving, spinning out, like the Big Bang, like a sudden eruption of energy, an alternate organizational scheme. His audience moves over the dark and the deep of his "in the crossing," separating day from night; the world would begin again and again and again with seduction; and his congregation would be taken in by the seduction of his performance to the climax of exigent exuberance, by his jazz-like improvisation: his spunk, his jasm, his gism.

> *Ptah*—he spoke, and the world was.
>
> *
>
> *But,*
> *could he*
> *really*
> *seduce*
> *his way*
> *to*
> *freedom?*

Scene Five: The Life and Loves of Mr. Jiveass Nigger

Cecil Brown lays out the leitmotif of George Washington's jiveass nigger performance in the crossing, as the sexing his sex, early in the novel. It is announced at the same time that Washington expresses his fear of being his father, realizes that he cusses just like his father, and theorizes himself as a constantly changing, constantly shifting force gale wind as a response to his father's ever presence in him, and the condition of the nigger ever around him. As part of his lying performance of himself, George Washington has left the United States for Copenhagen, Denmark. And this is where the story picks up.

We are told that George Washington has jived everyone he has met since arriving in the city; he has given each one a different name, a different history, a different reason for his being in Copenhagen. Eventually, he finds himself low on funds, and intending to stay in the city, he has resolved that he will go to the U.S. embassy to get the money he needs. His other expat, black male friends, each in Copenhagen for his own reasons, though jive themselves, marvel at George Washington's confidence in his performance and doubt his capacity to jive at a level that will get the money from the embassy. "So you think . . . they gonna give you some money? . . . You're naïve, man. You don't understand that you're living in an International Racist Environment" (*Life and Loves*, 19–20). But George Washington, a jiveass nigger, knew that he would get the money because he *needed* the money, and the need would necessitate whatever lie he would tell, what he would need to become in order to get it. The problem these other black male expats suffered was their unwillingness to become whatever they needed to become—whatever, not whoever—their jiving was limited by their lack of courage or their actual belief in meaning in the world.

George Washington, though, knew "he'd have to think up some lie to tell them, knew he had to play some phony role," and that he would be up for the task (*Life and Loves*, 22). He knew he would be up to the infinite transformation wherein need, want, desire would constitute and underpin his condition and would provide the structure for the narrative he offered. And he knew deep down he "might use a gun," or he "might use his cock" (*Life and Loves*, 21).

I. The Structure

The novel's structure is allegorical. And though the understanding of allegory is usually in terms of a description of the meaning or subtext of a narrative, it must be remembered that Brown's structure *is* the meaning of his narrative; that is, how the story itself unfolds *is* the argument much more than any particular moment in Washington's fictive life. But this is not to say that Washington himself is just a metaphor for the novel itself and that we should read him as something other than a man or a singular individual. Rather, it is to note a larger and more significant point that Brown is making with the novel.

Because Washington is a jiveass, a self-avowed jiveass, and Brown's novel is about a jiveass, it is a jive novel. Like a jazz improviser, George Washington and the novel break down form and challenge the very basis of storytelling. While there are details of the plot and details of Washington's daily experiences throughout, these are incidental, like the individual notes in improvisation. *But they are also critically significant*, because they are what make improvisation possible and necessary. What we experience in Brown's novel, then, is like a jazz improvisation: you have a central melody that establishes a baseline or story line in order to disrupt and dismantle it for another baseline, another story line and another and another.

We are following George Washington throughout the novel and discover with him what he needs to become and what each situation means for him. We also discover that the narrative, as improvised, is not as centrally organized as with usual narrative arcs but is scattered as he subverts and *becomes* on the fly. To the extent that we understand and recognize that George Washington is a jiveass performer who must perform, who has "promised a performance,"[62] we will understand that the story may be read as discordant with itself because Washington is improvising much of it, and Brown, following Washington, is also improvising much of it. As such, we should think of the novel "not as a simple linear narrative, but as a fractured, exploded one."[63] But we should not look at the exploded elements as just fragmented pieces; rather, just as with each jazz performance, there is still an underlying pattern to the performance; and as with the text, there is still a narrative plot, but it is one concerned not with coherency but with the technical aspects of evocation and the craft of feeling.

For the rest of this chapter, we will be looking through a snapshot of moments or shards of Washington's story, attempting to gather from them a meaning that Washington himself is also trying to gather about his own life. We will see assertions of fact—which may or may not ring as true—and failures of identity. We will be moving along through the story with Washington and gathering along with him the fragments of "the exploded narrative[s]" that may "reveal a mosaic with a discernable underlying pattern."[64]

II. The Arrival

George Washington arrives at the U.S. embassy, armed with the performative American idea that, "with important people, audacity is the only policy" (*Life and Loves*, 34). He must outwardly and audaciously demand the money to confuse and disorient them with his boldness. This is the first of the beta tests to take place. An initial sizing up is certainly expected: a black man enters the U.S. embassy, asking—no, demanding—to meet with the consulate. The American consulate, a white woman, enters the room, unsure of what to expect from a black man who would walk into the embassy and make such a demand. George Washington tells her he is an American in Copenhagen: "Just, just living . . . spending all my money . . . writing a few lines of verse," having just graduated from Princeton University (*Life and Loves*, 35–36). She is confused but delighted that he has graduated from Princeton. Washington projects an image of one who is erudite and carries within himself the air of a black man who might have done such a thing—his boldness is the expression of this truth.

He sees and "sees" that she is drawn into the seduction of his lie—and the boldness of its execution; he sees and "sees" that she wants to believe. But she unexpectedly shifts ever so slightly from the expectation of his frontal attack. She queries him as to why he is wasting his education "loafing around in Copenhagen" when he could be back home helping to fix the "race problem." George has misjudged her investment and her interest. His seductive beta test has revealed that she is the sort of liberal who not only believes that "we need more colored leaders like Martin Luther King" and that he could be such a leader but that *she* has the right to make this sort of demand on his life (*Life and Loves*, 35–36). He has to recover and switch his seductive lie; he must offer new stimuli and test the response. He knew that a conflicting response would not secure him the money he had demanded, for "the woman was brooding over a problem that had long ago become something personal."

He would sit there, silent. He knew that it was important for her to demonstrate who she is to him. He was the erudite Negro, the Princetonian Negro, the statesman, the lawyer, the man of infinite possibility, and she needed to demonstrate her own vigor. And so rather than offering "his own views, he changed the subject" in the manner of a request (*Life and Loves*, 36–37).

> "I want to borrow four hundred crowns from the embassy, which I will repay when my father send me money in a couple of weeks."
> "You want to *borrow* four hundred crowns," she laughed, in half disbelief.
> "Yes," George said.
> "Four hundred crowns," she repeated, saddling her chin mockingly into her hand. . . .
> "We have precedents established here for this kind of situation. . . . We never just give out cash, not even lend cash, not even to our own staff . . . Did you know our policy?" (*Life and Loves*, 38)

Washington certainly knew the policy—those who could not seduce reality succumbed to it. Yet Washington is somehow and ironically put off by what seems to be her dishonesty—there were no policies anywhere in the world; there were meted out decrees, like ideas of freedom, liberation, independence, and those who were naïve enough to believe in them became the suppliant for others' projected illusions. Though his initial offer was a lie—he had not gone to Princeton—he was offended by her lie: he was only jiving; she was being dishonest. She seemed to have real commitments and real views, ones that would establish her as a particular kind of person, and she seemed to be equivocating. Perhaps, though, maybe she did not know what "policy" really meant; he could not exactly tell. Perhaps she was just negotiating the terms of the beta testing of race contact and interracial conflict to see and "see" if he would walk across the tightrope from the Princeton graduate to the ominous threat of the nigger. In either case, Washington decided that the erudite existential Negro had not triggered the desired response and decided that enacting the possibility of the nigger might work.

"If you can't give me the money," he heard himself—crossing the Delaware, ice cracking beneath his feet, the eyes of the fish below looking up, puzzling—"I'd have to find some other way." He was not quite performing the nigger who would reach across the desk and take the money by force, but he could no longer be mistaken for Martin Luther King either. George Washington had raised the flag, half mast. Initially, it seems that this beta-testing trial, too, failed. "I am afraid I can't help you," the consulate returned, looking at him now "with her cold, unblinking eyes" (*Life and Loves*, 38–39).

What the consulate does offer George is a job—first as a window washer, then as a bartender—an opportunity to work, to earn the money she could have simply given him. It is not clear in this moment of the beta test if the

American consulate is attempting to reduce him to brute labor, attempting to resituate him according to his color rather than his education, or if she is genuinely wanting to help, and all she has is wage labor (*Life and Loves*, 39–40). Perhaps, she is "*testing him* for something else she had in mind, but what it was he could not guess" (*Life and Loves*, 40–43). Yet it would soon become clear what she has in mind.

In the first beta-testing trials, George Washington has shown himself to be the erudite Princetonian existential-tightrope-walker-Negro and, then, the potential aggressor, ominous and ambiguous threatening nigger. The consulate has shown herself a liberal, willing to take risks in pronouncing the necessary progress of the race. In the first trial, George Washington does not get what he came for, but their exchange is not over.

III. The Adjustment

Despite the rocky start and the coldness that George Washington perceives in the American consulate, she offers to take him to dinner—an open gesture from the embassy to Americans abroad. They go to an expensive restaurant, and Washington's jiveness is reintroduced: he is out of his environment, but given the infinitely seductive capacity of his jiveness, he is able to "rapidly adapt to any new environment" and "immediately gained his balance," escorting the consulate to her seat with an "air of self-assurance" that "had one not been previously acquainted with his true history . . . one would have been greatly persuaded that George Washington had been accustomed to this kind of style all of his life" (*Life and Loves*, 45–48). He knows how and what to order, but he is still unsure of their exchange: Why had she invited him to dinner? Were all Americans who were down on their luck and abroad entitled to a fancy dinner? Were all Americans abroad *really* abroad? Was this a brush-off from the earlier exchange—the offer of a menial job that, had he really gone to Princeton, would have been an insult; and as far as she was concerned, he really *had* attended Princeton, so it *was* an insult—or making amends for their initial exchange? Was it *her* white American performative gesture? Was this the prolongation of their interracial contact, their interracial conflict?[65]

George Washington aggressively intends to find out. He orders lobster and cauliflower. He and the consulate exchange small talk, and when she has enough wine, something between them begins to loosen up. "Do you have a girlfriend here in Copenhagen?" "My close friends call me Ruth, so why don't you do the same" (*Life and Loves*, 46). At the end of the dinner, the American consulate hands George Washington an envelope with her home number written on the outside. When he opens it, "some Danish currency sailed out": one hundred kroner, one-fourth of the money he had demanded.

The beta testing so far has been inconclusive. He had gotten the money demanded but only a portion of it. What was the exchange? Had he taken the money, or had she actually given it? Had she been seduced by the threat of the nigger? Had she found this threat a more seductive performance of his sex, more than the erudite Princetonian? Was the seduction in his capacity to move from one to the other—in the crossing, between the two? Or had she given the money as her seduction? Was he being seduced by her, the American consulate? Was there more to be performed for the rest of the money? The scene ends in confusion, confusion as to how to proceed.

IV. The Secret to Having Modern Western Sex

After taking or receiving some of the money, George Washington celebrates his newfound wealth at the Drop Inn, where one would go to "meet the 'intellectual' bloods," and the Casanova, "which is usually filled with servicemen" (*Life and Loves*, 19). These are the two establishments where expat black men frequent for European, usually Danish, women. "One could say that the Drop Inn comes close to being the Big House and Casanova has the smell of the slave quarters, but, really, such a distinction is misleading because brothers kept a very heavy traffic going from one to the other" (*Life and Loves*, 19). The past is never passed, and the present is never quite present; rather, we are somewhere in between, in the crossing between what has happened and what will happen—between the Big House and slave quarters. And black manhood is this intersection, even in this contemporary moment, still a throwback to a primitive.

We find George Washington in between the slave quarters and the Big House, in the midst of a secret American exchange, perhaps always already present because it remains secret—the heavy traffic flowing from one to the other was not just white men visiting black women in their slave quarters but was also white women sneaking out across the grounds, across the icy crossing, to visit, in the impossible secrecy of their white womanhood, black men.

On this particular night, George Washington finds himself again in between, in the crossing of a secret, yet on this night, the secret is a bit unexpected. He meets a woman, "very black hair that was tied at the nape of her neck, . . . newly suntanned" (*Life and Loves*, 68). He asks her to dance, and immediately, without reflection, he lies; he lied "so naturally that it surprised him. . . . He told lies so fast that he wondered if he could ever tell the truth" (*Life and Loves*, 69). Usually his lies were crafted toward some determined end— because you lie to people when you "don't trust *them*," when you "don't feel right" with them or when you want to take something from them (*Life and Loves*, 30–31). But this lie is automatic and has no functional purpose—it seems to emerge from him, like his father's own voice cussin'. And it makes him pause. There is something different about this woman: she appears the same as the other Danish women, she appears in this same place as all the other Danish women in the midst of black male expats, but she does not fully seem to be there in the same room as the other Danish women.

She invites George back to her apartment under the false impression of his initial lie of homelessness and under the auspice that she could tell him the truth, her truth, her secret—not that secret between the Big House and the slave quarters but something else, the secret that is "all wrapped up" in her identity. It has to do something with the past and the present—and she is dangling in between the two, in the flesh (*Life and Loves*, 73). She cannot directly tell Washington her secret but only gives him hints: "It is about your family and my family. . . . It has to do with You and Africa and Me. A long time ago" (*Life and Loves*, 75). Her secret is transhistorical and, somehow, also intraracial, even though she appears to be white.

Part of the secret, though, is that she can only tell him her secret once they begin to have sex. And as she begins to seize from the sex, she is able to tell him her transhistorical, intraracial secret, somehow involving him, somehow not, and somehow involving Africa as well. But instead of just telling him, she needs to shout it to him, at him: "I—AM A NIGGER, I AM A NEGRO." There is something about her secret, something about the fact that she appears white but has black lineage that requires that she "synchronize the revelation with her organism" (*Life and Loves*, 76); something about being a part of some wild, precivilized past yet having the appearance of the civilized present and future; something about the monstrous intersection in her own flesh that can only be released through the intimacy between his black flesh and her "white" flesh—the crossing, not between the Big House and slave quarters but between her sex and his.

Their exchange is similar to the American minstrel act, in which white American men and women would dress themselves in blackness to enact the deeper, more "savage" parts of their personality under the guise that it was not them doing the action but this blackness that has enraptured them. This blackness that sits between Washington and the woman is central to her reconciliation of her past and present in her own flesh but also to Washington's own act: they are twin pillars of a single action that is and is in the American scene—for his performance depends on their desire for blackness and their inability to become this blackness itself. In this moment, she and Washington are somewhere in the crossing together in the skin of another: he in the skin of his projected image, she in the skin that sank just below the surface—the "beast with two backs."[66]

* * *

"Later, when the room was much lighter . . . he looked at her carefully. She had the large lips, yes, the slightly coarse hair." She tells him her backstory, her history—"her great-grandmother had a baby by a black man from Africa; . . . some members of her family had . . . coarse hair and dark skin" (*Life and Loves*, 76)—but why the need to confess? Why the need to tell him? Why not continue the jive—he, the nigger, and she, the white Dane? Why break the cycle, the tradition of the Big House and the slave quarters? And why is it that she can only tell him her secret—her lineage, her family, her brother, who "looked like an American Negro," only after they begin to have sex? What is it about race and blackness (and *his* blackness) that necessitates such a psychoanalytic breakdown that can only be blasted away through fucking?

There is something chaotic here, something that George Washington had attempted to evade in the crossing, in his lies, in his performances, that she demands be revealed, placed before them, and exercised. She needs to scream out, "nigger," and so does he; and they do so as they have sex and as they climax—this chaos before them, unveiled in her disclosure of her past, which could not be read on her body, every detail easily explained away: her hair, lips, nose, skin; she could be Italian and, like most of her family, had passed for Danish.

She and George Washington fuck again in the morning, only this time, he is afraid. He fears that the ecstasy will have worn away, that, with the secret now revealed, their relations will now be normalized, the "fuck would be normal." But as they fuck again, "fast, quick, like animals, she screamed nigger, and he said it softly in her ear, they both came several times, several impulsive, satisfying times" (*Life and Loves*, 77).

The exchange, the modulation between "Negro" and "Nigger" in their first sexual act (like that of George Washington's own act, shifting from erudite Negro to threatening nigger) and the satisfaction of the continuing abnormality of their second sexual act—centered on the discovery of her blackness and the ecstasy of shouting "nigger" in this disclosure and on the pure delight that the power of "nigger" still exists even in disclosure: these two moments are their entrance into the sex itself. What they fuck is not each other but the idea of the nigger-as-fucker; they fuck each other through fucking the nigger. This is the site and source of desire and thought, of the establishment of the material world and the physiological response.

Here we have the relation between deception and desire, between jiving and fucking, replication and reproduction at the level of the phoneme, in the iteration of the nigger at the moment of ecstasy. In the "deeper level, where hate and disrespect and violence were dynamite for blasting one's way into the unconscious where orgasms live" (*Life and Loves*, 74), we have to ask, what is it about this word—of the reproduction and replication of self and desire in it—that triggers such a response, that has such a physiological reality? What, in other words, does the biocentric analysis of the word "nigger" reveal to us about the anthropology of the American?

> Why,
> in other words,
> do *fucking*
> and the
> *nigger*
> go hand-
> in-
> hand?

V. When Thy King Was a Boy

That night, George Washington dreamt about the American consulate, except the year was 1593, and she was Queen Elizabeth and he was both Spenser and Sir Walter Raleigh. In the dream, George Washington, as Raleigh, reaches under Queen Elizabeth's gown to discover that she is not wearing panties and that her pussy "smelled just like ordinary pussy" (*Life and Loves*, 78). She tells George, now Spenser, that she has a secret: "his head was to be cut off." George, as Spenser, is given two options: he can kill the queen and blame someone else, or he can "forceably fuck the queen, and fuck her so well that she would pardon him, would spare his head because he had a golden dick" (*Life and Loves*, 78).

Washington, as Spenser, is trapped between death and fucking, between order (of the pardon) and disorder (of his death), which demands his performance. Yet, unlike his own jive, this fucking is not his own; it is coerced. And, unlike his other performances, he would not be doing the fucking—though he would be performing the act—but would be fucked by her demand. And, although to the onlooker—any guard or court official—it would seem that he is aggressor, he is really the suppliant.

George Washington, named after the founding father of the American nation, disguised as Sir Walter Raleigh and Spenser, members of the British royal court, has to fuck the queen of England for his own liberty. He, named after the founding father but not the founding father; she, the American consulate appearing as the queen of England—both are caught in the cycle of representation that demands presentational action. Again, the distinction between being and doing is drawn out. This George Washington, as Sir Walter Raleigh, is also trapped between British expansionism and American liberty, for as George Washington disguised as Sir Walter Raleigh, he is never actually himself, never actually black; yet, nevertheless, he is called to order as if he were black, as if he were in the slave quarters and she were in the Big House. The transhistoricality of the night before emerges transracially and again centers on his liberation, their liberation, enacted through his cock.

After George Washington, as Spenser, is done fucking the queen and receiving the pardon, he looks down at the "slug of lead" in his lap, to discover "it was the gold of the sun" (*Life and Loves*, 78). George Washington finally thinks he understands: first enslaved by his fucking, he must now fuck to gain his freedom. This is his revelation from the night with the woman and from his dream: he must make his fucking his—not history's, the consulate's, or the nation's. His revelation is the consulate's secret: "he could have had a Golden cock if he were willing to risk—'willing to work with your hands'—to risk his neck" (*Life and Loves*, 79).

VI. Run Boy Run

Some unaccounted-for time has passed since George's dinner with the consulate. He has received a number of phone calls from the embassy but has not returned the calls. He finally calls back and speaks to the consulate. He has missed an appointment and the possibility of a job. She demands to know where he has been. She is both furious and disappointed—the Princeton graduate, who could be a voice and a leader for his people; the Princeton graduate in whom and with whom, having believed his many lies, she has invested emotional and cognitive energy. "I didn't *give* you that money," she tells George Washington. "You owe that money to the embassy, and you are obliged to, at least, to be courteous and to show some interest in getting a job to pay it back" (*Life and Loves*, 81; emphasis in original). He now has his answer.

"Owe," "obliged": similar words to "policy," beta-testing words, which are meant as containers for a sort of pattern of behavior, a certain typescript of expectations, especially around his black manhood; similar ideas to that of being made to fuck for another's pleasure or your freedom but never your own pleasure and design. America is everywhere, even abroad—and although he is not physically on American soil, with the embassy, an extension of America, comes the condition of the nigger, the one who must run when called, who must reveal when questioned, who must be accountable when called to account, who must fuck on command.

Washington begins magnanimously: "I am very sorry, Miss Smith, I was under the impression that—," the erudite Negro making his appearance to keep down the possibility of interracial conflict by minimizing the struggle for power and control, willingly suppliant but toward his own ends. Yet, when he hears "owe" and "obliged," something in him resists, something like his father comes out. Something in him expresses a genuine emotion—the performance is temporarily suspended: "I don't *owe* you anything. You *gave* that money to me, as far as I am concerned" (*Life and Loves*, 82). He has now asserted that the money was given, which means it was taken by him under the auspice of her giving it.

This, though, is not part of beta testing. The emotion is genuine. It emerges from somewhere inside him uncontrolled, and as such, this interracial conflict is not staged, is not a test to see where the consulate is on a matter: this is a real conflict. George Washington's unwillingness to remain prone to the American consulate has triggered hostility between them. After informing Washington of the sort of job she has waiting for him, to "help the delivery men with the unloading," George informs her that he is not interested in that sort of a job, to which the American consulate returns, "Are you above this kind of work . . . just because you went to college?" Does he believe that his education—even if fictitious—places him above work designated for black men? "You're fucking right," he says, and he hangs up the phone (*Life and Loves*, 82).

Although he had not actually gone to college, had in fact turned down college scholarships, imagining college to be "inferior to his innate ability," wondering if it "would hamper his growth," the American consulate has insulted him, perhaps more than if he had actually gone to college (*Life and Loves*, 8). Really, the American consulate has not insulted him, for he is not Paul Winthrop, the Princeton graduate, and he has not become a true believer of his own illusions. She has not really insulted his lie either, for it is merely functional. Somewhere she has insulted his "innate ability," his aesthetic performance, the dexterity and technique of his jazz improvisation. She has reminded him that even his hypothetical world is still constrained by his black male racialization—even if he goes to Mars, there might be a white American already there to remind him, though now Martian, that he will always remain black.[67]

In hanging up the phone, George Washington attempts to reorient the order by redirecting relationality—"owe" and "obligation" only exist within a framework of debt, when something has been given, but Washington wants to believe that what she has given has been taken. And though George Washington cannot be sure that the money has been surrendered, he is nevertheless going to act as if it has been. George Washington has temporarily cut his tie to her, to the embassy, to America. That seems to be it. But it is another break in the continuing action.

VII. *Drakaina*

Later in the afternoon, when George Washington returns home, he discovers two police officers with his bag in tow waiting for him, refusing him entrance. He is told that he is behind on the rent, and because of that, that he has been evicted. But, more than that, because he does not have the money to pay for his stay, the officers will keep his passport until he proves to them that he has a job and a place to stay so that he does not "cause trouble for Danish citizens" or "for other people, too" (*Life and Loves*, 87). He tells the officers that he does have a job, as a bartender for the embassy. Nevertheless, they keep his passport as insurance of this job. As just like that, George Washington, Sir Walter Raleigh and Spenser, and his Golden Cock are brought back before the American consulate, Queen Elizabeth, to fuck to ensure his pardon and to protect the "head remaining on his shoulders" (*Life and Loves*, 88):

> "I am sorry about what happened this morning," he said. She said nothing back. He waited long enough.
> "I was picked up by the police a few minutes ago," he said. Still, she said nothing back. . . .
> "I told them I had a job at the embassy as a bartender; you think I could still get the job?"
> "I'll see what I can do, but you'd better come right over here immediately. You'd better *run*." (88–89; emphasis in original)

And just like that, the situation has been reversed—perhaps was always reversed. Perhaps in running from his father, he was always running to her, always on that path in the crossing between the slave quarters and the Big House. He is now her supplicant. He must run for her, to her—with her instituting the set of relations by which he is to operate, "the nigger running like a puppet on a string" (*Life and Loves*, 89). But he is also committed, somehow, someway, to "fix her ass like it was never fixed before," but for right now, "she could save him, like no one else could" (*Life and Loves*, 89).

He arrives at the embassy to find the consulate seated on her desk, "leaning back in her chair," with a "glint of victory in her eyes," seemingly younger, refreshed, wearing the "clothes of a coquette—a white silk blouse with a nice dip into her surprisingly full breast, a necklace that accentuated the dip by falling lazily into the valley between the mounds, and a lipstick that left her mouth glistening with juice, and a bit more full than usual" (*Life and Loves*, 91). It seems that her reorienting their relationship has invigorated her and that she, the American consulate, has gained her energy by supplicating his black manhood. She is smoking a cigarette, "spraying smoke from her nostrils, like a female dragon" (*Life and Loves*, 91). She, the mythical creature, is admonishing and warning him of what he already knows.

This monstrosity, she, the female dragon, is different from the one noted earlier. With the girl of hidden origin, the monster they created, the beast with two backs, brought together their shared in the crossing condition of racialization; but she, the female dragon, having trapped him, demanding of him his performance, offers to him not only an admonishment and a warning but also advice, direction of where he already knows he is going. And she, giving him an envelope containing his passport, "strutted to the swivel chair, and threw herself in it" (*Life and Loves*, 91–92). "Dragon," from *drak*, stem of *derkesthai*: "to see clearly" and "the one with the deadly glance."[68] What we are to see clearly, though, is the darkness that both is and requires the imagination to render reality, the darkness that he is and the darkness between them: the American consulate, a white woman, a dragon and the black man.

This is the reestablishment of the colonial order. Queen Elizabeth had Sir Walter Raleigh or Spenser. He would go conquering the world and satirizing it, on her order, on her command. She has made of him what she wanted, revealing something critical about the American context. White women, usually understood as the supplicant of a dominant imperial order, are, under the cover of patriarchy, the unknown quantity of force and authority. She could be the seducer, the aggressor, the fucker, and go undetected, for he, even pliant in relationship to her, would always be both that which is docile and that which needs to be domesticated, always potentially the aggressor. She, seated at her desk, blowing smoke through her nostrils like a lady dragon, would be seen and "seen" as the nonpredatory victim of this phenomenological exchange, just as Queen Elizabeth would have appeared to be assaulted by Spenser if anyone would have walked into their exchange.

And this is what angers him: "She had pulled her dress up on him; she was showing him her thighs and there was nothing he could do about it. . . . It was as if she had thrown off all her clothes and was sitting there pretending nothing was wrong" (*Life and Loves*, 91). She is looking across her desk, across the crossing from the Big House, and is not there, in the crossing with him, as the other woman had been. She weaponizes the crossing, has used the ambiguity between them, the distance between them—his source of power—against him, has thrown her hands down onto the ice just to hear it crack, and he has to sit there and take it and still give himself to her. His golden cock is hers.

And, just like that, he has become his nemesis, Bigger Thomas, a "living masochistic nightmare," tragically bounded to the reality of another's imagination, trapped within his sex, within himself as the designated fucker. (*Life and Loves*, 22–23). It was Bigger that was the inversion of his own father and contested Washington's jiving improvisation. For Bigger revealed to Washington the opposite of his own revelatory dream and the meaning of this situation: the one who creates the reality others have to live, replicates him- or herself as its living structure—these are the real fuckers, not the ones who are made to physically fuck. He revealed to George that one could never be free in fucking—that was the real jive, to think the queen would ever pardon him, that his head would ever be safe. He could never be free by fucking because his fucking was never his.

Bigger revealed to Washington that the beloved, the one receiving the action, was "nobody's God but the weakling's, the suppliant," and that "the God of the strong was the Lover, the Seducer. The only living force in the world was that of the Seducer" (*Life and Loves*, 90). Just because you fucked did not make you the seducer. Miss Smith, sitting on the desk, smoking her cigarette, dress pulled up, throwing herself back into her chair, with his passport in tow—she has demonstrated that not only can she make him run but she can also upend his life, regardless of his lies, regardless of his seduction. With one phone call, she could have him arrested and deported or pardoned. And though he knows that "the only way to keep your strength is to give; never to accept anything from anybody," he nevertheless has to take what she has given because he is cornered, like Bigger Thomas. She would give him his passport, give him his freedom, and in exchange take from him all that he is. The American consulate has become what she always was: the fucker. And as Washington's dream had indicated that his vulnerability, the compossibility of his sex, could perhaps never be inverted into his power but had become, would always be, not an asset but a trap. But what else could he do? What else can a musician do when the music leaves you, and you are left playing birthday parties and corporate events that never call for alterations to the sound but one long note?

Had Washington gotten Bigger all wrong? Is there really no dignity in being the fucker—that is, fucking at all, even if he thinks it is for his own ends?

Could he ever really sex his sex? Could he ever really fuck her so good that "she would have gotten a glimpse into the immortal soul of the universe . . . so beautifully that she would have come away feeling he was a man, that his fucking (his humanity) had brought out that core of goodness which is in the worst of thieves, that she would come away feeling he was a man, and not a nigger or an animal or an ex-gorilla or something"? (*Life and Loves*, 22–23). Could he ever cross the divide between the Big House and the slave quarters, the divide of the transhistorical, transracial past and present through his capacity to upend space and time, with the special relativity of his golden cock? Or, was he trapped, imagining that he had fucked each and every white woman when he, like Bigger, had only managed to steal a kiss from a white girl, "a kiss which should have awakened her from a thousand years' sleep" but had not (23)? Had he inverted Bigger's fear of "The Great White Man" and taken his crossing as a mode of transgressing this ubiquitous, anonymous force waiting on the other side and not taken seriously enough the real, imposing force of white women, perhaps pretending to be asleep, waiting to be kissed, pretending to awaken themselves as their own empowerment? Was George's problem that he thought he could invert the condition of the nigger to his own benefit, that he could outfuck the fucker and turn this vulnerability into an advantage—because he knew he was vulnerable—and use it to wage a full-frontal attack?

>Could he ever
>really *cross*
>the Delaware and surprise
>the waiting soldiers,
>for they always already knew he was coming?

Could he ever really remain in the crossing, remain on the tightrope for all time? And is this the freedom that he wanted—to remain suspended above and in between? But if he was to leap, to cross to the other side, the Hessian army awaiting him, would he ever be liberated, independent like the original George Washington, or would he discover, even then, *especially* then, that the lies of niggers are never really believed, that his mythology could never really be the foundation of reality like they had been for the original, and that something else was required, something else demanded?

>*There comes that time.*
>*It is called "The End."*
>*You know*
>*the Atlantic Ocean is beneath your feet.*
>*You know you are going home.*
>*Home. Home. Home? Home!* (*Life and Loves*, 213)

An Elegy for Apophansis

> They will interpret your ass nigger. Knowing they will have it all wrong. And will not believe you when you rise from the grave on the day of resurrection.
> —Cecil Brown, *The Life and Loves of Mr. Jiveass Nigger*

Cecil Brown's *Life and Loves of Mr. Jiveass Nigger* may leave readers a bit unsettled, without a definite direction or answer as to the possibility of George Washington's existence in the crossing, of whether he ever actually sexed his sex, or whether he ever really was able to restore the power of his compossible black manhood in the American context. What we know is how the novel ends—with George Washington headed home, feet dangling above the Atlantic, in between Europe and the America he thought he had left behind. He is literally in the crossing, in between the old world and a possible new world. The end is fragmented, the novel is fragmented, and George Washington is fragmented.

But it must be remembered that, like Ellison's narrator who began his narrative in a hole and ended his narrative in the same hole, nothing has happened. Actions have been taken, but really nothing has occurred. And like a jazz improvisation, it must be remembered that no matter how long the solo, you still have to return to the source, to the melody, in order to begin again. And so this is why it is not really an ending but an elegy, for the return of George Washington to himself, to his source, no longer certain of either side, or in the crossing, but knowing that he must be somewhere. This is a lament but not one of regret or sorrow or love but a lament for the tightrope performer who is no longer certain of his performance.

This is an elegy for a man who straddled himself on the tightrope and could never quite get off the rope, could never quite give the crowd what it was looking for. This is an elegy for a man who has grown tired of existing in the crossing and is looking for the shore, an elegy for a man who recognizes that whichever shore he finds, there will be some "newspaperman" and "his twenty-three-year-old niece, a sociology student at the University of Chicago," and they will use biceps and precepts to "interpret your ass nigger." And they will do so, "knowing they have it all wrong . . . but they need to understand you. *Need* to. If they fail to understand how you live they'll kill your ass and call you a 'dead man'" (*Life and Loves*, 213).

It is an elegy for remembering that what they want is not you, never you, but the you that they will construct, that they have woven out "a thousand details, anecdotes, stories";[69] and, when you attempt a surprise attack on the other side of the icy crossing, they will see *it* coming, precisely because they do not see or "see" *you*. And that is why you need to die, so that they can "turn your dead cock over with the tip of [their] Scripto looking for 'meaning.'" But you know they will not find it there, just as their prescience was not prescience but just a system that understands its glitches, for there is never a there there (*Life and Loves*, 212).

This is an elegy to remind us that, in the end, there are no truths to be gathered, a reminder that we already think we know all that we need to know and that those who have something else to offer will be ignored and killed. This is an elegy for actual jazz improvisation—for Brown's Washington was not actually improvising; none of us are. This is an elegy to remind us that our choreographed compositions are only meant to *appear* improvised. This is an elegy to remind us of what is meant when someone says an "existential Negro," to remind us that all it means is an analysis of the black body and black death and the mangled black body on the sidewalk of some city street of one who might have leapt, might have fallen, or might have been pushed from the highest heights of a tightrope. This a reminder that on the day of resurrection, when you stand up, announce your existence, correct their scientific notions, tell them that "*your creator is not some white man, but a black brother, a nigger, a jiveass,*" they will not know what you mean because *you* do not quite know what you mean (*Life and Loves*, 212).

This is an elegy to lament that on that day that you refuse the black body, black death, or the black existentialist credo, choose to focus a bit on blackness, your own blackness, not their blackness, and realize that to "only see blackness, that doesn't mean you're blind" (*Life and Loves*, 212); you're just a man, crying out in the wilderness, no longer in the crossing but underneath the frozen water. This is also an elegy for a world that does not really exist, inside or out, a world in which "*living out of your insides*" seems an impossibility (*Life and Loves*, 212). This an elegy for impossibility. But we are told by Brown that we "*can go farther. You must*" (*Life and Loves*, 212). So here you have this elegy, at long last, for the wild, an elegy for blackness, an elegy for incompleteness, an elegy for clarity, an elegy for truth, an elegy for the synoptic image, and

> a
> hope
> that you
> know
> how
> to hold
> your
> breath.

Conclusion

✦

An Etiology of an Ending

> Ain't it too bad, y'all said
> Ain't it too bad, such a nice boy always kind to his motha
> Always say good morning to everybody on his way
>   to work
> But that last time before he got locked up and hurt, real bad
> I seen him walkin' towards this house and he wasn't smiling
> And he didn't even say hello
> But I knew he'd seen something
> Something in the way of things that it worked on him like it
>   do and will
> And he kept marching faster and faster away from us
> And never even muttered a word
> Then the next day he was gone
> You wanna know what
> You wanna know what I'm talkin' about . . .
>   —Amiri Baraka, "Something in the Way of Things (in Town)"

Frederick Douglass, Ralph Ellison, and Colson Whitehead have offered their insight—black male literature is sleight of hand—and Cecil Brown has offered his critique. It is a committed action of discovery through concealment. But must it be? It is an attempt at an intentional act without an intentional actor. But must it be? It is an attempt to give shape to something subtle and imperceptible. But can it be direct, ostentatiously direct? In either case, what is true about much of black male literary works is that they present to the reader fragments of a life, fragments of a story that need to be pieced together, and it is in this that the reader is pivotal. As witness, as audience, the reader becomes the reassembler of broken parts, of fractured narrative accountings—if even to document and record ostentatiousness.

We reflect here on Ishmael Reed's poem "Dragon's Blood," in which he writes about the paradox of bearing witness to an actorless action and the beguiling character of audacity.

> just because you
> cant see the stones dont
> mean i aint building
>
> you aint no mason. how
> d fuck would you know[1]

Reed gives us a paradox, "building without stones," that is parallel to that of Ralph Ellison's narrator's opening-line assertion, "I am an invisible man," as the self-assertion of self-negation—I am (an assertion of being) an invisible man (acknowledgment of nonbeing)—Frederick Douglass's assertion of the possibility of a "heroic slave," a seemingly oxymoronic title suggestive of heroism, a conscious act of intentional selflessness and slavery, a condition of selflessness in which there can be no intentional act on the part of the enslaved; Whitehead's *Apex Hides the Hurt* is simplistically and deceptively complex—it is about a nameless nomenclature specialist who discovers, through naming the world, that the "Apex" of social and linguistic control does not liberate him or reveal anything true about the world, but, "hides the hurt" in himself and in the world; and Cecil Brown's *Life and Loves of Mr. Jiveass Nigger*, a novel with an ironically self-deceptive title, for its form as a novel at once suggests to readers that they are to learn something, arrive at something new, yet also suggests that there is nothing to be learned, for though it is a story of life and love, it is the life and love of an actor who is inherently unreliable and unrelatable: a jiveass and a nigger, leading one to ask, How can you tell a story about a jiveass nigger? To build without stones, to be an invisible man, to be a heroic slave, to be an unnamed namer of things, to be a jiveass nigger are suggestive of alternate modes of logic and alternate forms of conceptual understanding—building, being, manhood, personhood, self-knowledge, and freedom.

But there is an additional layer to the texts and to Reed's poem. The last line of Reed's poem, "how d fuck would you know," both suggests that there is something to know that alludes the reader and also challenges the reader who has come to a conclusion about Reed's life or Reed himself. There is something that is both elusive and audacious about his poem, much like the works of Douglass, Ellison, Whitehead, and Brown. These works suggest by their very existence a kind of audaciousness and ask alongside Reed's poem about the best way of offering this truth to the world.

Reed here seems to suggest an answer to the question posed earlier in the introduction of this book as the leitmotif of the text: What does black male vulnerability look like within narrative form? Black male vulnerability, in Reed's poem, finds its expressive form as the paradox of self-assertive self-negation, as an elusive audacity. If one is building with stones that others cannot see, what sort of building are we discussing, and what is being erected?

In Douglass's, Ellison's, Whitehead's, and Brown's formulations, what is being erected is a being whose action are in tension with its normative existence—an "I am" that is invisible, a hero that is enslaved, a nameless nomenclature specialist, a jiveass nigger with a life and loves. In each of these formulations, there is not really a subject in any traditional sense—for there is no one doing the action or receiving the action. Rather, the "I am," the hero, unnamed namer, or the jiveass is different constitutionally from what is said of or about him: an invisible man, slave, a namer, or one who experiences a life and loves. And yet in each of these, the phrase somehow hangs together, in taut conflict, holding black male vulnerability between each of these conflicting elements, mocking and baiting readers into trying to figure out the puzzle—how to reassemble the pieces, the fragments from the tension, as if to tell them, "stop fucking looking; how d fuck would you know if you found it?" In attempting to reassemble the pieces, the reader discovers the sort of building that Reed is referencing—just how these discordant elements actually meditate on one another, nourish one another.

What readers also discover in their attempt at reassembly is what is required of them to do so. The cryptic line of Reed's poem "you aint no mason" is at once a declaration of who the reader is and a challenge of who the reader needs to become to see what is being built, how it is being built, and from what it is being constructed. It is a challenge to readers to abandon their preconceived ideas, their preconceived notions, and, in doing so, to become different readers, become other to themselves in order to see and "see" what is being built invisibly. In other words, one needs to become a mason and, if not, "stop fucking looking."

But this is not a solution, just a way into the landscape of building without stones. This self-assertive affirmative negation is meant to show something—a contradiction that cannot be solved, one that is not meant to be solved but one that is meant to be experienced, one that still has meaning. It is not so much a theory of being—we lose ourselves immediately if we are trying to discover the subject in normative forms—but a specific set of directions leading the reader somewhere else. It requires an active relationship for a full encounter—to leave oneself, evacuate the space of one's own embodied world, and relearn reading and listening, to really hear closely for what is spoken and unspoken, to know what is being cast out and what is waiting for a response. This is what is meant by relearning for "hearing and seeing around corners" and "on the lower frequencies" for different harmonic realities. It requires what the poet Ed Roberson calls for: "i must be careful about such things as these. / . . . the quiet grizzlies scared / into the hills by the constant tracks squeezing / in behind them closer in the snow," "not to shake / anything in too wild an elation" and to "set the precarious / words. like rocks. without one snowcapped mistake."[2] What is being called for in Roberson's and Reed's poems is for one to exist in and alongside this other landscape without altering its world with expectations or desires or the obligation for the clarity of language.

To understand to what Reed or Douglass or Ellison or Whitehead or Brown is referencing, it is not enough merely to look to the spectacle of the articulated and disarticulated black body—cut to shreds with the precision of taxidermist language and stitched back together with the some Frankenstein language; one will not find access points in this black body. One has to go under, beneath this black body to where language is born and takes its shape. The poetic here speaks to and through the fragments left from the tensions—building without stones, invisible man, heroic slave, jiveass nigger, affirmative negation—and steps into the breaks, the pauses, into thought, into language, to approach black male experiences without shaking "anything in too wild an elation," without killing the patient with the cure—without, in other words, turning black men into objects of investigation to be vivisected with traditional forms of knowledge and traditional theories of investigation. This new thought, this new language, must be composed from the rubble of old thoughts—words composed of old ideas, broken apart.

What is needed, then, are ways to sift through rubble to detect those moments when language has been broken to see these new arrangements, these new forms of thinking. Following Ishmael Reed and Ed Roberson, what we have to do is to look for signs of things, hints of subterranean life: "the spines of fish who look up and stare with their eyes pressed to the ice";[3] those who have learned to hold their breath. This means that we have to redefine what "life" itself means and what to look for as the signs of it.

Douglass, Ellison, Whitehead, and Brown offer themselves through their characters as signs of black male life in hypervisible invisibility—to be articulated and consumed, to be understood or perhaps misunderstood by an audience, to be reassembled and perhaps misassembled by a reader.

Perhaps this is all that we can have, to come full circle and admit to ourselves that this is what has always been talked about in various ways, at various levels: black male life is hypervisible invisible and audaciously subtextual, there but somehow and somewhere taken away. Perhaps this is what we have always somewhere, somehow already known and what shows up in black male literary works: an invisible man, a heroic slave, a nameless creator, a jiveass nigger looking for life and love. This is not so much an argument as it is a realization. There is more that can be said of this and more that will be. And still there is less and less to really say about it other than a reformulation of this truth, sometimes hidden within literary prose or a poetic phrase, sometimes set to a break beat, sometimes set to the abstraction of bent and broken note and melody, sometimes within the confines of a cryptic presidential speech reminding us that he does not in fact have a son but if he did. . . . Sometimes it will be beautifully written or beautifully spoken. Sometimes it will confront and light the air afire. But it will always be there, in totality, in parts, in (the) darkness, in (the) bright-as-day sunlight,

>*riding*
>*on top of the car*
>*peering through*
>*the windshield*
>*for his cue*[4]

Epilogue

Petite Marionette in the Black Box

"Professor?"

"Huh." He is startled out of his daydream and out of his leaning-back, feet-on-desk position. He was dreaming of his secretary and the loud whisper over microwaved lunch of his having arrived before the cleaning crew—"must've been 7–7:30"; each time it gets earlier to emphasize his heroism—and how, although he is here so early, he is always chipper. "You wouldn't even know he's a full professor." Humility is always expected and always rewarded.

"Professor? I know I'm early, but I wanted to speak with you privately."

"Yes, come in." He has something of a polished accent, the sort attached to those elite colleges and upbringings. He has practiced his to sound second nature, to add an air of mystery when he tells his stories of his poverty-stricken background. "Yes, what is it?" He moves his cursorily glanced book back to the pile of rotated texts, next to his desk lamp and office phone.

He is shaping the imagination of the next generation. This is what he tells himself. And these children will go home and confront their brothers and sisters, mothers and fathers, uncles and aunts and cousins, and those with whom they spend their sweated breaths about the vagaries of their lives—for most of the students he teaches have these sorts of lives. He will teach them how to confront the stabilizing and hyperrational responses of the past and current conditions, of race and racism and classism and inequality and parochialism and xenophobia and those who they imagine work for them. He imagined strained Thanksgiving dinners and uncomfortable Christmas Day dinners and screwed, tightened necks pretending to watch football games, avoiding eye contact with these newly minted idea hounds hunting and treeing all antiquated thought. He will give them all of the literature to pass out to their loved ones—they will become Christmas cards filled with diatribes and fashionable phrases; Christmas gift wrapping made of these books, decoupage of liberal insolence. He imagines it all. He is zoomed back to staring eyes awaiting his response. He had not heard what the student had said. But it does matter anyway—he would answer the question the same as if he had heard it. Socratic: he asks students what *they* thought about the problem, how *they* would solve it, if they were him.

"Well, I guess, I would confront my friend. I would tell them that I don't like them using *that* word around me and that I know the damage it has done in the past and continues to do."

He is reminded of a Chris Rock joke. "So the question is, can white people say 'nigger'? And the answer's the same: 'Not really.' Oh, there's some exceptions like. . . . Lot of white women trying not to laugh in front of their husbands right now. 'Honey I was in college! I had to see what it was about! He *made* me say it!'"[1] He tries not to laugh out loud and so laughs himself into a cough in his hand. But halfway through, he is reminded of his own wife and the discomfort of having her say that word to him under similar circumstances and how that made him cum effortlessly and painlessly and for a long time. He startles himself into another cough, for now *he* is the husband that is uncomfortable, and he is also the one who "made her say it"—he is the experiment in college. Nevertheless. Back to the student.

"Well, I imagine most whites don't really see the problem because there's something about the word that intrigues them, attracts them really. There's something primal about blackness that is critical to their own identity. So, when they say the word, they're really calling forward something hidden in themselves. I really do believe that. Freud's *Totem and Taboo* should really have been written by a black person. Fire does not show the primal rage instinct of destruction. It is that very word and what it stands for. It's the black flesh itself, the black body." And there you have it: the entrance of the black body as the center of all conversations. It always comes back in so many forms—black politics of the body, black body politics, necropolitics, prison politics—to this figure, object, subject, concept, metaphor, tax evasion, refusal to be inducted into a white man's war, "we are now closed" as soon as you come up to the window, the first cup of coffee in the morning, the conversation with the neighbors, and the secretary and arriving early to sit and stare at the wall with the door closed in hopes she may mention you. This is where all his conversations end. But the students never see it coming.

The quickness with which his black melandrama adapts to his ever-shifting environment is astounding—it is a reaction so quick as to border on precognition. No sooner than a black body hits the pavement is a text produced analyzing what this means for whiteness and blackness, colonial desires and racial expectations. It always begins the same way: flesh is opened up, and there are chants; and our man here trudges through *gehanna*, the crossing, or that lost place we often mistakenly refer to as hell, but he is always successful. In his hand, and weighting one branch of his bookshelf, are the artifacts of his success—his books. At times when the secretary closes the office door too tightly, one of the books tumbles over with a thud, with a sound like another body dropping. And he always somehow makes sure that the last book on the shelf does not have a bookend and always somehow says to himself, "I should really get that taken care of. Someone could get really injured." But he never does; it always floats away. He keeps his territory safe, in critical reprisal of appropriation; these fleshlings, his books, are determinatively loyal, and though he has not been shot and only by appointment related, nevertheless they are his call-to-arms, his charge, translating his secretaries' thoughts, neighbor's waiving gestures, men in tufted chairs grins and nods, all of it as affect, though, anecdotal, still evidence of his own superior precognition.

"You're probably right," the student answers. "Right now, they're dating a black person." He always gets these students to confess their desires. And like a priest who cannot dabble in the flesh but thrives in hearing about flesh, he sits rather stoically, looking at the student, with a slight smirk across his lips. "This is what I will return home to your parents," he thinks. It is through acting on white guilt, and by knowing how far to carry their threats, that Negroes might achieve the greatest revenge. It should be the end of a primitive, but it is only the beginning.

Their back-and-forth exchange goes on for another ten or fifteen minutes. Neither of them seems to notice that this is a weekly meeting. He is always surprised when they come by earlier than office hours with this problem—maybe not the word being said but some question of some fact learned in class and how their friends or family have been dealing with it and so on—and the student looks ever intrigued with his references to the attic of stored knowledge he offers to them. He is even considered a genius for it.

And he is being devoured, by such truculence, a new theory of the metabolic rate and digestive capacity. And like the field mouse under the windowsill, in a bed of flowers, unaware of just where the smell is coming from and how, in the silence of a breath, he finds himself at such a nonpoetic end, one that has no elegance or sophistication but just the chance of a passing cat—with a passing appetite of a just-missed prior opportunity with a more well-appointed chipmunk in the yard two doors down—whose owner, another housewife with her own kitchen window, her own pie to cool, and her own yard, upon opening the window lets it out into the world to satisfy its urges.

[End of scene.]

The final curtain closes to an empty theater. The lights flash on, and the chairs squeak their way slowly back to their fully closed position. The stage now looks barren, almost abandoned or haunted with a break in the action. It will sit empty for weeks between set breakdown and the design and installation of the new set. Theaters can be promiscuous this way—one day this, next day that, without any consistency. The Negro slowly turns around to the house, expecting an audience to confirm his act, to confirm his general feelings:

How did things go? Was he believable in his role?
Did he achieve the dramatic effect of the years of study in coffeehouses, museums, and the various benefits and socials?

And, finally, did it prepare him to play the man he always thought he would be?

[*Stage direction*] The room is silently being broken down behind him; he ventures toward the back door near the dressing room. His foot rests halfway through a stride as he looks back over his shoulder at the emptiness of the landscape, now segmented in boxes being carted off by men who appear indifferent to anything but their clipboards. He wonders to himself, "What's next? Was it all worth it?" The black, scuffed floor creaks softly beneath his foot as it is carried forward in the completion of a step.

NOTES

Prologue
1. Chester Himes, *My Life of Absurdity: The Autobiography of Chester Himes* (New York: Thunder's Mouth, 1995), 1.

Introduction
1. Andrew B. Leiter, *In the Shadow of the Beast: African American Masculinity in the Harlem and Southern Renaissances* (Baton Rouge: Louisiana State University Press, 2010), 15.
2. Ibid.
3. One of the reasons that this interpretation is prevalent is due to what is written about black men: how they have been perceived by and in white society, how they have been perceived by black and general feminist literatures, but also how they have been perceived by queer literatures. In short, black men have been perceived, in one way or another, as problems themselves—whether in their black maleness as hypersexual threat or their black maleness as hypermasculine threat. In other words, much of the texts written on black men have not really been on black men—what they have written about themselves, not as problems to be solved but how their reception existentially, linguistically, and heuristically structure a text. *The Buck* does not concern itself with questions of black men as problems within or for society. Rather, it is my contention that we should be studying the texts by black men in themselves to have a larger discussion of how the conscious mind projects itself onto the material world through the specific form of literature. Rather than bringing to the text explicit ideas to mine from the text, *The Buck* mines the texts directly to discover in them the specific mode of existence inherent in them.
4. Richard Wright, *American Hunger* (New York: HarperCollins, 1982), 135.
5. More will be said of the relationship between hearing and reading later in the introduction.
6. Richard Wright, "Big Boy Leaves Home," in *Uncle Tom's Children* (New York: Harper and Row, 1965), 24; emphasis mine.
7. Ibid., 27.
8. Richard Wright, "The Man Who Killed a Shadow," in *Eight Men: Short Stories* (New York: HarperCollins, 1996), 192–93.
9. Ibid., 164–65.
10. Richard Wright, *Black Boy* (New York: HarperPerennial, 1966), 281–82; emphasis mine.
11. In short, one can look to many of Wright's fictional works concerning this notion of flight. In addition to *Black Boy* and *American Hunger*, which are

ostensibly about the Great Migration (and are influencers of texts such as Isabel Wilkerson's *The Warmth of Other Suns*), one can see this term in use in Wright's other works as well (*Native Son* and *The Outsider*, to name two). One could also read Wright's nonfiction works as concerned with this theme, from *12 Million Black Voices*, which is ostensibly another analysis of the Great Migration but is actually about the ecological development of human personality, to *Black Power*, Wright's powerful, albeit unconscious flight from himself (as American) to discover himself (as American) in his unconscious biases toward Africans, to *White Man, Listen!*, which is largely concerned with the development of an aesthetic expression of internal or self-estrangement of black Americans in the modern Western world. An important and influential text on Wright in this regard is *Richard Wright: Critical Perspectives Past and Present*, ed. Henry Louis Gates Jr. and K. A. Appiah (New York: Amistad, 1993).

12. David Marriott, *On Black Men* (New York: Columbia University Press, 2000), vii.

13. For an excellent usage of existentialism and phenomenology in theorizing a black male literary work, see Lewis Gordon, "George Lamming the Existentialist" (Center for Africana Studies Working Papers Series Working Paper 006, Johns Hopkins University, 2008).

14. For more on the history and philosophical foundation of race and sexuality, especially concerning black men, see Arthur Flannigan Saint-Aubin, "Testeria: The Dis-ease of Black Men in White Supremacist, Patriarchal Culture," *Callaloo* 17, no. 4 (1994): 1054–73; Marlon Ross, "An Anatomy of the Straight Black Sissy as Theoretical Intervention," in *Blackness and Sexualities*, ed. Michelle Wright and Antie Schumann (Berlin: Forecast, 2007); William F. Pinar, "Black Men: You Don't Even Know Who I Am," *Counterpoints* 163 (2001): 855–938; Vincent Woodard, *The Delectable Negro: Human Consumption and Homoeroticism within US Slave Culture* (New York: New York University Press, 2014); Tommy J. Curry, "Ethnological Theories of Race/Sex in Nineteenth-Century Black Thought: Implications for the Race/Gender Debate of the Twenty-First Century," in *The Oxford Handbook of Philosophy and Race*, ed. Naomi Zack (Oxford: Oxford University Press, 2019), 565–76; Kyla Schuller, *The Biopolitics of Feeling: Race, Sex, and Science in the Nineteenth Century* (Durham, N.C.: Duke University Press, 2017); Keith Clark, *Black Manhood in James Baldwin, Ernest Gaines* (Champaign: University of Illinois Press, 2002); Oyeronke Oyewumi, *The Invention of Women: Making an African Sense of Western Gender Discourses* (Minneapolis: University of Minnesota Press, 1997); Sylvia Wynter, "1492: A New World View," in *Race, Discourse, and the Origin of the Americas: A New World View*, ed. Vera Lawrence Hyatt and Rex Nettleford (Washington, D.C.: Smithsonian Institution Press, 1995), 5–58; Darieck Scott, *Extravagant Abjection: Blackness, Power, and Sexuality in the African American Literary Imagination* (New York: New York University Press, 2010).

15. Frantz Fanon, *Black Skin, White Masks* (New York: Grove, 2008), 154–56. Specifically, Fanon writes, "I have said that the Negro is phobogenic. . . . This object does not come at random out of the void of nothingness; in some situation it has previously evoked an affect in the patient. His phobia is the latent presence of this affect at the root of his world; there is an organization that has been given a form" (155).

16. Calvin Warren, *Ontological Terror: Blackness, Nihilism, and Emancipation* (Durham, N.C.: Duke University Press, 2018), 25. For more on consumption of black male bodies, see Vincent Woodard's *The Delectable Negro*, in which he argues that the concept of consumption emerges from black life on the plantation and ranges from the traditional understanding of utilizing food as social control to "other intersecting issues," such as "social consumption," "ritualized hunger," or "cannibalistic masters" (5). Also see Tommy J. Curry, "This Nigger's Broken: Hyper-masculinity, the Buck, and the Role of Physical Disability in White Anxiety toward the Black Male Body," *Journal of Social Philosophy* 48, no. 3 (2017): 321–43.

17. James Baldwin, *No Name in the Street* (New York: Vintage, 2000), 61–62.

18. James Baldwin, "The Black Boy Looks at the White Boy," in *Nobody Knows My Name* (New York: Vintage, 1992), 217.

19. For more on this topic, see John S. Lash, "Baldwin Beside Himself: A Study in Modern Phallicism," *CLA Journal* 8, no. 2 (1964): 132–40.

20. Marlon Ross has argued that "the Jim Crow regime," or racial subordination in the United States, "itself is a *sexual* system of oppression." That is to say, for his particular study on the formation of black masculinity in the United States, the very presence of black men "unwittingly exposes the arbitrariness of the gender line that is supposed to separate all men from women as a natural division in culture" (2). What I am interested in theorizing, here, are the ways in which this arbitrariness, which for Ross manifests itself in the "violence, intimidation, coercion, and the sadistic manipulation of the courts, schools, public transport," and so on, was expressed aesthetically. For more on this, see Marlon B. Ross, *Manning the Race: Reforming Black Men in the Jim Crow Era* (New York: New York University Press, 2004).

21. Darieck Scott reminds us, "Whereas the initial political impulse animating reclamations of the term *queer* emphasizes a liberatory dissolution of fixed boundaries between genders, sexualities, and races, the queerness of blackness entails a confrontation with the likelihood that a historical context that provided for the defiance of conventions of sexual propriety and for the relatively unpoliced expression of sexual variation—racialized slavery in the Americas—was a practice of physical and psychic domination . . . to fix the human beings whose racialized bodies made the enjoyment of a certain kind of freedom possible in a particularly bound identity rather than release the fluid possibilities of that identity formation" (*Extravagant Abjection*, 8). In other words, if blackness is the boundary through which sexual normativity is constituted, how, then, can a queering of this boundary replicate the same outcome—conceptually or materially—as it can for whiteness?

22. Harriet Jacobs, *Incidents in the Life of a Slave Girl* (New York: Dover, 2001), 46.

23. Although focusing on relationships between black women and white men during slavery is important, as noted earlier, it can work to occlude not so much the other important relationships—such as those between black men and white men and between black men and white women—but the metatheoretical elements that undergird all of these relationships. That is to say, opening up our discussions of enslavement or of any of the other social, political, economic, or aesthetic relationships to include other experiences helps us to see what undergirds and

shapes the very embodied experiences we have within the material world. This is the focus and function of examining the literary voices of black men beyond the significance of their texts in themselves.

24. For more on the sexual economy of enslavement and, in particular, how it was visited differently on black male and female bodies, see Greg Thomas, *The Sexual Demon of Colonial Power: Pan-African Embodiment and Erotic Schemes of Empire* (Bloomington: Indiana University Press, 2007); Saidiya V. Hartman, *Scenes of Subjection: Terror, Slavery, and Self-Making in Nineteenth-Century America* (Oxford: Oxford University Press, 1997); and Katherine McKittrick, *Demonic Grounds: Black Women and the Cartographies of Struggle* (Minneapolis: Minnesota University Press, 2006).

25. Wright, "Man Who Killed a Shadow," 190–91.

26. Recently, there has been an interesting development and interest in the role of white women within the larger movement of white supremacy in the United States that suggests that the very idea of womanhood worked to conceal the consumptive practices and allowed them to occur and continue to occur undetected. For more on this, see William F. Pinar, "White Women in the Ku Klux Klan," *Counterpoints* 163 (2001): 555–619; Kathleen M. Blee, *Women of the Klan: Racism and Gender in the 1920s* (Oakland: University of California Press, 2008); Catherine E. Rymph, *Republican Women: Feminism and Conservatism from Suffrage through the Rise of the New Right* (Chapel Hill: University of North Carolina Press, 2006); and Stephanie E. Jones-Rogers, *White Women as Slave Owners in the American South* (New Haven, Conn.: Yale University Press, 2019).

27. For an interesting examination of race and listening, see Alex Weheyliye, *Phonographies: Grooves in Sonic Afro-Modernity* (Durham, N.C.: Duke University Press, 2005); Jennifer Lynn Stoever, *The Sonic Color Line: Race and Cultural Politics of Listening* (New York: New York University Press, 2016); and Nicole Brittingham Furlonge, *Race Sounds: The Art of Listening in African American Literature* (Iowa City: University of Iowa Press, 2018). A great example of the aesthetics of race and the politics of listening is W. E. B. Du Bois's seminal text *Souls of Black Folk*, which is concerned with articulating black life, prefiguring such an investigation through an analysis of sound—actual notation of sound to go along with written song lyrics. In this way, Du Bois's text demands that we hear and read simultaneously to understand the dualism of black life. *The Buck*, as a phenomenological examination, argues for the centrality of the body—not as the physiological thing, such as the ear, but as an array of intersecting forces, as the instrument through which we hear or listen to others. *The Buck* posits that listening and reading are dual and coconstituting activities. As such, both reading and listening have to be learned or cultivated, to hear or unhear, listen or unlisten to what is being said and unsaid by authors and within texts, especially those written by black men, who, it is argued are hypervisibly invisible, which means that their work, too, is both undertheorized and overtheorized, both overdetermined and underdetermined: what I have termed as "flight" and as "transitory becoming."

28. Maurice O. Wallace, *Constructing the Black Masculine: Identity and Ideality in African American Men's Literature and Culture, 1775–1995* (Durham, N.C.: Duke University Press, 2002), 2. Wallace's text is an attempt to think through the

manner in which modes of black male representation emerge within black male literary practices. Keith Clark, too, offers some insight, arguing, "when I attend lectures in which the speaker—irrespective of his or her sex—routinely uses the words 'patriarchy,' 'misogyny,' 'hegemony,' 'racist,' 'heterosexist,' and 'masculinist' interchangeably, . . . such tendentiousness, regrettably, glosses over their uniqueness, their distinctiveness, and their currency in different discourses" (*Black Manhood*, 3). Rather than analyzing the ways in which masculinity is understood as problematic, Clark is interested, in his analysis of James Baldwin and Ernest Gaines—that is, black male writers—in attending to "African-American male authors that thematically and narratologically foreground black men." My intention here, like that of Clark, is to "investigate how authors have grappled with questions surrounding voice, gender, sexuality, and community" (*Black Manhood*, 3), but while Clark is concerned with subjectivity in his analysis, my study is concerned with how narratology reveals, phenomenologically, the exchange between consciousness and the material order.

29. Frederick Douglass, "Pictures and Progress: An Address Delivered in Boston, Massachusetts, on 31 December 1861," in *Frederick Douglass Papers, Series One: Speeches, Debates, and Interviews, Volume 3: 1855–1863* (New Haven, Conn.: Yale University Press, 1986), 461.

30. This is where *The Buck* diverges from texts on the sociohistorical and existential situation of black men and black manhood, in that it is not a philosophical encounter with the metaphysics of black male identity or the existential contours that shape this historical reality. In this way, it does not fully engage works like Franz Fanon's *Black Skin, White Masks*, George Yancy's *Black Bodies, White Gazes*, or Lewis Gordon's *Existentia Africana*. As it is not directly concerned with black male subjecthood or subjectivity but is concerned with subjectivation, that is, the making of the subject; it is only interested in the phenomenological process on the formation of the subject as the unfolding relation between consciousness and the material within the specific framework of the literary object. As such, it does not fully engage works such as Orlando Patterson's *Social Death* or Abdul R. JanMohamed's *The Death-Bound-Subject: Richard Wright's Archaeology of Death*. And, given that this project is not directly concerned with the ontological status of black men as such but with the specific ways in which black men transfer this experience into expressive form, it will not directly engage with Afro-pessimism and texts like Fred Moten's "The Case of Blackness" and Nahum D. Chandler's *X—The Problem of the Negro as a Problem for Thought* or black male studies texts like Tommy J. Curry's *The Man-Not: Race, Class, Genre, and the Dilemmas of Black Manhood*. *The Buck* is as much a parallel project to these other projects, enriched by all of these insights, but in seeking to discover and create, it asserts itself into the argument about foundations for black male metatheory through an engagement with black male literary texts.

31. Ralph Ellison, *Invisible Man* (New York: Vintage, 1995), 354.

32. Charles Johnson, *Being and Race: Black Writing since 1970* (Bloomington: University of Indiana Press, 1988), 30.

33. *The Buck* argues, and in an explicitly phenomenological way, that discovery is a kind of creative praxis, which means that we cannot discover any text, especially texts written by black men, by bringing to them already-existing philosophical or

methodological approaches. Much of the scholarship on black men's literary voice attempts to bring to the text already-existing theoretical paradigms or philosophical arguments and attempts to mine the text through these paradigms and arguments rather than letting the text itself create its own method of reveal. Quite often what occurs is the idea that black men's literature, especially that of heterosexual black men, is seen as either toxic or derivative—either consumed with enacting patriarchal standards or, in failing to do so, revealing that the standards of manhood are not applicable to black men at all. In the process, though, what is revealed is that the text itself represents a kind of failing of critical self-reflective insight.

34. This is what W. Lawrence Hogue terms "polycentricism," that is, "the principle of advocating the existence of independent centers of power within a singular political, cultural, or economic system." Hogue, *The African American Male, Writing and Difference: A Polycentric Approach to African American Literature, Criticism, and History* (Albany: State University of New York Press, 2003), 2–3. I, though, interpret Hogue's categories "political, cultural, or economic" differently, focusing on a polycentric reading of each of these terms, where each is predicated not on "the dispersing of power, the empowering of the disempowered, and the reconfiguration of subordinating institutions, texts, traditions, and discourses" (ibid., 4) but on metaphysical supposition of "consumption" that shapes and gives rise to the specific arrangements we materially experience as systems or modes of exchange.

35. Ellison, *Invisible Man*, 13.

36. Ibid., 16.

37. Eldridge Cleaver, *The Book of Lives*, unpublished manuscript, reprinted in Tommy J. Curry, *The Man-Not: Race, Class, Genre, and the Dilemmas of Black Manhood* (Philadelphia: Temple University Press, 2017).

Chapter 1

1. There are over 170 remaining individual photographs of Frederick Douglass. This outpaces any other man in the nineteenth century by at least 20 photographs. With renewed interest and the publication and republication of many of his archival photographs and speeches on photography, we now know that this fact was neither accidental nor coincidental. For more on Douglass's photographs see David Brooks, "How Artists Change the World," *New York Times*, August 2, 2016, https://www.nytimes.com/2016/08/02/opinion/how-artists-change-the-world.html; and John Stauffer, Zoe Trodd, and Celeste-Marie Bernier, *Picturing Douglass: An Illustrated Biography* (New York: Liveright, 2015).

2. Maurice O. Wallace and Shawn Michelle Smith, introduction to *Pictures and Progress: Early Photography and the Making of African American Identity*, ed. Maurice O. Wallace and Shawn Michelle Smith (Durham, N.C.: Duke University Press, 2012), 2.

3. The daguerreotype was an early type of photographic process invented by Louis-Jacques-Mande Daguerre in 1839. What made the invention significant was its inexpensive cost, which made it widely available to the public. This photographic technology democratized the replication of the personal image, which until that point had been only the singular privilege of the very wealthy, given the

high commission costs of painterly or photographic portraits. Douglass himself argues that with the daguerreotype, "men of all conditions may see themselves as others see them. What was once the exclusive luxury of the rich and great is now within reach of all. The humbled servant girl whose income is but a few shillings per week may now possess a more perfect likeness than noble ladies and court royalty, with all its precious treasures could purchase fifty years ago." Frederick Douglass, "Pictures and Progress," 454. For more on daguerreotypes, see Mary J. Dinius, *The Camera and the Press: American Visual and Print Culture in the Age of the Daguerreotype* (Philadelphia: University of Pennsylvania Press, 2012).

4. Wallace and Smith, introduction to *Pictures and Progress*, 2.

5. A great example of this sort of propaganda is the drawing "Slavery as it exists in America. Slavery as it exists in England." Published by John Haven in 1850, the drawing depicts two scenes. In one scene, enslaved Africans are depicted as well taken care of and generally happy. In the other scene, white workers in London are depicted as downtrodden. The point of the drawing was to create the idea in white Americans living in the North that enslavement was really beneficial for Africans, while wage labor was fundamentally harmful to the human spirit. For more on this drawing, see John Haven, "Slavery as it exists in America. Slavery as it exists in England," Library of Congress Prints and Photographs Division, Washington, D.C., http://hdl.loc.gov/loc.pnp/pp.print.

6. An example of how the photographic image cuts through the propaganda of the drawing/etching is the famous image "The Scourged Back." For more on this photograph, see Joan Paulson Gage, "A Slave Named Gordon," *New York Times*, September 30, 2009, http://www.nytimes.com/2009/10/04/books/review/Letters-t-ASLAVENAMEDG_LETTERS.html.

7. John Stauffer, *The Black Hearts of Men: Radical Abolitionists and the Transformation of Race* (Cambridge, Mass.: Harvard University Press, 2004), 52–54; emphasis in original.

8. For more on this, see John Stauffer, "Frederick Douglass and the Aesthetics of Freedom," *Raritan* 25, no. 1 (2005): 114–36, reprinted in *Ideology and Aesthetics in American Literature and Arts*, ed. Jaroslav Kusnir (Hanover: Ibidem Verlag, 2006), 21–50.

9. Brooks, "How Artists Change the World."

10. Maurice Merleau-Ponty, *The Visible and the Invisible* (Chicago: Northwestern University Press, 1968), 3.

11. Douglass argues that it was not the issue of slavery or abolitionism that was tearing the nation apart but that the nation through enslavement, through the subjugation of humanity under the image of the Negro, was unable to fully realize its glorified possibility.

12. Julia Faisst, "Degrees of Exposure: Frederick Douglass, Daguerreotypes, and Representations of Freedom," *PhiN Beiheft*, supp. 5 (2012): 77, 79.

13. Frederick Douglass, *The Heroic Slave*, in *Three Great African-American Novels: The Heroic Slave, Clotel, and Our Nig* (New York: Dover, 2006), 10–11; emphasis added. Subsequent citations to this source refer to this edition and appear parenthetically in the text.

14. For more on marronage, see Neil Roberts, *Freedom as Marronage* (Chicago: University of Chicago Press, 2015).

15. Cynthia S. Hamilton, "Models of Agency: Frederick Douglass and 'The Heroic Slave,'" *American Antiquarian Society* 114, no. 1 (2004): 90.

16. There is ample evidence that Douglass was both aware of and held in great esteem each of these figures. For example, Douglass wrote an essay on Toussaint Louverture for Victor Schoelcher's American edition of *Vie de Toussaint-Louverture* in 1889. For more on this, see *The Portable Frederick Douglass* (New York: Penguin Classic, 2016), 527–39. He also published articles on Denmark Vesey and Nat Turner in his newsletter *Frederick Douglass' Paper*. For more on this, see Stauffer, *Black Hearts of Men*, 252. And while recruiting black men for the Fifty-Fourth Massachusetts Regiment, he gave speeches on Joseph Cinque and other freedom fighters. For more on this, see Peter Burchard, *Frederick Douglass: For the Great Family Man* (New York: Atheneum, 2003), 155.

17. Frederick Douglass, *My Bondage and My Freedom*, in *The Essential Douglass: Selected Writings and Speeches*, ed. Nicholas Buccola (Indianapolis: Hackett, 2016), 17–19.

18. Frederick Douglass, *Narrative of the Life of Frederick Douglass, an American Slave* (Hollywood, Calif.: Simon and Brown, 2013), 2.

19. Ibid.

20. One can search through the numerous philosophical essays on Frederick Douglass to discover the scene with Covey as central to the scholarship, with no mention of his photography lectures or his historical fiction. See, for example, George Yancy, "The Existential Dimensions of Frederick Douglass' Autobiographical Narrative," *Philosophy and Social Criticism* 28, no. 3 (2002): 297–320; Lewis R. Gordon, *Existentia Africana: Understanding Africana Existential Thought* (New York: Routledge, 2000), especially chapter 3, "Frederick Douglass as an Existentialist"; Bernard Boxill, "The Fight with Covey," in *Existence in Black*, ed. Lewis Gordon (New York: Routledge, 1997); Frank M. Kirkland, "Is an Existentialist Reading of the Fight with Covey Sufficient to Explain Frederick Douglass' Critique of Slavery?," *Critical Philosophies of Race* 3, no. 1 (2015): 124–51.

21. For more on the relationship between Washington and his wife, see Ellen Weinauer, "Writing Revolt in the Wake of Nat Turner: Frederick Douglass and the Construction of Black Domesticity in 'The Heroic Slave,'" *Studies in American Fiction* 33, no. 2 (2005): 193–202.

22. For more on this, see Hamilton, "Models of Agency."

23. What we have to remember is that Tom Grant was on the hook for the escaped slaves and could have been interpreted as motivated by his own legal proceedings to validate Washington's heroics to the utmost extent. Douglass writes,

> "Well, betwixt you and me," said [Jack] Williams, "that whole affair on board of the Creole was miserably and disgracefully managed. Those black rascals got the upper hand of ye altogether; and, in my opinion, the whole disaster was the result of ignorance of the real character of darkies in general. With half a dozen resolute white men (I say it not boastingly) I could have had the rascals in irons in ten minutes. . . ."
>
> This speech made quite a sensation among the company, and a part of them indicated solicitude for answers which might be made to it. Our first mate replied, "Mr. Williams, all that you've said sounds

very well here on shore, where, perhaps, you studied negro character. I do not profess to understand the subject as well as yourself; but it strikes me, you apply the same rule in dissimilar cases. It is quite easy to talk of flogging niggers here on land, where you have the sympathy of the community, and the whole physical force of the government, State and national, at your command. . . . It is one thing to manage a company of slaves on a Virginia plantation, and quite another thing to quell an insurrection on the lonely billows of the Atlantic. . . ."

"In that, too," said Grant, "you were mistaken. I did all that any man with equal strength and presence of mind could have done. The fact is, Mr. Williams, you underrate the courage as well as the skill of these negroes, and further, you do not seem to have been correctly informed about the case in hand at all."

"All I know about it is," said Williams, "that on the ninth day after you left Richmond, a dozen or two of the niggers ye had on board, came on deck and took the ship from you; had her steered into a British port, where, by the by, every woolly head of them went ashore and was set free. Now I take this to be a discreditable piece of business, and one *demanding explanation.*" (*Heroic Slave*, 55)

24. For more on slave insurrection and ethics, see Leonard Harris, "Insurrectionist Ethics: Advocacy, Moral Psychology, and Pragmatism," in *Ethical Issues for a New Millennium*, ed. John Howie (Carbondale: Southern Illinois University Press, 2002).

25. Albert Murray, *The Hero and the Blues* (New York: Vintage, 1973), 5.

26. Ibid., 9.

27. Ibid., 11–12; emphasis added.

28. Ibid., 28.

29. W. E. B. Du Bois, *The Souls of Black Folk* (Mineola, N.Y.: Dover, 1994), 2.

30. Ralph Ellison, *Invisible Man* (New York: Vintage, 1995), 3, 581.

31. Frantz Fanon, *Black Skin, White Masks* (New York: Grove, 2008), 12.

32. Murray, *Hero and the Blues*, 25–26.

33. Douglass, *My Bondage and My Freedom*, 17–19; emphasis added.

34. Murray, *Hero and the Blues*, 29.

35. Ibid., 17.

36. For more on Murray's notion of the modern social science narrative—what Murray terms "social science fiction fiction," see Albert Murray, *Omni-Americans: New Perspectives on Black Experience and American Culture* (New York: Da Capo, 1970), especially "A Clutch of Social Science Fiction Fiction," where he writes, "Fiction about Negroes offers an obvious example. Instead of the imaginative writer's response to the infinitely fascinating mysteries, contradictions, and possibilities of human existence, what fiction about U.S. Negroes almost always expresses is some highly specialized and extremely narrow psycho-political theory about American *Negro* existence" (122). Which, in our take, explains why philosophy always begins, when thinking about blackness, with the DuBoisian retort in the form of a question, "How does it feel to be a problem?" The black individual, unbeknownst to the philosophical writer, becomes the Negro *type*. Douglass, though, is not giving a fiction of the Negro type but a metacritical aesthetic

statement about the structural analysis of character and plot development and its relation with and to political organizing and political action. As such, his fictional narrative is tied aesthetically and politically to his photography lectures.

37. Murray, *Hero and the Blues*, 23.

Chapter 2

1. Ralph Ellison, "Change the Joke, Slip the Yoke," in *The Collected Essays of Ralph Ellison*, ed. John Callahan (New York: Modern Library, 2003), 108.

2. Ibid.

3. Ibid., 107.

4. There is a long history of theater and philosophy when discussing reality, or the ontology of existence within the realm of experience. Alain Badiou, for example, argues that the relationship between philosophy and the theater is "an ambiguous one, from its very origins." Rosie Warren, "An Interview with Alain Badiou: Theatre and Philosophy, an Antagonistic and Complementary Old Couple," *Verso Books Blog*, September 9, 2014, https://www.versobooks.com/blogs/1697-an-interview-with-alain-badiou-theatre-and-philosophy-an-antagonistic-and-complementary-old-couple. Badiou, though, is only discussing philosophy beginning with Plato and staying within the European tradition and interpretation of this origin. Yet, if we do not keep the idea of philosophy as Western and adopt the view, like that of Kwame Anthony Appiah, that "Western civilization" is a falsified construction, then we come to the conclusion that any discussion, whatsoever, of Western philosophy itself is a theatrical display—that is, expresses a theatrical attitude toward reality in which because it is taken to be *actual*, it becomes tragic. Appiah, "There Is No Such Thing as Western Civilization," *The Guardian*, November 9, 2016, https://www.theguardian.com/world/2016/nov/09/western-civilisation-appiah-reith-lecture. For Ellison, America is theatrical because it does not realize that it *is* theatrical—that it is an appearance of cultivated forms enacted on the stage of existence. That is, picking up on what David Krasner says, "theater and philosophy shed light on thought, behavior, action, and existence while simultaneously enhancing our comprehension of the world and ourselves." Krasner, *Staging Philosophy: Intersections of Theater, Performance, and Philosophy* (Ann Arbor: University of Michigan Press, 2006), 3. I am interpreting Ellison's theory of theatricality of America and the West itself as the dramatic performance and staging of reason.

5. Ralph Ellison, *Invisible Man* (New York: Vintage, 1995), 581. Subsequent citations refer to this edition and appear parenthetically in the text.

6. Simon During, *Modern Enchantments: The Cultural Power of Secular Magic* (Cambridge, Mass.: Harvard University Press, 2002), 1.

7. Darwin Ortiz, *Designing Miracles* (The Netherlands: Magical Media, 2006), 15, quoted in Jason Leddington, "Magic: The Art of the Impossible," in *Aesthetics: A Reader in Philosophy of the Arts*, ed. David Goldblatt and Lee B. Brown (New York: Routledge, 2016), 373–81. Also see Jason Leddington, "The Experience of Magic," *Journal of Aesthetics and Art Criticism* 74, no. 3 (2016): 253–64.

8. Philosopher Charles Mills has argued convincingly that the Western social contract that takes us from our natural state into a social and political state is not consummated through the enactment of laws, as is traditionally argued, but through race and racialization. He argues that it is a racial contract. While I do

agree that race is central to the social contract, I want to add that race itself and the act of racialization are theatrical in nature. For more on the racial contract, see Charles W. Mills, *The Racial Contract* (Ithaca, N.Y.: Cornell University Press, 1999).

9. Frederick Douglass, *The Heroic Slave*, in *Three Great African-American Novels: The Heroic Slave, Clotel, and Our Nig* (New York: Dover, 2006), 62.

10. Douglass, *Heroic Slave*, 12.

11. Lawrence Jackson, *Ralph Ellison: Emergence of Genius* (New York: Wiley, 2002), 340. Quoted in Ralph Ellison, letter to Richard Wright, August 24, 1946, Box 97, Folder "Ellison, Ralph," RWP.

12. For more on realism and surrealism in Ellison's *Invisible Man*, see Richard Purcell, *Race, Ralph Ellison and American Cold War Intellectual Culture* (New York: Palgrave Macmillan, 2013).

13. For more on the unreliability of Ellison's narrator, see Michel Fabre, "The Narrator/Narratee Relationship in *Invisible Man*," *Callaloo* 25 (Autumn 1985): 535–43. Fabre pays special attention to the last line of Ellison's novel—"Who knows but that, on the lower frequencies, I speak for you?"—as a declarative statement not only of intent but also of voice. For Fabre, this line alludes to the fact that "matters may be more complicated than they appear, especially regarding the implied identity of that certainly hypocritical reader" (535). I point this out to note that the narrator is more complicated than he initially appears and embodies both omniscient narrator and subject of the famous literary device "little does he know"—which, one can argue, is replicated in Ellison's first and last lines. For more on Ellison's famous last line, see Leon Forrest, "Luminosity from the Lower Frequencies," in *Speaking for You: The Vision of Ralph Ellison*, ed. Kimberly W. Benston (Washington, D.C.: Howard University Press, 1990), 308–21.

14. Ellison, "Change the Joke," 109.

15. For more on the grandfather as trickster, see Joseph F. Trimmer's "The Grandfather's Riddle in Ralph Ellison's *Invisible Man*," *Black American Literature Forum* 12, no. 2 (1978): 46–50.

16. Frantz Fanon, *Black Skin, White Masks* (New York: Grove, 2008), 135. For Jean-Paul Sartre's critique of black consciousness, see his "Black Orpheus," *Massachusetts Review* 6, no. 1 (1964–65): 13–52, where he argues that "since he [the black man] is oppressed within the confines of his race and because of it, he must first of all become conscious of his race" (18). But Sartre notes of black consciousness or Negritude that "it is not a matter of his [the black man's] *knowing*, not of his ecstatically tearing himself away from himself, but rather of both discovering and becoming what he is" (29). And, finally, Sartre argues that Negritude is itself not an end for consciousness but a moment in which universal consciousness finds itself within a raceless society. As such, "it aims at preparing the synthesis or realization of the human being in a raceless society," even if it is not consciously aware of this goal (49). Yet this view is only possible if one takes a teleological view of human history. And as Fanon points out, Sartre's own point of departure in this teleological argument is not an African but a European: Hegel. Even Sartre's universalism is itself culturally situated. Sartre, here, does not quite realize that European culture, even European philosophy, is a kind of ethnic self-referencing of identity that must be replenished at all times, must be brought back to itself through its mythos and the reification of its mythos as fact. In other

words, Sartre, it seems, does not think of European thought as developing, as constantly referencing and devouring itself as part of its self-actualization. Rather, he seems to think of it as a finished product that is constantly discovering itself as part of its telos. But, as Fanon reminds us, colonialism as a system demands reification of itself; and, as such, in a colonial situation, knowledge on both sides is uncertain, and this is what a theatrical reading of racism reveals that a totalizing view of colonialism obscures.

17. Ralph Ellison, "What America Would Be Like without Blacks," *Time*, April 6, 1970; emphasis added.

18. Lewis R. Gordon, "On Reasoning in Black: Africana Philosophy under the Weight of Misguided Reason," in *I Am Because We Are: Readings in Black Philosophy*, ed. Fred Lee Hord and Jonathan Scott Lee (Amherst: University of Massachusetts Press, 2016), 287; emphasis in original. This question is of critical importance to Gordon's work overall and could be said to be the animating element of his distinction between black and traditionally European existentialism. But it could also be what constitutes Gordon's phenomenological and heuristic projects as well. For more on this, see Gordon, *Introduction to Africana Philosophy* (Cambridge: Cambridge University Press, 2008); Gordon, *Existentia Africana* (New York: Routledge, 2000); and Gordon, *Fanon and the Crisis of European Man: An Essay on Philosophy and the Human Sciences* (New York: Routledge, 1995). Also see the edited collection *Black Existentialism: Essays on the Transformative Thought of Lewis R. Gordon*, ed. Danelle Davis (Lanham, Md.: Rowman and Littlefield, 2019).

19. Ralph Ellison's *Invisible Man*, as well as his work overall, exists in different registers. That is, one cannot simply read his work; one also has to hear it. As Ellison instructs in *Invisible Man*, one has to "see" and "hear" around corners, which means one must approach the text with one's whole body and not just the mind. Reading is, in other words, a phenomenally embodied experience. One of the challenges, then, of reading Ellison is hearing his tone. Tone here implies the undercurrent elements implicit and explicit in a text as a multilayered, polyvalent artifact. Tone, then, suggests the detailed, anthropological undercurrents of aesthetic expression much more than it does race. For more on this, see Nina Sun Eidsheim, *The Race of Sound: Listening, Timbre, and Vocality in African American Music* (Durham, N.C.: Duke University Press, 2019); Horace A. Porter, *Jazz Country: Ralph Ellison in America* (Iowa City: University of Iowa Press, 2001); and Kenneth W. Warren, *So Black, So Blue: Ralph Ellison and the Occasion of Criticism* (Chicago: Chicago University Press, 2004).

20. For more on this, see Ralph Ellison, "The World and the Jug," in *The Collected Essays of Ralph Ellison*, ed. John Callahan (New York: Modern Library, 2003), 155–88; and Joseph T. Skerrett Jr. "The Wright Interpretation: Ralph Ellison and the Anxiety of Influence," in Benston, *Speaking for You*, 217–30.

21. Rather than speaking of causation, I argue that the better way to think of the relationship between Ralph Ellison and European and Anglo-American thought is in terms of ancestry or influence. For more on the relationship between Ellison and European thought as ancestry, see "Part Four: Choosing Ancestors: The 'Possibilities' of Literary Tradition," in Benston, *Speaking for You*, 187–284.

22. Thinkers such as Paul C. Taylor have worked to theorize the meaning of "blackness" from the expressive objects of black art. It is on this point that I

agree with Taylor's assessment of black culture as expressive. For more on this, see Taylor, "Assembly, Not Birth," in *Black Is Beautiful: A Philosophy of Black Aesthetics* (Malden, Mass.: Wiley-Blackwell, 2016), 1–31.

23. For more on this, see James B. Haile, "The Cultural-Logic Turn in Black Philosophy," *Radical Philosophy* 18, no. 1 (2015): 129–50.

24. Walter Kaufmann, *Existentialism from Dostoevsky to Sartre*, ed. Walter Kaufmann (New York: Plume Books, 1975), 11.

25. Martin Heidegger, *Being and Time* (Albany: State University of New York Press, 2010), 33 (par. 13).

26. Jean-Paul Sartre, "Existentialism Is a Humanism," in Kaufmann, *Existentialism*, 350, 353.

27. Martin Heidegger, *What Is Philosophy?* (Lanham, Md.: Rowman and Littlefield, 1956), 30–31.

28. Nahum Chandler theorizes this failure of ontology or the ontological project itself in terms of "paraontology," where blackness is a ghost of sorts in relation to pure being or normatively constructed Truth. For more on this, see Chandler, "Originary Displacement," *Boundary 2* 27, no. 3 (2000): 249–86; and J. Kameron Carter, "Paratheological Blackness," *South Atlantic Quarterly* 112, no. 4 (2013): 589–611.

29. Sartre, "Existentialism Is a Humanism," 362.

30. Rene Descartes, *Meditations on First Philosophy* (Cambridge: Cambridge University Press, 2017), 1.

31. For more on this, see Tommy J. Curry, "Derelict and Method: The Methodological Crisis of African-American Philosophy's Study of African-Descended Peoples under an Integrationist Milieu," *Radical Philosophy Review* 14, no. 2 (2011): 139–64.

32. Here I disagree with theorists like Randal Doane, who argues that Ellison's usage of "light" and "dark," "civilization" and "culture" expresses a "dialectic of appropriation and refusal." Doane, "Ralph Ellison's Sociological Imagination," *Sociological Quarterly* 45, no. 1 (2004): 166. Rather, I am arguing that Ellison is playing with the self-certainty of a "science of history" itself. Later in *Invisible Man*, Ellison utilizes the figures of "zoot suitors" to blur the lines of history and to assert that, rather than a rational process, history may be a madman. More will be said of this later. For more on Ralph Ellison's zoot suitors, see Larry Neal, "Ellison's Zoot Suit," in Benston, *Speaking for You*, 105–24.

33. Martin Heidegger, "Nur noch ein Gott kann uns retten," *Der Spiegel* 30 (May 1976): 193–219.

34. Ellison, "Change the Joke," 103.

35. Ibid., 101.

36. For example, Jack Taylor argues that "Ellison's *Invisible Man* characterizes black existence as a struggle for recognition." Taylor, "Ralph Ellison as a Reader of Hegel: Ellison's *Invisible Man* as Literary Phenomenology," *Intertexts* 19, nos. 1–2 (2016): 136. Drawing on Hegel's theory of recognition from *Phenomenology of Spirit*, especially the master-slave dialectic, Taylor argues that Ellison's novel can be read through the lens of this moment of struggle. This reading, though, does not take seriously the idea that Hegel's master-slave dialectic was an early stage of consciousness for Hegel and thus is not an adequate idea of what Hegel meant by Spirit's own self-understanding. Rather, this is a primitive version of

consciousness, for it is dependent on another and not the self-cultivated internal light of one's own self-recognition in and as the foundation of the meaning of the world (world history, culture, etc.). That is to say, the denouement of Ellison's novel cannot be the primitive stage in Hegel's consciousness. But if, like the end of Hegel's text, Spirit has found itself as self-recognizing, not still in the primitive struggle for recognition from another, Taylor would need to say exactly where this occurs in Ellison's novel. At the end of Ellison's *Invisible Man*, he recognizes that the other is useless in defining himself and acknowledges that he will be invisible even when he comes out of his hole—but he is still materially engaged with the other, if existentially separate. The difference between the end of Hegel's text and Ellison's novel is that for Ellison this realization entails social and political responsibilities to engage with the world. But, what is more, Ellison has come to the realization that because history is chaotic, it cannot be predicted and controlled, as does Hegel's absolute knowing, in which consciousness is the fundamental formation in the meaning of the world. The question that is revealed in this reading of Ellison is, Does black consciousness ever have any other issues other than white recognition? Is this the only lens through which to understand and view "recognition" and "consciousness"? In other words, what is the frame used to interpret Ellison's novel? This, though, is not meant to single out Taylor's work but to highlight an example of this sort of reading.

37. An interesting and important point must be made here. My point is one of nuance, not of distinction. That is to say, while the Marxist dialectical materialism arose out of and in critique of the Hegelian dialectic as too abstract, I think it is important to note the metatheoretical grounds and formative elements of Hegel's dialectic that is implicit in Ellison's critique. It is important to note Hegel's understanding of history as the movement of consciousness within the material world before engaging in the dialectical materialism of Marxism and, later, communism in which social class marks the distinction of history and historical becoming.

38. J. P. Lovecraft, *The Call of Cthulhu and Other Weird Stories*, ed. S. T. Joshi (New York: Penguin Books, 1999), 148. For more on Ellison and Chthonian, see Alan Nadel, "Tod Clifton: Spiritual and Carnal," in *Ralph Ellison*, ed. Harold Bloom (New York: Bloom's Literary Criticism, 2010), 5–28.

39. It is instructive here to note Hegel's lectures on history and his views on Africa's participation. For Hegel, Africa does not directly participate in world history or the unfolding of consciousness onto the material world plane but only as "fuel" in the machine of consciousness's own development. For more on Hegel, world history, and Africa, see G. W. F. Hegel, *Lectures on the Philosophy of World History* (Cambridge: Cambridge University Press, 1981); for critiques of Hegel and Africa, see Susan Buck-Moss, *Hegel, Haiti, and Universal History* (Pittsburgh: University of Pittsburgh Press, 2009); Achille Mbembe, *Critique of Black Reason* (Durham, N.C.: Duke University Press, 2017); Michael Monahan, ed., *Creolizing Hegel* (Lanham, Md.: Roman and Littlefield, 2017); and Babacar Camara, "The Falsity of Hegel's Theses on Africa," *Journal of Black Studies* 36, no. 1 (2005): 82–96.

40. Ellison, "Change the Joke," 108.

41. Kevin Bell, "The Embrace of Entropy: Ralph Ellison and the Freedom Principle of Jazz Invisible," *Boundary 2* 30, no. 2 (2003): 22.

42. For more on Ellison and visual iconography (in particular the Sambo dolls), see Lena M. Hill, "The Visual Art of *Invisible Man*: Ellison's Portrait of Blackness," *American Literature* 81, no. 4 (2009): 775–803.

43. Recall from the conversation about Richard Wright in the introduction that flight is the demarcation of black male life.

44. A. Timothy Spaulding, "Embracing the Chaos in Narrative Form: The Bebop Aesthetic in Ralph Ellison's *Invisible Man*," *Callaloo* 27, no. 2 (2004): 482.

45. Kevin Bell similarly argues that "American jazz" is "of its own structural devastation . . . sonorous explorations" that lend themselves to an "aesthetic risk" of "symphonic formalizing of abyss" ("Embrace," 21). And while this may be informative of the music itself, in particular for Bell, it is especially poignant for Ralph Ellison's narrative construction in *Invisible Man*, which, like the music, is an "endless improvisation upon traditional materials." Ralph Ellison, *Shadow and Act* (New York: Vintage Press, 1995), 234.

46. Søren Kierkegaard, *Fear and Trembling / Repetition*, vol. 6 of *Kierkegaard's Writings* (Princeton, N.J.: Princeton University Press, 1983), 9.

47. Ibid., 10–12.

48. Ibid., 7.

49. Ibid., 22.

50. See note 28.

51. Similarly, Cooper Harris argues that the leap of faith "does not offer a 'solution,' or provide an 'answer [to] the question' outside of 'its precondition, the state of nothingness.' Instead, the leap of faith stands as the acceptance of despair." Harris, *Ralph Ellison's Invisible Theology* (New York: New York University Press, 2017), 92.

52. Ralph Ellison, "Richard Wright's Blues," in *The Collected Essays of Ralph Ellison*, ed. John Callahan (New York: Modern Library, 2003), 129.

Chapter 3

1. Saul Williams, "Sha Clack Clack," *Slam: The Soundtrack* (Sony, 1998), CD.

2. John 1:23.

3. Colson Whitehead, *Apex Hides the Hurt* (New York: First Anchor, 2006). Subsequent citations refer to this edition and appear parenthetically in the text.

4. For more on the metaphysics of language and its relation to social and political institutions, see Charles Mills, *The Racial Contract* (Ithaca, N.Y.: Cornell University Press, 1997); also see Tommy J. Curry, "On Derelict and Method: The Methodological Crisis of African-American Philosophy's Study of African-Descended People," *Journal of Black Studies* 42, no. 3 (2011): 314–33.

5. Charles Mills, *Blackness Visible* (Ithaca, N.Y.: Cornell University Press, 2014), 3.

6. Countee Cullen, "Saturday's Child," in *My Soul's High Song: The Collected Writings of Countee Cullen* (New York: Anchor Books, 1991), 91.

7. Immanuel Kant, *Critique of Pure Reason* (Cambridge: Cambridge University Press, 1998), 20.

8. G. W. F. Hegel, *Phenomenology of Spirit* (Oxford: Oxford University Press, 1977), 485.

9. Ibid., 493.

10. Daniel C. Dennett, *Kinds of Minds: Toward an Understanding of Consciousness* (New York: Basic Books, 1997), 32.

11. Jeremy Bentham, *An Introduction to the Principles of Morals and Legislation* (Mineola, N.Y.: Dover, 2007), 11.

12. Alain Locke, *Race Contacts and Interracial Relations* (Washington, D.C.: Howard University Press, 1992), 20.

13. W. E. B. Du Bois, *Souls of Black Folk* (Oxford: Oxford University Press, 2007), 3.

14. Sylvia Wynter, *On Being Human as Praxis*, ed. Katherine McKittrick (Durham, N.C.: Duke University Press, 2014), 26.

15. Ibid., 26–27.

16. Ibid., 27.

17. James Baldwin, "Stranger in a Village," in *The Norton Reader: An Anthology of Nonfiction* (New York: Norton, 2007), 389.

18. James Baldwin, *No Name in the Street* (New York: Vintage, 2007), 55.

19. Lewis Gordon, "Four Kinds of Invisibility of Euromodernity" (TEDx talk, January 3, 2019).

20. Bob Dylan, "Shelter from the Storm," *Blood on the Tracks* (Columbia Records, 1974), CD.

21. For more on this, see Wynter, *On Being Human as Praxis*.

22. Derek C. Maus argues that this neglect is a kind of bad faith surmised by a "physical manifestations of an underlying ethical corruption," in which the narrator has to know that the injury is getting worse each time he "reapplies Apex after Apex, [but] he deludes himself that his 'hurt' is not worsening." In this way, his condition becomes largely the self-inflicted consequence of carelessness. Maus, *Understanding Colson Whitehead* (Columbia: University of South Carolina Press, 2014), 38.

23. Stephanie Li has argued that the irony at the heart of Whitehead's novel, named after a bandage, is that "healing wounds will not sell more adhesive bandages; rather the consumer must always be left in a state of perpetual injury." Taken to its end, then, the novel is about covering over that which is not supposed to be healed. For Lin [Li], the question is not so much one of neglect but one of "the deceptive quality of the product [that] actually aggravates the wound" rather than healing it. Li, *Signifying without Specifying: Racial Discourse in the Age of Obama* (New Brunswick, N.J.: Rutgers University Press, 2011), 92.

24. Jesse S. Cohn, "Old Afflictions: Colson Whitehead's *Apex Hides the Hurt* and the 'Post-Soul Condition,'" *Journal of the Midwest Modern Language Association* 42, no. 1 (2009): 16.

25. For more on this, see Alan P. Merriam and Fradley H. Garner, "Jazz—The Word," in *The Jazz Cadence of American Culture*, ed. Robert O'Meally (New York: Columbia University Press, 1998), 20–21. More will be said of this in the next chapter.

Chapter 4

1. Cecil Brown, *The Life and Loves of Mr. Jiveass Nigger: A Novel* (New York: Farrar, Strauss and Giroux, 1969), jacket flap. Subsequent citations refer to this edition and appear parenthetically in the text.

2. Vijay Iyer, "Improvisation: Terms and Conditions," in *Audio Culture: Readings in Modern Music*, ed. Christoph Cox and Daniel Warner (New York: Bloomsbury, 2017), 399–400.

3. Ralph Ellison, *Invisible Man* (New York: Vintage, 1995), 7.

4. Toru Kiuchi and Yoshinobu Hakutani, *Richard Wright: A Documented Chronology, 1908–1960* (Jefferson, N.C.: McFarland, 2014), 4.

5. Amiri Baraka, *The Dutchman and the Slave* (New York: Harper Perennial, 2001), 35.

6. Kenneth W. Warren, "Does African American Literature Exist?," *Chronicle of Higher Education*, February 24, 2011, https://www.chronicle.com/article/Does-African-American/126483.

7. Kenneth W. Warren, "On *What Was African American Literature?*," *Amerikastudien* [American Studies] 55, no. 4 (2010): 739–42.

8. Kenneth W. Warren, *What Was African American Literature?* (Cambridge, Mass.: Harvard University Press, 2012).

9. Warren, "On *What Was African American Literature?*," 739.

10. Ibid.

11. See page <X> in the prologue of this text.

12. Quoted in Kiuchi and Hakutani, *Richard Wright*, 3–4. Reprinted in *Conversations with Richard Wright*, ed. Keneth Kinnamon and Michel Fabre (Jackson: University of Mississippi Press, 1993), 46.

13. Charles Johnson, *Being and Fiction: Black Writing since 1970* (Bloomington: Indiana University Press, 1983), 30.

14. Hortense J. Spillers, "The Crisis of the Negro Intellectual: A Post-Date," *Boundary 2* 21, no. 3 (1994): 67.

15. Vijay Iyer, "Exploding the Narrative in Jazz Improvisation," in *Uptown Conversation: The New Jazz Studies*, ed. Robert O'Meally, Brent Hayes Edwards, and Farah Jasmine Griffin (New York: Columbia University Press, 2004), 395.

16. Iyer, "Improvisation," 401.

17. Fred Moten, *In the Break: The Aesthetics of the Black Radical Tradition* (Minneapolis: University of Minnesota Press, 2003), 26.

18. Brent Hayes Edwards, *Epistrophies: Jazz and the Literary Imagination* (Cambridge, Mass.: Harvard University Press, 2017), 4.

19. Ibid.

20. Ibid. Reprinted in Alessandro Portelli, *The Death of Luigi Transtulli and Other Stories: Form and Meaning in Oral History* (Albany: State University of New York Press, 1991), 52.

21. Ibid., 51; emphasis in original.

22. Ibid.

23. Ibid.; emphasis in original.

24. Ibid.

25. Ibid.

26. Ibid., 26.

27. See, for example, Dany Laferrière, trans. David Homel, *Why Must a Black Writer Write about Sex?* (Toronto: Coach House Press, 1994); and Darius James, *Negrophobia* (New York: St. Martin's Press, 1993). See introduction, James Baldwin.

28. Edwards, *Epistrophies*, reprinted in Portelli, *The Death of Luigi Transtulli and Other Stories*, 26.

29. Ibid.

30. Ibid., 5.

31. Edwards, *Epistrophies*, reprinted in Michael Ondaatje, *Coming through Slaughter* (New York: Vintage, 1976), 37. This is where liner notes are so important. In commercial jazz albums, liner notes are guide posts "instructing the listener, in subtle ways, what it means to be a jazz fan" (13). In the case of black men's literature, we are still looking for "liner notes" or guide posts to understand and appreciate a jazz structured ontology or existence.

32. Ibid., 13.

33. Ibid., 4.

34. It is important to note here the distinction between creation and jazz improvisation. Bruce Ellis Benson distinguishes between creation and improvisation, arguing that creation is "to produce where nothing was before," while improvisation means to "fabricate out of what is conveniently on hand." Benson, "In the Beginning There Was Improvisation," in *Oxford Handbook of Critical Improvisation Studies*, vol. 2, ed. George E. Lewis and Benjamin Piekut (Oxford: Oxford University Press, 2016), 157–58. While I grant Benson this distinction, what must be kept in mind is the cosmology out of which his distinction emerges. Within his chapter "In the Beginning There Was Improvisation," Benson heavily relies on a Western cosmology of creation and a Western idea of a creator God. In Brown's novel, though, this cosmological view is challenged. If the "Negro" is the foundation for cosmology itself—what I have termed the cosmological constant—of Western modernity, then it too undergirds how we have chosen to interpret religious texts. As I have argued in the introduction of this text and in other places, blackness is not specifically about color or ethnic identity but is about ambiguity and uncertainty. In this view, creation is less about producing what was not there before and more about the existential ambiguity of facing the not-thereness of absence as an ontological horizon—like the being of nothing. In this reading, the nothing actually structures the something of reality, and when one creates, one is actually creating out of this being. In this cosmological view, there is no nothing; everything has being of different sorts. Blackness in the modern West has come to embody this being of nothing, and as such, when Brown's Washington jives, when he riffs, when he is improvising on this nothing, on the fact that this nothing grounds everything else, he is jazzing himself and creating the world. In Brown's novel, creation and improvisation are one and the same.

35. Andrew Levy, "Frederick Douglass, Benjamin Franklin, and the Trickster Reader," *College English* 52, no. 7 (1990): 743–55.

36. Ethridge Knight, "Cell Song," in *The Essential Ethridge Knight* (Pittsburgh: University of Pittsburgh Press, 1986), 9.

37. Kevin Young, "I Am Trying to Break Your Heart," in *Dear Darkness: Poems* (New York: Knopf, 2010), 145–47.

38. Iyer, "Improvisation: Terms and Conditions," 400.

39. Ralph Ellison, "Change the Joke, Slip the Yoke," in *The Collected Essays of Ralph Ellison*, ed. John Callahan (New York: Modern Library, 2003), 107–8.

40. Ernest Hemingway, *The Green Hills of Africa* (New York: Simon and Schuster, 2015), 28.

41. Ralph Ellison, "Hidden Name, Complex Fate," in *Collected Essays*, 192.

42. James Baldwin, "Take This Hammer," interview by National Educational Television by the KQED film unit, San Francisco, 1963.

43. Franz Fanon, *Black Skin, White Masks* (New York: Grove Press, 2008), 84.

44. Ibid.

45. Immanuel Kant, *Observations on the Feeling of the Beautiful and Sublime* (Oakland: University of California Press, 2004), 255.

46. For more on this, see Sylvia Wynter, "1492: A New World View," in *Race, Discourse, and the Origin of the Americas: A New World View*, ed. Vera Lawrence Hyatt and Rex Nettleford (Washington, D.C.: Smithsonian Institution Press, 1995).

47. Mircea Eliade, *The Sacred and the Profane: The Nature of Religion* (New York: Harcourt, 1987), 22.

48. Nahum Chandler, *X—The Problem of the Negro as a Problem for Thought* (New York: Fordham University Press, 2014), 1.

49. Ibid., 3.

50. Ibid., 25.

51. Eliade, *Sacred and the Profane*, 23.

52. Ibid., 25.

53. Ellison, *Invisible Man*, 16.

54. Ibid., 30–31; emphasis mine.

55. Friedrich Nietzsche, "Thus Spoke Zarathustra," in *The Portable Nietzsche* (New York: Penguin Books, 1982), 126–27.

56. James Baldwin, *Going to Meet the Man* (New York: Vintage, 1995), quoted in Joe Gorman, "Oppression through Sexualization: The Use of Sexualization in 'Going to Meet the Man' and 'The Shoyku Kid,'" *Undergraduate Review* 5 (2009): 271.

57. For example, blackface actor, Bert Williams chose to wear blackface arguing that, "Nobody in America knows my *real* name and, if I can prevent it, nobody ever will. That was the only promise I made to my father." Quoted in Ann Charters, *Nobody: The Story of Bert Williams* (New York: Macmillan, 1970), 14.

58. As depicted in Michelle Wright's *The Physics of Blackness: Beyond Middle Passage Epistemology* (Minneapolis: University of Minnesota Press, 2015); Michelle D. Commander's *Afro-Atlantic Flight: Speculative Returns and the Black Fantastic* (Durham, N.C.: Duke University Press, 2017); and in many other black works, the ship of transatlantic enslavement, on the one hand, was the physical and metaphysical marker of the spatiotemporal exchange of the old and new world, binding together these two worlds and the chaotic crossings between them; on the other hand, the ship marked the ironic dispensation of the void of the Atlantic ocean itself as at once the unavoidable reality that the space and time of enslaved men, women, and children had been ruptured, but also this same space and time, for the European merchants, marked the creation and continuation of a world where black bodies were property.

59. John Coltrane, with McCoy Tyner, Jimmy Garrison, Art Davis, and Elvin Jones, *Ascension* (Impulse!, 1965), LP.

60. Iyer, "Exploding the Narrative," 395.

61. Thomas F. Slaughter, "Epidermalizing the World," *Man and World* 10, no. 3 (1977): 307.

62. Nietzsche, "Thus Spoke Zarathustra," 131.
63. Iyer, "Exploding the Narrative," 395.
64. Ibid.
65. For more on race contact and interracial conflict, see Alain Locke, *Race Contacts and Interracial Relations: Lectures on the Theory and Practice of Race* (Washington, D.C.: Howard University Press, 1992).
66. William Shakespeare, *Othello* (St. Paul, Minn.: EMC/Paradigm, 2005), 11.
67. For discussions on the permanence of race as a recurring theme in science fiction texts, see Douglas Turner Ward, "Day of Absence," in *"Happy Ending" and "Day of Absence": Two Plays by Douglas Turner Ward* (New York: Dramatists Play Service, 1996); Ray Bradbury, "The Other Foot," in *The Illustrated Man* (New York: Doubleday, 1951); Derrick Bell, "Space Traders," in *Faces at the Bottom of the Well* (New York: Basic Books, 1992), 158–95; George Schuyler, *Black No More* (New York: Penguin, 2018).
68. *Online Etymology Dictionary*, s.v. "dragon," https://www.etymonline.com/word/dragon, accessed June 18, 2019.
69. Fanon, *Black Skin, White Masks*, 84.

Conclusion

1. Ishmael Reed, "Dragon's Blood," in *New and Collected Poems, 1964–2007* (1988; repr., New York: Thunder's Mouth, 2007), 72.
2. Ed Roberson, "be careful," in *Black Nature: Four Centuries of African American Nature Poetry*, ed. Camille T. Dungy (Athens: University of Georgia Press, 2009), 29.
3. Ibid.
4. Amiri Baraka, "Something in the Way of Things (in Town)," *Phrenology* (MCA Records, 2002), CD.

Epilogue

1. Chris Rock, *Kill the Messenger*, directed by Marty Callner (HBO, 2008).

INDEX

Abraham and Isaac, biblical story of, 83, 87–94
absurdity, 3, 36, 57
Along the Way (Johnson), 9
American exceptionalism, 37
American Hunger (Wright), 10, 191n11
American identity, 149–50
Apex Hides the Hurt (Whitehead), 22–23, 98, 99, 182; earning of names in, 117–19; functionality of names in, 116–17; fundamental neglect in, 133–37, 142, 206nn22–23; history of enclosure and erasure in, 107–10; imposition of names in, 114–15; naming process and black maleness in, 103–5; our inner world and names in, 121–24; ourselves and our names in, 128–31; plot summary of, 105–7; science of names in, 119–21; science of the word in, 124–28; setting of, 102–3; specter of excess in, 131–33; things evoke and become their names in, 111–14. *See also* Whitehead, Colson
Appiah, Kwame, 200n4

Baldwin, James, 15–16, 18, 132, 140, 150, 156, 162
Baraka, Amiri, 141, 181
Being and Fiction (Johnson), 143
Bell, Kevin, 205n45
Benson, Bruce Ellis, 208n34
Bergson, Henri, 143
"Big Boy Leaves Home" (Wright), 10, 11–13
bio-mythoi, 126–28
Black Boy (Wright), 13, 191n11
black consciousness, 73–74, 201n16, 203n36, 204n39. *See also* black existentialism
Black Culture and Black Consciousness (Levine), 25
black existentialism, 74–77, 191n3, 203n36, 208n34. *See also* black consciousness

Black Hearts of Men, The (Stauffer), 29
black male hypervisible invisible vulnerability, portrait of, 3–7, 17–20, 23, 140, 146, 182–83
Black Power (Wright), 192n11
Boedeker, Edgar, 73
Book of Night Women (James), 140
Brooks, David, 31–32
Brown, Cecil: on freedom and liberty, 147–50, 165; on "Nigger," as condition and function, 143–44, 146, 150, 151–63, 171–72, 179. *See also Life and Loves of Mr. Jiveass Nigger, The* (Brown)
Brown, Claude, 140

Camus, Albert, 75
Chandler, Nahum, 153, 203n28
"Change the Joke, Slip the Yoke" (Ellison), 72
Clark, Keith, 195n28
Cleaver, Eldridge, 23
Cohn, Jesse S., 136
colonial oppression, 151, 176, 202n16
Colored Man's Reminiscences of James Madison, A (Jennings), 39
Coltrane, John, 164
Constructing the Black Masculine (Wallace), 194n28
consumerism and naming process, 103–4
consumptive authority, 15–18, 81, 113–14, 151, 193n16
Covey, Edward, 40, 45, 46, 48, 56–57, 198n20
Crisis of the Negro Intellectual, The (Cruses), 140
Cruses, Harold, 140

daguerreotype, 196n3
"Degrees of Exposure" (Faisst), 35–36
Descartes, Rene, 76–77
dialectical thinking and dialectical history, 77–86, 203n32, 203n36, 204n37
Doane, Randal, 203n32

211

"Does African American Literature Exist?" (Warren), 141
Douglass, Frederick: on daguerreotype, 196n3; on fight with Covey, 40, 45, 46, 48, 56–57, 198n20; on freedom and liberty, 21, 37–42, 47–49, 51–52, 101, 142; as metaphysician of language, 101–2; *My Bondage and My Freedom*, 29, 31, 39; *Narrative of the Life of Frederick Douglass: An American Slave*, 35, 39, 40–41, 45; on "Negro" as image and idea, 27–36, 97; "Of Pictures and Progress," 20–21, 26–36; photographs of, 25–26, 196n1; "Why Is the Negro Lynched?," 142. See also *Heroic Slave, The* (Douglass)
"Dragon's Blood" (Reed), 61, 181–83
dreamwork, 14
Du Bois, W. E. B., 55, 153–54, 194n27
During, Simon, 63
Dutchman, The (Baraka), 141

Eliade, Mircea, 153, 155
Ellison, Ralph, 3; "Change the Joke, Slip the Yoke," 72; on freedom and liberty, 66, 101; on identity of America, 149; on literary representation, 19; as metaphysician of language, 100–102; on performance of "Negro/Nigger," 67, 73; on reading and listening, 202n19; *Shadow and Act*, 25. See also *Invisible Man* (Ellison)
Erasure/fuck (Everett), 96, 140
escape. See flight; freedom and liberty
Everett, Percival, 96, 140
exceptionalism, 37
existentialism, 69, 74–77. See also black existentialism

Fabre, Michel, 201n13
Faisst, Julia, 35–36
Fanon, Franz: on black consciousness, 73, 201n16; on black existentialism, 76; on "Negro" as idea and image, 76, 150–51, 153–54; on phobic object of black male, 15, 192n15
Fear and Trembling (Kierkegaard), 86–87
flight, 13, 84, 191n11, 205n43
freedom and liberty: Brown on, 147–50, 165; Douglass on, 21, 37–42, 47–49, 51–52, 101, 142; Ellison on, 66, 101; Scott on, 193n21; Whitehead on, 101–2, 104, 110, 113–14, 126, 133. See also flight
French existentialism, 69
Fugitive Slave Act (1793), 44

Gates, Henry Louis, Jr., 146
gender divisions, 26, 193nn20–21
Glidden, George, 29, 31
Going to Meet the Man (Baldwin), 162
Gordon, Lewis, 73, 132–33, 202n18
"Grandfather's Riddle, The" (Ellison), 71, 72
Great Migration, 191n11

Hamilton, Cynthia S., 37–38
Harris, Cooper, 205n51
Hegel, Georg Wilhelm Friedrich, 77, 78, 80, 201n16, 203n36, 204n37, 204n39
Heidegger, Martin, 74, 75, 76
Hemingway, Ernest, 140, 149–50
Henry, Patrick, 36–37, 66
Hero and the Blues, The (Murray), 36, 53–56
Heroic Slave, The (Douglass), 20–21; Faisst on, 35–36; Listwell, as character in, 39, 67; slave rebellion in, 39, 48, 49–51; Washington, as character in, 21, 37–38, 65, 67; Washington, as hero in, 36–37, 47–52, 182. See also Douglass, Frederick
heroism, 36–37, 47–52, 53–59, 182. See also *Heroic Slave, The* (Douglass)
Himes, Chester, 3–4, 140
Hogue, W. Lawrence, 196n34
How to Make Love to a Negro without Getting Tired (LaFerriere), 140
hypervisible invisible vulnerability, portrait of black male, 3–7, 17–20, 23, 140, 146, 182–83

Incidents in the Life of a Slave Girl (Jacobs), 15, 16–17
In the Shadow of the Black Beast (Leiter), 9
Invisible Man (Ellison), 3, 21–22; on black existentialism, 74–77; construction of the self in, 156–59, 182; dialectical thinking and dialectical history in, 77–86, 203n32, 203n36, 204n37; Fabre on, 201n13; story of Abraham and Isaac in, 83, 90–94; theatricality in, 62–72, 97, 142. See also Ellison, Ralph

Index

irony: Brown's use of dramatic, 23, 152–53; Douglass's use of controlled, 21, 44–45, 49, 58, 65, 72; Ellison's use of, 20, 22–23, 67; Murray on, 36; Whitehead's use of, 104, 111, 206n23
Isaac and Abraham, biblical story of, 83, 87–94
Iyer, Vijay, 143

Jacobs, Harriet, 15, 16–17
James, Darius, 140
James, Marlon, 140
jazz improvisation, as form, 86, 137, 143–46, 148, 164–67, 179, 205n45, 208n34. *See also Life and Loves of Mr. Jiveass Nigger, The* (Brown); literary aesthetics; theatricality
Jennings, Paul, 39
Johnson, Charles, 19, 143
Johnson, James Wheldon, 9

Kaufmann, Walter, 74
Kierkegaard, Søren, 72, 77, 86–92, 94
Knott, Josiah, 29, 31

LaFerriere, Dany, 140
Leiter, Andrew B., 9
Levine, Lawrence W., 25
Li, Stephanie, 206n23
liberty. *See* freedom and liberty
Life and Loves of Mr. Jiveass Nigger, The (Brown), 23–24, 98, 136–37; black male vulnerability in, 146–47; construction of the self in, 151–61, 179–80; consulate encounters in, 167–70, 174–78; historical influence and context of publication, 140–43; performance of self in, 161–66; plot summary of, 139, 143; portrait of main character in, 147–50, 151; sexual acts in, 170–73; structure and form of, 143–46, 166–67. *See also* Brown, Cecil
liner notes, 208n31
listening and reading, politics of, 18, 98, 183, 194n27, 202n19
Listwell, Mr. (literary character). *See Heroic Slave, The* (Douglass)
literary aesthetics, 53–55, 62, 193n20, 194n27. *See also* theatricality
literary representation of black men, overview, 9–10, 191n3

Madison, James, 38–39
magic, 63–64, 67–69
"Man Who Killed a Shadow, The" (Wright), 10, 12–13, 17
Marriott, David, 14
Maus, Derek C., 206n22
Merleau-Ponty, Maurice, 33
Mills, Charles, 102, 200n8
minstrelsy, 171, 209n57
Modern Enchantments (During), 63
Moten, Fred, 144
Murray, Albert, 36, 53–59, 199n36
music. *See* jazz improvisation, as form
My Bondage and My Freedom (Douglass), 29, 31, 39

naming principles and process. *See Apex Hides the Hurt* (Whitehead)
Narrative of the Life of Frederick Douglass: An American Slave (Douglass), 35, 39, 40–41, 45
Native Son (Wright), 192n11
"Negro," as idea and image: Douglass on, 27–36, 97; Ellison on, 67, 73; Fanon on, 76, 150–51, 153–54; Murray on, 199n36
Negrophobia (James), 140
"Nigger," as condition and function: Baldwin on, 150; Brown on, 143–44, 146, 150, 151–61; Ellison on, 67; Fanon on, 150–51; Whitehead on, 128, 131
nomenclature. *See Apex Hides the Hurt* (Whitehead)
No Name in the Street (Baldwin), 15

"Of Pictures and Progress" (Douglass), 20–21, 26–36
Once You Go Black (Reid-Pharr), 52–53
Ortiz, Darwin, 64
Outsider, The (Wright), 192n11

Parker, Charlie, 164
perception–perspective, 31–32, 71
performance. *See* theatricality
phenomenological perspective, 19–20, 70–71
photography, Douglass on. *See* "Of Pictures and Progress" (Douglass)
Pictures and Progress: Early Photography and the Making of African American Identity (Wallace and Smith), 28
Plato, 61
polycentrism, 20, 196n34

queerness, as concept, 193n21

reading and listening, politics of, 18, 98, 183, 194n27, 202n19
reality, 63, 97–98, 200n4
Reed, Ishmael, 61, 181–83
Reid-Pharr, Robert, 52–53
Republic (Plato), 61
Revolutionary War (1775–83), 36–37
Roberson, Ed, 183
Ross, Marlon, 193n20
"Running Commentary to Being and Time" (Boedeker), 73

Sartre, Jean-Paul, 74, 76, 201n16
Scott, Darieck, 193n21
secular magic, 63–64, 67–69
semiotics, 184
sexuality and desire, 12, 15–16, 23, 170–73
Shadow and Act (Ellison), 25
Sickness unto Death (Kierkegaard), 72, 86–92
slave rebellions, 21, 39, 48, 49–51, 198n23
slavery, 16–17, 149, 193n23, 197n5, 197n11
Smith, Shawn Michelle, 28
"Something in the Way of Things (in Town)" (Baraka), 181
Souls of Black Folk (Du Bois), 153–54, 194n27
specters, 134, 160, 203n28
Spillers, Hortense, 143
Stauffer, John, 29

Taylor, Jack, 203n36
Taylor, Paul C., 202n22
theatricality, 20–23, 62–72, 97, 161–65, 200n4, 200n8. *See also* jazz improvisation, as form; literary aesthetics

trauma, 9–10
12 Million Black Voices (Wright), 192n11
Types of Man (Knott and Glidden), 29, 31

Visible and the Invisible, The (Merleau-Ponty), 33

Wallace, Maurice O., 18, 19, 28, 194n28
Warmth of Other Suns, The (Wilkerson), 192n11
Warren, Kenneth, 141
Washington, George (historical person), 39, 147, 148–49, 151
Washington, George (literary character). See *Life and Loves of Mr. Jiveass Nigger, The* (Brown)
Washington, Madison (historical person), 21, 37–38
Washington, Madison (literary character). See *Heroic Slave, The* (Douglass)
Western modernity and black maleness, 69, 79, 86, 98, 101–4
What Was African American Literature (book by Warren), 141
"What Was African American Literature?" (essay by Warren), 141
Whitehead, Colson: on Douglass and Ellison, 102; on freedom and liberty, 101–2, 104, 110, 113–14, 126, 133; on "Nigger," as condition and function, 128, 131. See also *Apex Hides the Hurt* (Whitehead)
White Man, Listen! (Wright), 192n11
"Why Is the Negro Lynched?" (Douglass), 142
Williams, Bert, 209n57
Williams, John, 140
Wright, Richard, 10–14, 17, 140, 142, 191n11
Wynter, Sylvia, 125

www.ingramcontent.com/pod-product-compliance
Lightning Source LLC
Chambersburg PA
CBHW032034290426
44110CB00012B/799